KAFKA'S *THE TRIAL*

OXFORD STUDIES IN PHILOSOPHY AND LITERATURE

Richard Eldridge, Philosophy, Swarthmore College

PUBLISHED IN THE SERIES

Ibsen's *Hedda Gabler*: Philosophical Perspectives
Edited by Kristin Gjesdal

Shakespeare's *Hamlet*: Philosophical Perspectives
Edited by Tzachi Zamir

Kafka's *The Trial*: Philosophical Perspectives
Edited by Espen Hammer

KAFKA'S *THE TRIAL*

Philosophical Perspectives

Edited by Espen Hammer

OXFORD
UNIVERSITY PRESS

OXFORD
UNIVERSITY PRESS

Oxford University Press is a department of the University of Oxford. It furthers
the University's objective of excellence in research, scholarship, and education
by publishing worldwide. Oxford is a registered trade mark of Oxford University
Press in the UK and certain other countries.

Published in the United States of America by Oxford University Press
198 Madison Avenue, New York, NY 10016, United States of America.

© Oxford University Press 2018

Library of Congress Cataloging-in-Publication Data
Names: Hammer, Espen, editor.
Title: KAFKA'S the Trial : philosophical perspectives /
edited by Espen Hammer.
Description: New York, NY : Oxford University Press, 2018. |
Series: Oxford studies in philosophy and literature |
Includes bibliographical references and index.
Identifiers: LCCN 2017031714 (print) | LCCN 2017042972 (ebook) |
ISBN 9780190461461 (online course) | ISBN 9780190461478 (updf) |
ISBN 9780190461485 (epub) | ISBN 9780190461447 (pbk. : acid-free paper) |
ISBN 9780190461454 (cloth : acid-free paper)
Subjects: LCSH: Kafka, Franz, 1883–1924. Prozess. | Kafka, Franz,
1883–1924—Philosophy. | Literature—Philosophy. | Law in literature.
Classification: LCC PT2621.A26 (ebook) | LCC PT2621.A26 P7656 2018 (print) |
DDC 833/.912—dc23
LC record available at https://lccn.loc.gov/2017031714

3 5 7 9 8 6 4 2

Paperback printed by WebCom, Inc., Canada
Hardback printed by Bridgeport National Bindery, Inc., United States of America

CONTENTS

CONTENTS

SERIES EDITOR'S FOREWORD

At least since Plato had Socrates criticize the poets and attempt to displace Homer as the authoritative articulator and transmitter of human experience and values, philosophy and literature have developed as partly competing, partly complementary enterprises. Both literary writers and philosophers have frequently studied and commented on each other's texts and ideas, sometimes with approval, sometimes with disapproval, in their efforts to become clearer about human life and about valuable commitments—moral, artistic, political, epistemic, metaphysical, and religious, as may be. Plato's texts themselves register the complexity and importance of these interactions in being dialogues in which both deductive argumentation and dramatic narration do central work in furthering a complex body of views.

While these relations have been widely recognized, they have also frequently been ignored or misunderstood, as academic disciplines have gone their separate ways within their modern institutional settings. Philosophy has often turned to science or mathematics as providing models of knowledge; in doing so it has often explicitly set itself against cultural entanglements and literary devices, rejecting, at least officially, the importance of plot, figuration, and imagery in favor of supposedly plain speech about the truth. Literary study has moved variously through formalism, structuralism, post-structuralism, and cultural studies, among other movements, as modes of approach to a literary text. In doing so it has understood literary texts as sample instances of images, structures, personal styles, or failures of consciousness, or it has seen the literary text as a largely fungible product, fundamentally shaped by wider pressures and patterns of consumption and expectation that affect and figure in non-literary textual production as well. It has thus set itself against the idea that major literary texts productively and originally address philosophical problems of value and commitment precisely through their form, diction, imagery, and development, even while these works also resist claiming conclusively to solve the problems that occupy them.

These distinct academic traditions have yielded important perspectives and insights. But in the end none of them has been kind to the idea of major literary works as achievements in thinking about values and human life, often in distinctive, open, self-revising, self-critical ways. At the same time readers outside institutional settings, and often enough philosophers and literary scholars too, have turned to major literary texts precisely in order to engage with their productive, materially, and medially specific patterns and processes of thinking. These turns to literature have, however, not so far been systematically encouraged within disciplines, and they have generally occurred independently of each other.

The aim of this series is to make manifest the multiple, complex engagements with philosophical ideas and problems that lie at the hearts of major literary texts. In doing so, its volumes aim not only to help philosophers and literary scholars of various kinds to find rich affinities and provocations to further thought and work but also to bridge various gaps between academic disciplines and between those disciplines and the experiences of extra-institutional readers.

Each volume focuses on a single, undisputedly major literary text. Both philosophers with training and experience in literary study and literary scholars with training and experience in philosophy are invited to engage with themes, details, images, and incidents in the focal text, through which philosophical problems are held in view, worried at, and reformulated. Decidedly not a project simply to formulate A's philosophy of X as a finished product, merely illustrated in the text, and decidedly not a project to explain the literary work entirely by reference to external social configurations and forces, the effort is instead to track the work of open thinking in literary forms, as they lie both neighbor to and aslant from philosophy. As Walter Benjamin once wrote, "new centers of reflection are continually forming," as problems of commitment and value of all kinds take on new shapes for human agents in relation to changing historical circumstances, where reflective address remains possible. By considering how such centers of reflection are formed and expressed in and through literary works, as they engage with philosophical problems of agency, knowledge, commitment, and value, these volumes undertake to present both literature and philosophy as, at times, productive forms of reflective, medial work in relation both to each other and to social circumstances and to show how this work is specifically undertaken and developed in distinctive and original ways in exemplary works of literary art.

Richard Eldridge
Swarthmore College

ACKNOWLEDGMENTS

I owe a great debt of gratitude to the book's contributors, all of whom enthusiastically agreed to write while holding to tight deadlines. I should also like to thank Carmen Fosner for her invaluable editorial assistance. The support I have received from series editor Richard Eldridge and Oxford University Press's Lucy Randall has been both helpful and inspiring.

CONTRIBUTORS

Howard Caygill is Professor of Philosophy at the Centre for Research in Modern European Philosophy at Kingston University and Visiting Professor in the Department of Philosophy at the University of Paris 8. He is the author of *Art of Judgement* (Blackwell, 1989), *A Kant Dictionary* (Wiley-Blackwell, 1995), *Levinas and the Political* (Routledge, 2002), *Walter Benjamin: The Colour of Experience* (Routledge, 2005), *On Resistance: A Philosophy of Defiance* (Bloomsbury Academic, 2015), and *Kafka: In Light of the Accident* (Bloomsbury Academic, 2017).

Anne Fuchs is Professor and Director of the Humanities Institute at University College Dublin. She has published widely on German cultural memory, modernist and contemporary literature, and time and temporality. Her monographs include *After the Dresden Bombing: Pathways of Memory, 1945 to the Present* (Palgrave Macmillan, 2012), *Phantoms of War in Contemporary German Literature, Films and Discourse* (Palgrave Macmillan, 2008, 2nd ed. 2010); *Die Schmerzensspuren der Geschichte: zur Poetik der Erinnerung in W. G. Sebalds Prosa* (Böhlau, 2004). Recent edited volumes are: *The Longing for Time: Ästhetische Eigenzeit in Contemporary Film, Literature and Art*, eds. Anne Fuchs and Ines Detmers, Oxford German Studies 46/2 (2017) and 46/3 (2017); (with J. J. Long), *Time in German Literature and Culture, 1900—2015: Between Acceleration and Slowness* (Palgrave Macmillan, 2016).

John Gibson is Professor of Philosophy and Director of the Commonwealth Center for Humanities at the University of Louisville. He works on topics in aesthetics and the philosophy of literature with particular focus on connections between these areas and issues in the philosophy of language and the philosophy of the self. He is the author of *Fiction and the Weave of Life* (Oxford University Press, 2012), editor of *The Philosophy of Poetry* (Oxford University Press, 2015), and co-editor of *The Routledge Companion to Philosophy of Literature* (Routledge, 2015), *Narrative, Emotion, and Insight* (Penn State University Press, 2011), *The Literary Wittgenstein* (Routledge, 2004), and *A Sense of the World: Essays on Fiction, Narrative, and Knowledge* (Routledge, 2009). He is currently writing a book titled *Poetry, Metaphor & Nonsense: An Essay on Meaning* (forthcoming with Oxford University Press).

Elizabeth S. Goodstein is Professor of English and the Liberal Arts at Emory University; she is also affiliated with the Department of Comparative Literature, History, and Philosophy. She is the author of *Experience Without Qualities: Boredom and Modernity* (Stanford University Press, 2005) and *Georg Simmel and the Disciplinary Imaginary* (Stanford University Press, 2017).

Peter E. Gordon is the Amabel B. James Professor of History at Harvard University; he is also Faculty Affiliate in the Department of Germanic Languages and Literatures, and Faculty Affiliate in the Department of Philosophy. He is the author of several books, including *Rosenzweig and Heidegger: Between Judaism and German Philosophy*

(University of California Press, 2003), *Continental Divide: Heidegger, Cassirer, Davos* (Harvard University Press, 2010), and *Adorno and Existence* (Harvard University Press, 2016). He has also co-edited a variety of books in philosophy and intellectual history, including *The Cambridge Companion to Modern Jewish Philosophy* (Cambridge University Press, 2007), *The Modernist Imagination: Intellectual History and Critical Theory* (Berghahn Books, 2008), and *Weimar Thought: A Contested Legacy* (Princeton University Press, 2013). He is co-editor, with Axel Honneth and Espen Hammer, of *The Routledge Companion to the Frankfurt School* (Routledge, 2018).

Espen Hammer is Professor of Philosophy at Temple University, Philadelphia. He is the author of *Stanley Cavell: Skepticism, Subjectivity, and the Ordinary* (Polity Press, 2002), *Adorno and the Political* (Routledge, 2006), *Philosophy and Temporality from Kant to Critical Theory* (Cambridge University Press, 2011), and *Adorno's Modernism: Art, Experience, and Catastrophe* (Cambridge University Press, 2015). He is the editor of *German Idealism: Contemporary Perspectives* (Routledge, 2006) and *Theodor W. Adorno II: Critical Assessments of Leading Philosophers* (Routledge, 2015). He is also a co-editor of *Stanley Cavell: Die Unheimlichkeit des Ungewöhnlichen* (Fischer Verlag, 2002), *Pragmatik und Kulturpolitik: Studien zur Kulturpolitik Richard Rortys* (Felix Meiner Verlag, 2011), the *Routledge Companion to the Frankfurt School* (Routledge, 2018), and the *Blackwell Companion to Adorno* (Wiley-Blackwell, 2018). His Norwegian translation of Immanuel Kant's *Kritik der Urteilskraft* came out in 1995, and he is the author of three Norwegian monographs.

Iain Macdonald is Professor of Philosophy at the Université de Montréal. He is the author of many articles in English and French on Hegel, Adorno, Heidegger, Nietzsche, Terrence Malick, and Paul Celan, among others, in the areas of metaphysics, epistemology, and aesthetics. He is co-editor of *Adorno and Heidegger: Philosophical Questions* (Stanford University Press, 2008) and of *Les normes et le possible: héritage et perspectives de l'École de Francfort* (Éditions de la maison des sciences de l'homme, 2013). His current work deals with the relation of possibility to actuality, especially in Hegel, Marx, Critical Theory, and Heidegger. He is also past president of the Canadian Society for Continental Philosophy.

Gerhard Richter teaches critical theory, aesthetics, and literature and philosophy at Brown University, where he is Professor of German Studies and Comparative Literature, as well as Chair of German Studies. Among his books are *Inheriting Walter Benjamin* (Bloomsbury Academic, 2016), *Verwaiste Hinterlassenschaften. Formen gespenstischen Erbens* (Matthes & Seitz Berlin, 2016), *Afterness: Figures of Following in Modern Thought and Aesthetics* (Columbia University Press, 2011), *Thought-Images: Frankfurt School Writers' Reflections from Damaged Life* (Stanford University Press, 2007), *Ästhetik des Ereignisses. Sprache—Geschichte—Medium* (Fink Verlag, 2005), and *Walter Benjamin and the Corpus of Autobiography* (Wayne State University Press, 2000). He also is the editor of seven additional books in the area of European critical thought and aesthetics, including volumes on Benjamin, Adorno, the relation between German music and philosophy, literary paternity and literary friendship, and Derrida on photography.

Fred Rush teaches philosophy at the University of Notre Dame. He is the author of *On Architecture* (Routledge, 2008) and *Irony and Idealism: Rereading Schlegel, Hegel, and Kierkegaard* (Oxford University Press, 2016). He has also edited *The Cambridge Companion to Critical Theory* (Cambridge University Press, 2004) and the *Internationales Jahrbuch des Deutschen Idealismus* (2004–14).

KAFKA'S *THE TRIAL*

Introduction

ESPEN HAMMER

Franz Kafka's *The Trial* stands as one of the most influential and emblematic novels of the twentieth century. Yet, as the overused adjective "Kafkaesque" suggests, rather than as a work of art in its full complexity, it has all too often been received as an expression of some vaguely felt cultural or psychological malaise—a symbol, perhaps, of all that we do not seem to comprehend, but that nevertheless is felt to haunt and influence us in inexplicable ways. Its plot, however, is both complex and completely unforgettable. A man stands accused of a crime he appears not to have any recollection of having committed and whose nature is never revealed to him. In what may ultimately be described as a tragic quest-narrative, the protagonist's search for truth and clarity (about himself, his alleged guilt, and the system he is facing) progressively leads to increasing confusion before ending with his execution in an abandoned quarry. Josef K., its famous anti-hero, is an everyman faced with an anonymous, inscrutable yet seemingly omnipotent power. For all its fundamental strangeness, the novel seems to address defining concerns of the modern era: a sense of radical estrangement, the belittling of the individual in a bureaucratically controlled mass society, the rise perhaps of totalitarianism, as well as the fearful nihilism of a world apparently abandoned by God.

Few novels more insistently invite philosophical reflection. Like its famous, contained parable of the doorkeeper, *The Trial* is itself a parable (or allegory) waiting to be interpreted. However, if a key to its overall meaning exists, then it is far from evident that it has been found. Searching for clues in such diverging fields as theology, psychoanalysis, sociology, and mythology, interpreters have not been able to agree on any overarching interpretive framework—and perhaps will it never emerge.

Unlike much commentary on Kafka, the contributors to this volume have not taken recourse to straightforward thematic analysis. Rather than looking for a unified meaning existing independently of the text, they have sought to highlight how its philosophical layers are shaped by literary form. Being attuned to how a literary text conducts its reflection qua literary is not an easy task. Yet the motivating hypothesis of this volume is that it can be done, in particular with works of high modernist writing such as *The Trial*.

A NOVEL EMERGES

It is sometimes assumed that *The Trial* had a relatively conventional origin, and that it was conceived, written, and finally published as the outcome of what can be characterized as a unified project. Nothing, however, could be further from the truth. From the author's own perspective, the writing of *The Trial* ended in failure and abandonment of the manuscript.

In July 1914, his brief engagement with Felice Bauer came to an abrupt end as Kafka, intensely committed to his writing, could not accept the conventional family life that marriage held in store for him. With the First World War erupting, the work on the manuscript for *Der Proceß* started in August 1914. Kafka's diary entries at the time speak of his high hopes for this novel, and how his efforts satisfy him.[1] During the first two months he managed to compose about two hundred handwritten pages. In November and December, however, he found it hard to continue; and at the end of January 1915, as he abandoned the work, he had barely been able to write another hundred manuscript pages.

Kafka does not seem to have believed that the manuscript for *The Trial* could ever be brought to a publishable state, and like *The Castle* and *Amerika* (*The Man Who Disappeared*), it was included in the author's list of works that, sometime before his death in 1924, he instructed his friend Max Brod to destroy. The only section he found worthy of publication is that of the doorkeeper from the chapter "In the Cathedral." Several times during Kafka's life this story, which also appeared under the separate title "Before the Law," was both read before audiences and published.

Rather than destroying the manuscript, Brod edited it and had it published. In his 1925 postscript to the published novel, he offers various reasons for his decision. Supposedly, he had made it clear to an at least implicitly obliging Kafka that he would not under any circumstances respect his request.[2] He had also witnessed how Kafka, contrary to the wishes being expressed in his list of works to be destroyed, had eventually agreed to publishing a number of the short stories. In addition, he states that he very strongly believed that, from both "a literary and from an ethical point of view," Kafka's *Nachlass*

---

1. Franz Kafka, *Diaries, 1910–1923*, trans. Martin Greenberg (New York: Schocken, 1976), 303. On August 15, 1914, Kafka writes the following: "I have been writing these past few days, may it continue. Today I am not so completely protected by and enclosed in my work as I was two years ago, nevertheless have the feeling that my monotonous, empty, mad bachelor's life has some justification. I can once more carry on a conversation with myself [*Ich kann wieder ein Zwiegespräch mit mir führen*], and don't stare so into complete emptiness. Only in this way is there any possibility of improvement for me."
2. In *Franz Kafka: The Necessity of Form* (Ithaca, NY, and London: Cornell University Press, 1988), 1n1, Stanley Corngold even claims that Kafka "knew" that his last will and testament regarding the manuscripts "would fall on deaf ears." On what basis Corngold claims to know this is not made clear.

was too valuable to be put to the fire, even if this had been what their author wanted.

We shall never know exactly what it was that motivated him. Of overriding significance is the simple fact of Brod's bold but in several respects quite problematic decision to make the work available to the public.

Editors do have a hand in most published work, and almost invariably in novels. However, Brod's impact was relatively large. Indeed, some scholars even view the Brod version as a kind of "collaborative" effort, a text that in any event should not exclusively be viewed as "written by Franz Kafka." One particularly noteworthy procedure he applied was to remove a number of the seemingly most unfinished chapters. Since Kafka did not write linearly but went back and forth, adding and erasing material, seven such chapters, appearing to Brod as particularly unfinished, were omitted in the first edition of the novel. To the remaining material, whose original order is not certain, Brod made a number of emendations, many of which carried semantic implications. There is an initial and a final chapter, framing as it were a narrative with considerable gaps, errors, and confusion in the middle. While Brod added the incomplete chapters as an appendix to the second edition, a critical edition based on the original handwriting was not published until 1990, and even here the ordering and selection of the chapters remain somewhat uncertain.[3] Indeed, rather than ordering them, Kafka wrote the various parts of the novel in ten separate notebooks. A philologically sound method of ordering

3. Ritchie Robertson, *Kafka: Judaism, Politics, and Literature* (Oxford: Clarendon Press, 1985), 88: "It is perhaps impossible to determine with any certainty at which points in the narrative the incomplete chapters belong. Even the completed chapters have not proved easy to arrange." The 1990 critical edition based directly on the handwriting is edited by Malcolm Pasley: *Der Proceß. Roman in der Fassung der Handschrift: Gesammelte Werke in Einzelbänden in der Fassung der Handschrift* (Frankfurt: Fischer Verlag, 1990). Another authoritative, very lightly edited, version of the text is Franz Kafka, *Der Proceß* (Frankfurt: Fischer Verlag, 2008). Contributors to this volume refer to two separate translations: Franz Kafka, *The*

might be based on the temporal order in which they were composed. However, the fact that the temporal order may have been haphazard, hard to trace, and ultimately unreflective of the progression of the narrative, suggests instead that one ought to reconstruct the internal coherence of the narrative. Yet, with so many of the chapters left unfinished, the ordering that appears to make this novel cohere is bound to be provisional. Thus, we shall never know exactly how Kafka would have developed his narrative had he not reached a writerly impasse some time in the early winter of 1914–15. Like his two other novels, *The Castle* and *Amerika* (*The Man Who Disappeared*), *The Trial* remains a fragment.

It is tempting to draw a wider set of conclusions from the fragmentary state of much of Kafka's writing.[4] Most notably, perhaps, the French critic Maurice Blanchot has highlighted the sense of dislocation associated with the fragment itself—the general uncertainty and skepticism it projects with regard to notions of totality, unity, finality, and reconciliation.[5] In a similar vein, the Hungarian philosopher Georg Lukács has referred to the fragment as the form that writing takes under conditions of "transcendental

Trial, trans. Mike Mitchell (Oxford and New York: Oxford University Press, 2011); and Franz Kafka, *The Trial: A New Translation Based on the Restored Text*, trans. Breon Mitchell (New York: Schocken, 1999).

4. Friedrich Schlegel and the Jena Romantics, for example, advocated a kind of fragmentary writing as the literary form required for any ongoing reflection on the absent absolute. For a modernist, or even deconstructivist, account of this deliberate auto-fragmentation, see Jean-Luc Nancy and Lacoue-Labarthe, *The Literary Absolute: The Theory of Literature in German Romanticism*, trans. Philip Barnard and Cheryl Lester (Albany: State University of New York Press, 1988).

5. Maurice Blanchot, "Reading Kafka," in *Twentieth Century Interpretations of* The Trial, ed. James Rolleston (Englewood Cliffs, NJ: Prentice-Hall, 1976), 16: "The principal narratives of Kafka are fragments; the totality of his works is a fragment. This lack might explain the uncertainty which makes the form and the content of their reading unstable without changing their direction. But this lack is not accidental. It is incorporated within the very sense that it mutilates; it coincides with the representation of an absence which is neither tolerated nor rejected."

homelessness."[6] The fragment is the extreme and ultra-modern antithesis of the synthesizing epic.

Suggestive as these claims may be, it should be noted that the text, although a torso and beset with editorial challenges, does in fact aim at being a fairly straightforward and tightly knit narrative. A great admirer of accomplished storytellers such as Flaubert, Dostoyevsky, Grillparzer, and Kleist, whom in September 1913 he had characterized as "my true blood-relations," Kafka wanted it, as he had done one year earlier with the manuscript of *Amerika* (*The Man Who Disappeared*), to attain narrative unity—to become a *story* with a definite narrative structure.[7] He did not deliberately leave it to posterity in its fragmented state.

The Trial is a novel, to be sure, but of what kind? How should it be approached?

From Cervantes and Fielding to Joyce and many contemporary novelists, the novel qua genre has been pervaded by the comic mode. As in classical comedy, K. is confused and challenged, and *The Trial* contains some outrageously funny (though also disturbing) scenes. However, unlike comedy, there is no resolution. Made up of what are often grotesque, dreamlike sequences (indeed, many critics have noted their affinity with nightmares), the plot follows a single, ever-present individual's confrontation with an incomprehensible order entirely beyond his control. K. meets his fate and

---

6. Georg Lukács, *The Theory of the Novel*, trans. Anna Bostock (London: Merlin, 1978), 118–119: "Compositionally speaking, a maximum of continuity is aimed at, since existence is possible only within a subjectivity that is uninterrupted by any outside factor or event; yet reality disintegrates into a series of mutually absolutely heterogeneous fragments which have no independent valency of existence even in isolation, as do the adventures of Don Quixote. All the fragments live only by the grace of the mood in which they are experienced, but the totality reveals the nothingness of this mood in terms of reflexion."

7. Franz Kafka, *Briefe an Felice und andere Korrespondenz aus Verlobungszeit*, ed. Erich Heller and Jürgen Born (Frankfurt: Fischer Verlag, 1967), 460. The translation is taken from Erich Heller, ed., *The Basic Kafka* (New York: Washington Square Press, 1979), 282.

is destroyed by it. The guilt seems to be objective. There is a tragic mismatch—an incommensurable breach—between consciousness and being, mental self-representation and the circumstances generative of objective guilt.

Unlike classical tragedy, however, there is in this novel neither tragic greatness nor any turning point and critical discovery from which true insight emerges. K. never has a clue. He asks questions (although questions are often asked *on his behalf*, reflecting his loss of autonomy) and presents demands, yet with an arrogance that, unlike that arch-tragic figure of Oedipus, is never, except possibly in the execution scene at the end, tempered by the occasion and transformed into humility.

While displaying elements of both comedy and tragedy, K.'s quest for truth, vindication, and redemption may seem to align the novel with the mystery genre. Like Joseph Conrad's *The Secret Agent*, any Raymond Chandler story, or for that matter, Kafka's two other novels, *The Trial*, tinged at times with the unbridled horror and grotesquery of the gothic tradition, is a mystery or even, as Ritchie Robertson has argued, a crime novel.[8] However, unlike the standard crime novel, it is the crime and not the supposed culprit that is unknown. Moreover, the mystery surrounding the transgression and its associated guilt is hardly of a conventional kind. Early in the story it becomes quite evident that whatever K. is claimed to be guilty of, it is neither robbery, nor assault, nor murder—the kinds of trespasses to which human law applies. *The Trial*, then, belongs to the more rare species of the *metaphysical* crime narrative, also cultivated by such authors as Edgar Allan Poe, Maurice Blanchot, and Jorge Luis Borges. As in their writings, Kafka seems to have a different and less tangible order in mind, a transcendent dimension of law that simultaneously seems both close and infinitely distant.

---

8. Robertson, *Kafka: Judaism, Politics, and Literature*, 90.

The metaphysical crime novel displays a number of character-istic features. Rather than employing a realistic setting, such novels indulge in symbolism; thus, everything in *The Trial*, including archi-tecture, dress codes, behavior, and formulations, seems pregnant with some sort of deep, yet also decisive meaning. K. finds himself in a labyrinth of signs whose significance has become lost to him and around which he does not know his way. In a space of incomprehen-sion of this kind, the psychology of the characters plays a subordi-nate role. It is not *who* Fräulein Bürstner, Leni, the lawyer, Titorelli, or Kaufmann Block is *psychologically* that matters. What matters is the role these figures play in the mysterious allegorical order of the story itself. They are, one might say, more or less indecipherable symbolic figures, existing within a larger, partly transcendent system.

As Robertson observes, the metaphysical crime novel (in this respect like film noir) tends to employ an urban environment in which slums and squalor are rendered in excruciating detail. Thus, the settings of K.'s nameless city are often shabby and stuffy. People joylessly inhabit attics with hardly any air, and office spaces reek of sweat and paint. Unlike James Joyce's *Ulysses* or Marcel Proust's *In Search of Lost Time*, in which urban surroundings at least occasion-ally promise joy and sometimes even redemption, these are spaces of decay, darkness, misery, and anxiety. In *The Trial*, they are also deeply confining: if leading anywhere, it is always into more confin-ing spaces, and never into spaces of excitement or opportunity.

In a relatively short span of both narrated and narrative time, the metaphysical crime novel presents readers with a quickly unfolding series of dramatic confrontations moving toward a climax. While driving the plot forward, these confrontations serve as stations of potential self-clarification. Ironically subverting this scheme of cog-nitive success, K. moves from one situation to the next, yet with each encounter promising an enlightenment that never occurs. Closely related to this epic of failure is the metaphysical quest itself, the way the metaphysical crime novel, rather than focusing on crime, police ingenuity, or psychology, sets up a dualistic (and sometimes gnostic) system of human and nonhuman (transcendent) orders.

As readers and critics have noted, there is undoubtedly a metaphysical backdrop to *The Trial*. However, it is not easy to identify its exact purport, let alone its function and significance within the narrative as a whole, and as Roberto Calasso argues, it may be impossible to properly distinguish the hidden, metaphysical world properly from the present, everyday world.[9] Despite their complexities, exemplary creations of European literature such as Dante's *Divine Comedy*, Milton's *Paradise Lost*, and Dostoyevsky's *Crime and Punishment* offer transparent religious narratives: the attentive and educated reader is never uncertain about how they employ Christian visions of sin, guilt, and redemption in order to weave their plots and design their characters. *The Trial*, however, while in various ways gesturing toward some sort of metaphysical horizon, seems to disallow any positive recourse to transcendence, and the operations and ultimate meaning of the transcendent or divine law remain beyond human reckoning.

What if K. simply is an innocent person being persecuted on a false pretext by an unjust system? If so, *The Trial* could perhaps be interpreted as an allegory, anticipating George Orwell's *1984*, of totalitarianism. A reading of this kind might be supported by the arrival of the guards in K.'s apartment while he is still in bed or the court's assumption that since K. has been arrested, he must be guilty—both

---

9. Roberto Calasso offers a number of fine passages regarding the "hidden world" in Kafka. See his *K.*, trans. Geoffrey Brock (New York: Vintage, 2005), 10–11: "What distinguishes both *The Trial* and *The Castle* is that, from the first line to the last, they unfold on the threshold of a hidden world that one suspects is implicit in this world. Never had that threshold been such a thin line or so ubiquitous. Never had those two worlds been brought so terrifyingly close as to seem to touch. We can't say for sure whether that hidden world is good or evil, heavenly or hellish. The only evidence is something that overwhelms and envelops us. Like K., we alternate between flashes of lucidity and bouts of torpor, sometimes mistaking one for the other, with no one having the authority to correct us."

well-known totalitarian practices. On the basis of these and other facets of the story, Bertolt Brecht, in particular, drew the conclusion that Kafka foresaw Nazism with its disrespect for the integrity of the individual and its travesty of law. Such readings are both suggestive and revealing. However, Kafka himself seems to have believed not only in the relative validity of human law (with which he worked as an insurance officer) but also in the absolute validity of a divine law. On the grounds of this latter law, both the Judaic and the Christian traditions view man as a fallen creature, guilty of the original sin of opposing God's command.[10] K. may be guilty in this more complete sense, and if so, he never stands a chance of being released from the court's grip. Indeed, the more he pronounces his innocence, the more he seems to evoke his guilt.[11] K. can admit to his guilt, but would then risk the consequences of doing so. Or, he can refuse to do so, but on his accusers' interpretation this would only demonstrate his guilt. For those living in hereditary sin, nothing seems more evident of guilt than its refusal.

Whether from a lack of knowledge or sheer arrogance, K. continues throughout the novel to be in denial. Although his execution is grisly, it may—even if hard to fathom—seem to satisfy the demands of absolute justice.[12] From the vantage point of human law, however, K.'s fate—the fate of a man who has not done anything wrong—may strike the reader as equally incomprehensible, entirely

10. For whatever they are worth in terms of approaching his narratives, Kafka's writings abound with brief entries referring to the necessary expulsion from paradise. See, for example, Franz Kafka, *Aphorisms*, trans. Willa Muir, Edwin Muir, and Michael Hofmann (New York: Schocken, 2015), 83: "We were created to live in Paradise, and Paradise was designed to serve us. Our designation has been changed; we are not told whether this has happened to Paradise as well."

11. For a complete rejection of the traditional emphasis on guilt in Kafka, see Gilles Deleuze and Félix Guattari, *Kafka: Toward a Minor Literature*, trans. Dana Polan (Minneapolis and Oxford: University of Minnesota Press, 1986).

12. Ingeborg Henel, "The Legend of the Doorkeeper and Its Significance for Kafka's *Trial*," in Rolleston, *Twentieth Century Interpretations of* The Trial, 50: "To . . . God there is no

unjustified—allegorical, perhaps, of human finitude as such, our life-long condemnation to death.

While conceptions of divine and human law structure many readings of *The Trial*, the themes of persecution, inscrutable authority, guilt, and sacrifice have led many critics to view the novel in psychoanalytic terms. Several of his other writings, including *Letter to the Father* and "The Judgment," indicate that Kafka harbored a deep resentment toward his own father. According to Sigmund Freud, resentment of this kind should be viewed in terms of the Oedipal complex, with its fear and hatred of the fatherly figure, its fantasy of rebellion, and its sense of guilt as the son eventually internalizes the paternal law. In *The Trial* there is no biological father. However, there are many paternal figures—*ersatz* fathers—and perhaps the whole court should be viewed as some sort of projection of K.'s paternally structured psyche.

The women in the novel play a different role. Rather than figures of potential persecution, at least some of them appear to promise a more anarchic relationship to desire than the men. Leni, for example, or the unruly girls in Titorelli's building, are highly sexual beings, difficult for K. to understand and undoubtedly belonging to the court, yet suggestive of a psychic economy different from that of aggression, repression, and guilt. In the first scene with Leni, the most overtly Oedipal one of the whole novel, K. begins an affair with the mistress of the one attorney who could conceivably have helped him. While passionate, it is both brief and wholly irrational. As a result, he ends up alienating three powerful father figures: Huld, his uncle Karl, and the Chief Clerk of the court.

relationship except that of antithesis and insuperable separation, which is expressed in human consciousness of guilt. Consciousness of guilt, then, must not be interpreted psychologically in Kafka, but must be understood in its central religious significance. Just as Kierkegaard declares that the human bond with God is repentance, so Kafka sees the only path to the 'law' or the 'highest judge' in the acknowledgment of guilt."

Every attempt to bring clarity and closure to his case takes K. one step closer to death. In psychoanalytic theory, we are never innocent but always entangled in a web of relations whose control over us can never be fully revealed.

LIFE AND WRITING

As already indicated, Max Brod's influence on Kafka's posterior reputation can hardly be exaggerated. Brod, whom Kafka met at the university, prefaced and edited substantial parts of his literary output and published both a biography and several larger works of interpretation and scholarship. Along with Gustav Janouch, whose 1951 *Gespräche mit Kafka* purported to offer an authentic view of the writer's thinking and intellectual commitments, Brod is largely responsible for the attribution of a *religious* persona to Kafka. The image we have of Kafka, Milan Kundera claims, is for this reason largely religious: it is the image of *der religiöse Denker*.[13]

Is this image adequate?

In strict biographical terms, the impact of Judaism on Kafka seems to have been vast and multifaceted. While somewhat alienated from their conventional middle-class values, Kafka grew up with Jewish parents, was taken to the synagogue, celebrated bar mitzvah, and later, as he settled into his life as a Prague insurance officer, developed a profound interest in Zionism, Yiddish culture and literature, and from Hasidic sources, the body of Jewish mystical thought called the Kabbalah. However, Kafka displayed an equally strong attraction to classical German culture and revered the writings of Goethe and

13. See Gustav Janouch, *Gespräche mit Kafka* (Frankfurt: Fischer Verlag, 1968); and Milan Kundera, *Les testaments trahis* (Paris: Gallimard, 1993), 55. For Brod's contribution, see in particular Max Brod, *Über Franz Kafka* (Frankfurt: Fischer Verlag, 1966).

Kleist.[14] It is true that Prague had gone through periods of aggressive anti-Semitism, and discrimination was rife. Yet in terms of education and cultural orientation, Kafka was fully assimilated into its German environment.[15] Indeed, since as early as the tenth century there had been Jews in this city, and from the eighteenth century on, they accounted for about a fourth of its population.

Until the end of the First World War, Prague belonged to the Kingdom of Bohemia, itself part of the vast and culturally complex Austrian-Hungarian Empire. Kafka's parents, Hermann and Julie, spoke a variety of German influenced by Yiddish. In addition to mastering German, Kafka communicated in Czech, knew quite a lot of Hebrew, and had studied Latin, Greek, and enough French to read Flaubert in the original. It is impossible to overestimate the impact that his studies and his extensive cultural interests had on him. Kafka was a ferocious reader, widely versed not only in European literature and philosophy but in law, science, art, technology, and politics as well. This in itself suggests that Brod's theological approach may have been too narrow.

If the image of *der religiöse Denker* must be qualified in light of the deeply cosmopolitan nature of Kafka's mind, then so must the equally well-known image (also solicited by Brod) of the desperately secluded writer be tempered by what is now known of his social and political activities. Kafka frequently refers to the solitude of his nightly writing sessions as uniquely fulfilling, the only possible passage to an authentic life. Placing him before a supreme tribunal and making possible an almost complete sense of self-oblivion, he describes them as tinged with a strong redemptive quality. He did, no

---

14. See Brod, *Über Franz Kafka*, 108: "Kafka mit Andacht über Goethe spechen zu hören,—das war etwas ganz Besonderes; es war, als spreche ein Kind von seinem Ahnherrn, der in glücklicheren, reineren Zeiten und in unmittelbarer Berührung mit dem Göttlichen gelebt habe."
15. In both 1897 and 1920, there were major anti-Semitic riots in Prague.

doubt, as Stanley Corngold emphasizes, seek to arrange his adult life such as to be able to devote himself as much as possible to writing.[16] However, Kafka also led a fairly active public life. He met with other writers (among them Franz Werfel and Hugo von Hofmannsthal) and publishers, traveled quite frequently, and took a strong interest in theater (in particular, the local Yiddish theater) and politics—in addition, of course, to performing his many professional duties as an insurance officer. While hardly an activist, Kafka was a Zionist and a socialist.

Scholars often remark on Kafka's bachelor existence. Although, in one biographer's view, "there was nothing he wanted more than to marry and have a family,"[17] his numerous relationships—with Felice Bauer, in particular, to whom he was twice engaged, and later with Milena Jesenská and Dora Diamant—never resulted in marriage. Despite their relative brevity, these relationships seem to have played a very important role in Kafka's life, impacting him not only romantically and erotically but also artistically. In part because the writing of *The Trial* took place in the aftermath of the first, turbulent ending of the relationship with Felice on July 23, 1914, a number of interpreters claim to have found close connections between this event and the novel itself. The guilt Kafka seems to have felt about the termination of the relationship, as well as the fear he appears to have had of a life in conformity with the kinds of petit-bourgeois, anti-literary expectations he had grown up with, may suggest a link between Kafka himself

---

16. Corngold, *Franz Kafka: The Necessity of Form*, 6: "[Kafka's] real life, it seems, has no other story to tell than the search for circumstances propitious for the leap out of it into the uncanny world of writing."

17. Ronald Hayman, *K: A Biography of Kafka* (London: George Weidenfeld and Nicolson, 1981), 121. Judging from his stormy relationship with Felice Bauer, and his reluctance to accept her desire for a settled bourgeois existence, one may feel that Hayman is going too far. Throughout his adult life, there seems to have been nothing Kafka wanted more than to write, and compared to that all other activities and commitments, while not without importance, seem to have taken second place.

and K., and possibly also between Felice and the novel's Fräulein Bürstner.[18] Perhaps, as Walter Sokel argues, the novel ultimately is a punishment fantasy.[19] Just as biographically oriented, yet with a different conclusion, Corngold, on the other hand, claims that Kafka, by means of "a scriptive suspension of the ethical,"[20] tried to establish distance and perhaps even indifference to Felice. Writing, Corngold suggests, became a kind of sacrificial act whereby the writer not only attained distance from experience but also managed to justify it.[21]

Throughout most of his adult life, Kafka struggled with health problems. The tuberculosis that would kill him on June 3, 1924, was diagnosed as early as 1917 when, for the first time, he spat blood. His final story, "Josephine the Singer, or the Mouse Folk," written in March 1924, presents the reader with a singing artist-mouse, Josephine, whose actual performance amounts to no more than a weak squeaking. At the end of the story, Josephine disappears and dies, leaving the narrator to ponder the weakness of memory when confronted with the destructive movement of history.

THE MODERNIST LEGACY

Like the central writings of Samuel Beckett, James Joyce, Marcel Proust, Robert Musil, and Hermann Broch, *The Trial* is frequently

---

18. See Hartmut Binder, *Kommentar zu den Romanen, Rezensionen, Aphorismen und zum Brief and den Vater* (Munich: Winkler, 1976), 187.
19. Walter Sokel, *Franz Kafka: Tragik und Ironie* (Frankfurt: Fischer Verlag, 1976), 140. For a fascinating biographical interpretation of the correspondence with Felice Bauer, see Elias Canetti, *Der andere Prozeß: Kafkas Brief an Felice* (Munich: Hanser Verlag, 1969).
20. Corngold, *Franz Kafka: The Necessity of Form*, 231.
21. Corngold, *Franz Kafka*, 295: "My understanding of Kafka's fiction is of an enterprise that aims to engage to the limit the being wholly centered on writing, whose mode is, in Kafka's word, *Schriftstellersein*, existence as a writer." The writer literally writes himself into existence.

referred to as belonging to a high modernist canon of European literature. On some views, modernism is simply the name for a writing of alienation in which literature aspires to explore the very conditions of sense-making in a world that has lost all sources of symbolic authority. Related more specifically to such views one frequently finds sociological claims about the transition from *Gemeinschaft* to *Gesellschaft*, from tightly knit communities to anonymous, atomized mass societies, and philosophical claims about nihilism, the forgetfulness of Being, the subjectivization of all value, and an onset of skepticism and uncertainty in all areas of human engagement. Much modernist writing thus displays skepticism about meaning in general; indeed, even ordinary language itself is at times considered to be potentially nonreferential, calling for an understanding of how words can be employed both to express the condition of nonreferentiality and to stake out new routes for achieving reference and intelligibility. According to some critics, modernism is the form writing takes when the dispossession of man in a cosmic scheme has become culturally available as a mere fact.[22] Ideally, the modernist writer wants more than to tell a story or construct a poem; he or she desires a new language, capable of retrieving or reinventing those deep layers of intelligibility otherwise lost in a nihilistic, skeptical modernity. In most cases, this project remains purely negative. The writer keeps circling

---

22. Irwing Howe, "The Culture of Modernism," in *Modernism: Critical Concepts in Literary and Cultural Studies*, vol. III: 1971–1984, ed. Tim Middleton (London and New York: Routledge, 2003), 26: "For the modernist writer the universe is a speechless presence, neither hospitable nor hostile; and after a time he does not agonize, as did nineteenth-century writers like Hardy, over the dispossession of man in the cosmic scheme. He takes that dispossession for granted and turns his anxieties inward, toward the dispossession of meaning from inner life. Whatever spiritual signs he hears come from within his own imaginative resources and are accepted pragmatically as psychic events. Romanticism is, among other things, an effort to maintain a transcendent perspective precisely as or because the transcendent objects of worship are being withdrawn; modernism follows upon the breakdown of this effort."

around a void, gesturing or falling silent rather than making straightforward claims or attempting to express or articulate.

One may find that writers such as Beckett and Paul Celan fit this latter characterization better than Kafka. After all, Kafka was mainly a *storyteller*, and his language, while at times formal and somewhat drained of emotion, gives the impression of being both extremely precise and versatile. He did not seem to have seen the need to conduct *experiments* with language.

Perhaps a better way to approach the modernism of Kafka would be via his general suspension of meaning. Nothing in a Kafka story seems to be what it purports to be: meaning is always deferred or displaced, and the reader is forced to search for a truth that appears wholly recalcitrant to representation. K. finds himself in a topsy-turvy world in which a judge's book of laws contains pornography, Leni turns out to have an amphibious hand, sadomasochistic scenes of torture take place right next to his office, and a "quite depraved," hunchbacked, thirteen-year-old girl is whirling round in the painter Titorelli's hand. Who are these people? Who are they *really*? The answers to these questions seem forever to elude the reader.

The overwhelming strangeness of this novel suggests that straightforward, thematic interpretations should be resisted. Whatever meaning may be assigned to the story as a whole must be related to its form and not simply to its content. Thus, according to Theodor W. Adorno's modernist account, *The Trial*, mediated by its form, unfolds a kind of cryptic commentary on the state of modernity itself, and how it presumably condemns us to an estranged existence, as all objects as well as agents are commodified.[23] Rather than expressing

23. Theodor W. Adorno, *Prisms*, trans. Samuel and Shierry Weber (Cambridge, MA: MIT Press, 1997), 255: "The crucial moment towards which everything in Kafka is directed, is that in which men become aware that they are not themselves—that they themselves are things." See also Adorno's comment on *The Trial* on p. 256: "It is the cryptogram of capitalism's highly polished, glittering late phase, which he excludes in order to define it all the more precisely in its negative."

a theoretical pronouncement on this condition, it allows its readers to experience, and identify with, the suffering associated with such alienation. Owing, moreover, to the detached tone of its prose, it counteracts the potential for empathy, the very existence of which would intimate the possibility of some sort of meaningful response to the state of the world. Instead, it utilizes its own devices of alienation, including not only its somewhat formal and regimented rhetoric (drawn in part from the legal domain) but also various types of shock and surreal moments of narrative interruption. The text tests, as it were, its own capacity for generating meaning. In a world devoid of meaning, it is not obvious that a literary text can be "meaningful." Its meaning, if available, must be constituted below the textual surface.

A different notion of literary modernism stems from phenomenology. Central to phenomenological reflection is the view that at least some literary texts are capable of truthfully disclosing the world to us—in particular, how it matters to us and comes to harbor significance. They do this not primarily by stating facts. Rather, they start from a knowing subject and try to account for the experience this subject has when generalized to become exemplary of all subjects. With reference to K.'s tribulations, *The Trial* discloses for us the relevant phenomena as they appear, thereby mercilessly dissecting what it is to experience the world in which we live. This is different from claiming that its meaning can be paraphrased. On the phenomenological view, disclosive truth is available only to those who painstakingly work their way through the text with a view to accounting for every single detail and how it interacts with, and helps to articulate, the text as a whole.[24]

24. For an example of phenomenological criticism, see Hans-Georg Gadamer's readings of Paul Celan in Hans-Georg Gadamer, *Gadamer on Celan: "Who Am I and Who Are You?" and Other Essays*, trans. Richard Heinemann and Bruce Krajewski (Albany: State University of New York Press, 1997).

Yet another influential understanding of what it means to say that a literary text is modernistic has its origin in ordinary language philosophy. The sustaining idea here is that meaningful speech is socially conditioned, dependent for its intelligibility on its use within a necessary yet fragile framework of normatively structured expectations as to the propriety of particular moves and strategies. On this view, the writer, critic, and philosopher are united in their endeavors to return words to the ordinary. Of course, while the language in *The Trial* seems straightforward, a closer analysis reveals a deep emptiness. Words such as "guilty," "justice," "punishment," and "law" are employed without any clear meaning, reference, or context; and no one seems to stand behind what they say and take responsibility for their own words by revealing to K. the real conditions of their use.[25] When he is informed by Titorelli, for example, about the various possible outcomes of his case, it is impossible to make out what it is that could make Titorelli's assertions rationally acceptable. Titorelli's words, as Ludwig Wittgenstein would put it, are idling: there is in this world of generalized skepticism no "friction."[26]

The contributors to this volume come from different yet mutually informing schools of literary and philosophical reflection, including those already mentioned. My own contribution explores the Wittgensteinian approach that I just outlined. Peter E. Gordon, Gerhard Richter, Iain Macdonald, and Elizabeth S. Goodstein, on the other hand, all draw on and discuss the writings of Adorno and Walter Benjamin, both of whom view Kafka's texts within a constellation of social-theoretic, theological, hermetic, and philosophical elements. Kafka becomes the critical modernist of a modernity that

---

25. In *The Claim of Reason: Wittgenstein, Skepticism, Morality, and Tragedy* (Oxford and New York: Oxford University Press, 1979), 337–338, Stanley Cavell applies such ideas of emptiness and idling to Kafka's "A Hunger Artist."

26. Ludwig Wittgenstein, *Philosophical Investigations*, trans. G. E. M. Anscombe, P. M. S. Hacker, and Joachim Schulte (Oxford: Wiley-Blackwell, 2009), §109.

has gone off the track. Gordon takes this approach in the direction of the question of transcendence, uncovering in Kafka an "inverse theology" different from, yet also more radical than, negative theology. With reference to Adorno and Giorgio Agamben, Richter, moreover, explores how meaning becomes dispersed in Kafka's refractory texts. Macdonald, on the other hand, looks at *The Trial* in the light of the concept of alienation, arguing that Kafka holds up for us a world—the modern world—that, in its estrangement, seems to hold no promise whatsoever. Its potentials for change, while undeniable, have been forsaken. A similar experience of modernity is central to Goodstein, who analyzes Kafka and his various shots at modernist myth-making from the vantage point mainly of Benjamin's work. While insisting on the modernity theme and the need to situate literary texts in their historical context of emergence, Anne Fuchs explores the temporal regime of *The Trial*. Can Kafka help us to disclose the temporality of modern life—and perhaps also point to its dissatisfactions and reveal modes of resistance? Consulting Kafka's notes as an insurance officer, Howard Caygill, moreover, finds new ways of thinking about transcendence. There is the vertical (Platonic) transcendence of the law. However, there is also a horizontal transcendence of repetition, promising opposition to the law. John Gibson asks: What is it for literature to have an ethical character? Although in ways rarely understood in the philosophical literature, which too often concentrates on representational content while neglecting its oblique, more indirect dimension, *The Trial*, he argues, is a deeply ethical text. Focusing on the famous parable of the doorkeeper and investigating it with the care of a phenomenologist or ordinary language philosopher, Fred Rush, finally, pleads for a reading that emphasizes the unfathomable yet universal demand of the law.

Uniting all the essays of this volume is an insistence on the continued importance of *The Trial*. By inviting and sustaining different methodological approaches, the contributors all find that this novel may help us to elucidate such issues as the fate of human subjectivity in modernity; the relationships between law, guilt, and subjectification; and the nature of literary discourse and its capacity to disclose essential features of human reality.

The Trial has exerted a tremendous impact on subsequent European and American fiction. Jean-Paul Sartre, Maurice Blanchot, and Alain Robbe-Grillet all tried their hands at the metaphysical *récit*, and novelists such as Don DeLillo, David Foster Wallace, and Thomas Pynchon have rehearsed Kafkaesque paranoia in postmodern garb. With their intense and surreal sense of individual resignation in the face of vast, anonymous structures, Pynchon's early works—*V, The Crying of Lot 49,* and *Gravity's Rainbow*—vividly demonstrate how Kafka's fears and sensibilities may successfully be transplanted into radically different settings.

In film, the legacy of Kafka is perhaps even more overt. The great modernist *auteurs*—Michelangelo Antonioni, Ingmar Bergman, and Robert Bresson—have created their own Kafkaesque universes, and the same is true of contemporary directors such as Lars von Trier, the Coen brothers, and Paul Thomas Anderson. While issues of guilt and alienation may not structure the Western psyche the way they seem to have done during the waning days of the European bourgeoisie when Kafka wrote his stories, the need for works of art that deal authentically with the most traumatic and fundamental features of modern psychic life is not likely to go away. Kafka was in many ways the most iconic writer of the twentieth century. As we return to him, he becomes our contemporary as well.

Chapter 1

Kafka's Inverse Theology

PETER E. GORDON

In what follows, I raise some questions about the status of religion in *The Trial*. Specifically, I explore the contrast between two distinctive modes of religion: the first is identified as "negative theology," and the second as "inverse theology." I suggest that the peculiar pathos of hopelessness in Kafka's novel is due chiefly to the way it *inverts* the religious longing for God, rather than merely affirming God's transcendent otherness in the conventional manner of negative theology. To explain this contrast in greater detail, I begin with some remarks on interpretations developed by Walter Benjamin, Gershom Scholem, and Theodor W. Adorno.

In a July 9, 1934, letter to his friend Walter Benjamin, the historian of Jewish mysticism Gershom Scholem mentions a "theological didactic poem" that he had written as a commentary on Kafka's novel *The Trial*.[1] Scholem had originally composed the poem for Robert Weltsch, the Prague-born journalist who grew up in the same circle

---

1. For comments and critical suggestions on this essay, I am deeply grateful to Judith Ryan and Espen Hammer. All deficiencies herein are naturally my own responsibility.

of German-speaking Jews as Max Brod and Franz Kafka.[2] The poem, which Scholem reproduces in his letter to Benjamin, reads as follows:

> Your trial began on earth.
> Does it end before your throne?
> You cannot be defended,
> As no illusion holds true here.
> Who is the accused here?
> The Creature or yourself?
> If anyone should ask you,
> You would sink into silence.
> Can such a question be raised?
> Is the answer indefinite?
> Oh, we must live all the same
> Until your court examines us.[3]

What first strikes us about this remarkable poem is its personal tone: it is composed as if it were directly addressed to God. The pronoun *Du* not only signals the intimate character of the appeal, it also repeats the conventional grammar of German-language liturgy (in which the supplicant speaks to God as *Du*—that is, without the straitened formalism of the pronoun *Sie*). Although Scholem resorts to traditional accouterments of divine majesty with references such as "your throne" and "your court," the poem's overall register could

2. Gershom Scholem, ed., *The Correspondence of Walter Benjamin and Gershom Scholem, 1932–1940*, ed. Gary Smith and Andre Lefevre (New York: Schocken, 1989). Letter 57, Scholem to Benjamin (July 9, 1934), 122–125, quote from 122–123.

3. "Dein Prozeß begann auf Erden; / endet er vor deinem Thron? / Du kannst nicht verteidigt werden, / Hier gilt keine Illusion. / Wer ist hier der Angeklagte?/ Du oder die Kreatur? / Wenn dich einer drum befragte, / du versänkst in Schweigen nur. / Kann solche Frage sich erheben? / Ist die Antwort unbestimmt? / Ach, wir müssen dennoch leben, / Bis uns dein Gericht vernimmt." Quoted from *The Correspondence of Walter Benjamin and Gershom Scholem, 1932–1940* (Letter 57), 124–125.

hardly be mistaken for a prayer. The speaker in the poem lacks a specified identity: we do not know if it is Kafka himself or, as seems likely,
the protagonist of his novel, Josef K. The speaker addresses himself
to God with the same bold manner that Josef K. adopts toward the
judicial system: "Who is the accused here?" he asked, "The Creature
or yourself?" The speaker doubts that God would respond to such a
challenge ("If anyone should ask you, / You would sink into silence"),
and he suspects that the question may be impermissible or may simply lack a satisfactory answer. Like the protagonist in *The Trial*, the
poem oscillates in its moods between righteous anger ("You cannot
be defended") and abject despair ("Oh, we must live all the same /
Until your court examines us"). Most striking of all is the speaker's
readiness to turn the judicial examination against the divine. The
ambiguous phrase "Your trial" (*Dein Prozeß*) raises an unresolved
question as to who is on trial and who sits in judgment. The poem
reads less like a prayer than an accusation.

Scholem's poem about *The Trial* invites us to confront anew the
status of theology in Kafka's novel.[4] The suggestion that theological
meaning, either cryptic or overt, might serve as a key for unlocking the mysteries of this always mysterious text is an old chestnut in
the critical literature on Kafka.[5] But it has often drawn fierce criticism, not least from Scholem himself, who wrote disparagingly

4. See also the detailed analysis by Sigrid Weigel, "Jewish Thinking in a World Without
God: Benjamin's Readings of Kafka as a Critique of Christian and Jewish Theologoumena,"
in *Walter Benjamin: Images, the Creaturely, and the Holy*, especially chapter 6, trans. Chadwick
Truscott Smith (Stanford: Stanford University Press, 2013), 130–163.
5. See, e.g., Ernst Pawel's suggestion that *The Trial* represents a "tension between faith and rea-
son" that lies "at the heart of the Jewish tradition." Ernst Pawel, *The Nightmare of Reason: A
Life of Franz Kafka* (New York: Vintage, 1985), 323. Recent interpretation has especially
focused on Kafka's relationship to Judaism and to Jewish culture in Prague. See, e.g., Sander
L. Gilman, *Franz Kafka: The Jewish Patient* (New York: Routledge, 1995); Ritchie Robertson,
Kafka: Judaism, Politics, and Literature (Oxford: Clarendon, 1985); and Evelyn Torton Beck,
Kafka and the Yiddish Theater: Its Impact on His Work (Madison: University of Wisconsin
Press, 1971).

of Kafka's "theological" interpreters. In his response to Benjamin, Scholem explicitly distances himself from what he calls their "somewhat harmless-idiotic theological quotations." Foremost among such interpreters was Max Brod, Kafka's friend and literary executor, who collaborated with the conservative Jewish nationalist writer Hans-Joachim Schoeps to edit the German-language collection of Kafka's short stories, *Beim Bau der Chineschischen Mauer*, first published in 1931.[6] In their co-authored afterword, Brod and Schoeps insisted on the religious significance of Kafka's universe, anticipating the far more elaborate theological interpretation of his friend's oeuvre that Brod would present in his highly personalized (and frequently disparaged) 1937 biography.[7]

In an exemplary passage from his biography, Brod assigned special importance to "the hopeful side" of his friend's work. He hastened to note that "this attitude of Kafka's is only an occasional flash, and that passages which describe man as powerless crowd in on the reader in an overwhelming majority." But he nonetheless insisted that "the propositions of freedom and hope *are there too!*" In Brod's opinion, such rare and unexpected moments affirm that Kafka's writing "rejoices in activity," that it draws sustenance from the appealing idea "that man, with his spark of reason, will, and ethical perception is not altogether the plaything of super-mighty powers, who judge according to other laws than his, which he does not understand and never can understand, faced with which he is lost, and only thrown unconditionally on God's mercy." Brod of course knew that this interpretation would encounter resistance, but he insisted on its absolute veracity even in the face of counterevidence. The "proposition" that

6. Max Brod and Hans Joachim Schoeps, "Nachwort," in Kafka, *Beim Bau der Chinesischen Mauer* (Berlin: Gustav Kiepeneuer Verlag, 1931); reprinted in Kafka, *The Great Wall of China: Stories and Reflections*, trans. Wila and Edwin Muir (New York: Schocken, 1946).

7. Max Brod, *Franz Kafka: eine Biographie* (1937); in English as Max Brod, *Franz Kafka: A Biography* (New York: Schocken, 1947), 171–172.

humanity has justified ground for hope may appear only with great rarity in Kafka's writing, he admitted, but its infrequency is no reason to deny its significance. Even "if only *one* such proposition is found," Brod reasoned, "in a religious thinker, it has the remarkable quality of decisively changing the whole picture of him." This argument led Brod to the remarkable conclusion that his friend may have sustained a personal faith in God and that this faith, like hope wrested from hopelessness, formed the "kernel" of what was "best and most characteristic" in Kafka's writing:

> *Just because the dispositions to faith were won from such a radical skepticism, they are in their truthfulness, refined by the ultimate tests, infinitely valuable, and powerful.* "Man cannot live without a permanent faith in something indestructible in himself," says Kafka. And adds, "At the same time this indestructible part and his faith in it may remain permanently concealed from him." Very significant is the following minor proposition which rejects the theism of the ordinary religious observance: "One of the forms in which this concealment may be expressed is the belief in a personal God."[8]

Brod's suggestion that his friend's work drew consolation from the unlikely persistence of some sort of personal religious faith has few advocates today. Critics such as Benjamin and Adorno have expressed their skepticism with special vehemence, and Scholem, too, declared himself immune to such interpretive trends. And yet Scholem could not share what he considered Benjamin's exaggerated hostility to the theological dimension in Kafka's universe. "I am still firmly convinced," he wrote, "that a theological aspect of this world, in which God does not appear, is the most legitimate of such

8. Max Brod, *Franz Kafka: A Biography*, 171–172.

interpretations." Benjamin's own interpretation of Kafka had gone too far, Scholem wrote, in promoting a wholesale "elimination of theology." This was an error that amounted to "throwing the baby out with the bathwater."[9]

Contestation over the legitimacy of a theological interpretation of Kafka's work will no doubt persist so long as there are readers who read it. In what follows I pursue one such line of interpretation, prompted by Scholem's paradoxical suggestion that, even if we resist attributing an overt religious faith to its author, we might identify a theological aspect to *The Trial* if we attend to the fact that it is a novel in which *God does not appear*. For Scholem, the simple fact of God's *absence* from the novel should not tempt us to conclude that the novel lacks all theological significance. For we cannot ignore the possibility that it is precisely the fact of God's *non*appearance that lends the novel its singular power. But even this idea does not capture the unusual sense of hopelessness and fatalism that pervades *The Trial* from beginning to end. For it is hard to avoid the impression that in Kafka's novel theology survives, if it survives at all, only as a memory-trace of once-living belief. What Scholem called its "theological aspect" still ascribes to the novel an unlikely persistence of a metaphysical God, even if it is a God who has grown remote or ineffective. Here, Scholem's interpretation runs into considerable difficulties. We must ask ourselves: At what point does divine *nonappearance* turn into thoroughgoing *absence*? Or, to put the matter another way: When should the striking *inefficacy* of anything like theism in Kafka's universe force us to conclude that God has moved irrevocably beyond the vanishing point, leaving behind merely the sense of something that has departed and an atmosphere of loss?

---

9. *The Correspondence of Walter Benjamin and Gershom Scholem, 1932–1940.* Letter 57 (July 9, 1934), 122–125, quote from 122–123.

These questions serve as an overture to the following medita-
tions on the vexed question of theology in Kafka's novel. In this
essay, I explore the contrast between Scholem's notion of God's nonappearance and a rather different interpretation first introduced by
the philosopher and social theorist Theodor W. Adorno, who attributed to Kafka's writings a highly unusual theologico-philosophical
orientation that he called "inverse theology." I suggest that in reading's Kafka's novel, we should keep in mind the distinction between
Scholem's model of a *negative* theology and an *inverse* theology in
Adorno's sense. This distinction is helpful chiefly because *The Trial*
occupies an uncertain middle ground *between* negative theology and
inverse theology, between theism and atheism, between hopeful-
ness and mourning. For even if Scholem is correct to suggest that the
novel is a meditation on God's nonappearance, it is no less true that
over the course of the novel the very fact of God's nonappearance
deepens the reader's sense that theism loses all metaphysical content
and becomes only a critical device by which to illumine the world's
unredeemed—and possibly irredeemable—condition.

A PARABLE OF IMPENETRABILITY

To understand what Adorno meant by an "inverse theology" and
how the term might serve as an apt characterization of Kafka's work,
we might begin by examining a letter that Adorno sent to Benjamin
on December 17, 1934. That same month, Benjamin had published
an essay in the *Jüdische Rundschau* in which he offered reflections on
the occasion of the tenth anniversary of Kafka's death.[10] Commenting

10. Walter Benjamin, "Franz Kafka: On the Tenth Anniversary of his Death" in *Illuminations*,
trans. Harry Zohn (New York: Schocken, 1969), 111–140. Originally published as "Franz
Kafka. Eine Würdigung," *Jüdische Rundschau*, December 21, 1934, and December 28, 1934.

briefly on the question of hope in Kafka's world, Benjamin proposed a contrast between the hopelessness of the accused and the hope that is typically reserved for marginal characters such as assistants or administrators: "From *The Trial*," Benjamin wrote, "it may be seen that these proceedings usually are hopeless for those accused— hopeless even when they have hopes of being acquitted. It may be this hopelessness that brings out the beauty in them—the only creatures in Kafka thus favored." Just why Benjamin might have associated the hopelessness of Josef K.'s predicament with anything like an enhanced beauty is a question that remains hard to fathom, but it does not deter his inquiry into the status of hope in the novel. Benjamin recalled a conversation between Kafka and his friend Max Brod concerning "present-day Europe and the decline of the human race."

> "We are nihilistic thought, suicidal thought that come into God's head," Kafka said. This reminded me at first of the Gnostic view of life: God as the evil demiurge, the world as his Fall. "Oh no," said Kafka, "our world is only a bad mood of God, a bad day of his." "Then there is hope outside this manifestation of the world that we know." He smiled. "Oh, plenty of hope, an infinite amount of hope—but not for us."[11]

This exchange motivates the thought that salvation in Kafka's world always lies elsewhere than in the main sphere of action. Hope is always on the other side of a door, or at the other end of a telephone; but we are rarely permitted even the most oblique glimpse of its reality. Nor could such hope in its painful remoteness offer genuine consolation for the central protagonist of the tale, who is condemned to oscillate between anger at the injustice of his own situation and longing for the peace others alone appear to enjoy but which he alone (or those of his station or kind) has been denied. Benjamin observed that such thoroughgoing hopelessness afflicts even the animals in Kafka's universe along with those "hybrids or imaginary creatures" (such as Gregor Samsa, the "Cat Lamb," and Odradek) who exist in a twilight space of uncanny domesticity and endure only so long as they remain "under the spell of the family." The sense of sheer fatalism that otherwise suffuses Kafka's tales leaves hope intact (if at all) only for the "assistants," those exceptional and marginal agents who have "escaped from the family circle."[12]

It is at this point that theology first makes its appearance. The overwhelming feeling that judgment emanates from an unapproachable *elsewhere* prompted Benjamin to cite Kafka's conversation with Brod, since it is Kafka's friend who wishes to explain this feeling of hopelessness and remote judgment by raising a religious analogy, the Gnostic distinction between the absent God and the fallen world. Against this rather edifying analogy Kafka offered a humorous retort: "Oh no, . . . our world is only a bad mood of God, a bad day." Clutching at solace no matter how small, Brod hastens to derive the optimistic lesson that "there is hope outside this manifestation of the world that we know." But Kafka dismisses even this qualified optimism: "Oh, plenty of hope, an infinite amount of hope—but not for us." Although the distinctively theological register of this conversation does not figure into Benjamin's own interpretation, it reinforces the essential distinction in Kafka's *Trial,* as in all his writings, between those who are locked into a world without salvation and those who figure as emissaries from a salvific beyond. In *The Trial,* even such messengers are likewise tainted by their official status as agents of the court. They do not, and perhaps *cannot*, comprehend the source of their own authority. According to court usage the lawyers are ranked, and they extend upward from the "unregistered" to

12. Benjamin, "Franz Kafka," 116.

the "petty lawyers" and finally to the "great lawyers" who exist as if in an inaccessible realm:

> "The great lawyers?" asked K. "Who are they? How do you approach them?" "So you've never heard of them?" said the corn merchant. "There's hardly a defendant who, once he's heard of them, doesn't dream of them for a while. But don't be tempted. I don't know who the great lawyers are, and I presume you can't get to them. I know of no case where it can be said for certain that they took part."[13]

Such gradations of social power seem to invite theological comparison, though one could argue that any such allusion to a hidden God serves only to enhance the mood of absolute fatalism that seizes all those who bid for admission to the higher orders of the law. The question we must ask ourselves is why such hopelessness should assume a distinctively theological character.

Upon reading Benjamin's Kafka essay, Adorno wrote to Benjamin in the December 17, 1934, letter with a declaration concerning "our agreement in philosophical fundamentals." Alluding to his own (no longer extant) interpretation of Kafka, Adorno writes that: "[Kafka] represents a photograph of our earthly life from the perspective of a redeemed life." Not unlike Kafka himself, Adorno resists the temptation to construe redemption as a stable *locus* or *vantage* from which one might gaze down in safety upon the unredeemed world. Instead, redemption appears only as a negative to our unredeemed condition, or in Adorno's intriguing simile, it appears only as "an edge of black cloth" that is draped over the "obliquely angled" apparatus of a traditional camera, through which one can view "the terrifyingly distanced optics of the photographic image." The logic of this analogy

13. Kafka, *The Trial*, 128.

has a twofold significance: first, it depends on the increasingly unfamiliar technique of a photographic negative in which light and dark are reversed; second, it suggests that redemption itself cannot appear within the optical frame—it serves merely as the *condition* by which the terror and hopelessness of the unredeemed world is brought into view.[14]

If this perspective qualifies as theological at all, we should not permit ourselves to exaggerate its metaphysical or doctrinal status as if it somehow implied the persistence of an actual divinity or divine realm. Not only does Adorno reject the proposal that redemption manifests itself directly *within* the bounds of human experience (that is, within the optical frame), he also seems to disallow even the minimalist consolation that redemption might qualify as a reality that lies *beyond* our experience or in some precinct *elsewhere-than-here* (a doctrine which Max Brod associated with Gnosticism).[15] According to Adorno, Kafka's world owes its critical power not to a theology in any conventional sense but, rather, to what he identifies as an "'inverse' theology." (In the German original of the letter, Adorno places the term *inverse* in quotation marks, thus: *"inverse" Theologie*.) Just what Adorno intends with this curious term becomes somewhat more intelligible when he remarks on the fact that his own book on Kierkegaard (originally submitted to Paul Tillich as his habilitation and first published in 1933) was essentially a study in inverse theology. But Adorno hastens to explain that his own interest in the connection between Kafka and Kierkegaard does not betray any hidden affinity with dialectical theology.[16] For unlike dialectical theologians

14. In Kafka's texts, Adorno claims, "the wounds with which society brands the individual are seen by the latter as ciphers of the social untruth, as the negative of truth." Adorno, "Notes on Kafka," 252.

15. On the importance of Gnostic themes in Kafka, see especially Stanley Corngold, *Lambent Traces: Franz Kafka* (Princeton, NJ, and Oxford: Princeton University Press, 2004), especially chap. 5, pp. 104, 108, and *passim*.

16. "But if I nonetheless still insist upon a relationship between Kafka and Kierkegaard, then it is decidedly not that espoused by dialectical theology, the representative example of

(such as Schoeps), Adorno conceives of Kafka's inverse theology as "directed against natural and supernatural interpretation alike."[17] The inverse theology found in Kafka's writing does not affirm but, rather, *vanquishes* hope: it locates the object of hope *neither* within the bounds of this-worldly experience *nor* beyond the world in an afterlife or metaphysical elsewhere. But what kind of hope would this be?

We can develop a better understanding of Adorno's concept of an inverse theology if we consider the 1953 essay "Notes on Kafka," where Adorno denies the relevance of conventional theological categories in the strongest terms.[18] "Nowhere in Kafka," Adorno writes, "does there glimmer the aura of the infinite idea; nowhere does the horizon open." If Benjamin was correct to characterize Kafka's stories as parables, they are parables that do not admit of interpretive elucidation but remain instead stubbornly fastened to factual report. The claustrophobic experience of reading these parables is due in part to the fact that they refuse the consolation of an interpretive space beyond themselves where all mysteries would be explained. "Each sentence is literal and each signifies." If Kafka's work qualifies as expression, it expresses itself "not through expression but by its repudiation, by breaking off. It is a parabolic system the key to which has been stolen." The very claustrophobia of these scenarios, poorly identified with the cliché of the "Kafkaesque" is precisely the feeling that they somehow signify even though their significance eludes

which is Schöps as far as Kafka is concerned." Theodor Adorno and Walter Benjamin, *The Complete Correspondence, 1928–1940*, trans. Nicholas Walker, ed. Henri Lonitz (Cambridge, MA: Harvard University Press, 1994): Adorno to Benjamin. (Berlin, December 17, 1934), 66–67.

17. Theodor W. Adorno and Walter Benjamin, *The Complete Correspondence, 1928–1940*. Adorno to Benjamin. (Berlin, December 17, 1934), 66–67.

18. Adorno, "Aufzeichnungen zu Kafka" originally published in *Die Neue Rundschau*, 64. Jg. 1953, Drittes Heft. In English as Adorno, "Notes on Kafka," in *Prisms*, trans. Samuel and Shierry Weber (Cambridge, MA: MIT Press, 1981), 243–271. Quotes from the original are from Adorno, *Gesammelte Schriften*, 10–11. *Kulturkritik und Gesellschaft* I. "Aufzeichnungen zu Kafka," 254–287.

capture. "Each sentence says 'interpret me,' and none will permit it."[19] Incidentally, this self-enclosed character of brute *literalness* without an interpretive key helps us to appreciate the strong continuity between Kafka and Samuel Beckett, the latter whose major works likewise reinforce the pathos of a much-awaited elucidation that will never arrive. Condemned to "waiting," Vladimir and Estragon exemplify the interpretive impossibility of understanding the drama in which they remain unredeemed. Not just Godot but meaning itself fails to appear. "They do not move."[20]

Perhaps better than any other work by Kafka, *The Trial* exemplifies the challenge of struggling for an elucidation of a world that seems to defy it. This resistance to meaning is evident in what is surely the most crucial fact about the entire novel: that Josef K. *does not seem to have done anything that would help to explain his condemnation.* It is not that the reader *knows* him to be wholly innocent, since the very category of innocence would seem to imply some criterion of blameworthiness from which he might not be exonerated. The problem is quite simply that neither Josef K. nor the reader *can get any grip at all on what such a criterion might even be.* Without exploring the problem at length, Adorno at least brings it to our awareness when he writes that "*if one is not to lose all ground on which to stand,* one must cling to the fact that at the beginning of *The Trial,* it is said that someone must have been spreading rumors about Josef K., 'for without having done anything wrong, he was arrested one fine morning.'"[21] Adorno

19. Adorno, "Notes on Kafka," *Prisms*, 246.
20. This is the interpretative predicament that unites the play's critics with its central protagonists:

    ESTRAGON: Let's go.
    VLADIMIR: We can't.
    ESTRAGON: Why not?
    VLADIMIR: We're waiting for Godot.
    ESTRAGON: (despairingly). Ah! (Beckett, *Waiting for Godot,* Act II)

21. Adorno, "Notes on Kafka," *Prisms*, 247 (my emphasis).

focuses our attention on these lines though he does not linger over the untrustworthiness of the so-called fact about Josef K.'s innocence. The reader may very well yearn for knowledge of this innocence, since such knowledge would make the entire narrative into an intelligible study of manifest injustice. But we are denied even this satisfaction. Throughout the novel innocence remains a status the reader can neither verify nor deny since it is presented in the epistemological limbo of what might after all be merely Josef K.'s own self-declaration. It should not escape our attention that the novel's opening sentence offers not the consolations of certainty but only speculation: "somebody *must have been* telling lies." Even the apparent certitude of K's innocence is offered to the reader only as a negation of a negation: he is arrested "*without* having done anything *wrong*."[22] It is as if the language that opens the dramatic action has already been evacuated of positive terms.

For Adorno, *The Trial* reinforces a modern sense of "universal suspicion" that Kafka, he claims, may have borrowed from the popular genre of detective fiction.[23] But even if this were the case, Adorno's suggestion ignores the occluded theological significance of a literary genre that is consumed with the explanation of death. The paradigmatic event in a detective story is the discovery of a corpse, which becomes the focal point for an unfolding inquiry. This is the structure of a secularized theodicy, which in Kafka's tale works backward from the mystery of an accusation to the production of a corpse. To be sure, the inversion borrows its mood of generalized paranoia from the popular genre: a detective, after all, must suspect nearly everyone and anyone, since otherwise there would be no mystery. But this very mood derives its power from a theological worldview in which the

---

22. Kafka, *The Trial*, 5.
23. Adorno, "Notes on Kafka," 265.

all-seeing eye of an unseen God spreads the possibility of guilt across all of society.

Adorno captures a crucial thought when he observes that the novel constantly evades our attempt at understanding precisely through a "principle of literalness." We are thrust, along with Josef K. himself, into a world that enjoys all the stark self-evidence of incorrigible fact but lacks the depth of available meaning. Adorno suggests (somewhat implausibly) that this principle is "probably a reminiscence of the Torah exegesis of Jewish tradition." While it could be argued that the Talmudic practice of textual interpretation exhibits a scrupulous concern for factual detail, this traditional practice draws sustenance from an unshakeable if typically unstated belief in the status of the text as divine revelation: guiding rabbinic interpretation is the expectation that divine meaning can be at least partially recuperated through the act of exegesis itself. In Kabbalistic interpretation this expectation reaches a point of hyperbolic confidence, for example, in the belief that if one were to actually *pierce* a page of the Torah with a pin one could discover a bridge of meaning between the exposed word and the one that lies beneath. Such a practice realizes in a quite literal way the religious belief that revealed meaning can be penetrated: a religious text has *depth*. The reader of Kafka's texts, however, can feel no such confidence in even the partial recuperation of deeper meaning. As Adorno notes, it is characteristic of Kafka's texts that "words, [and] metaphors in particular, detach themselves and achieve a certain autonomy."[24] The experience of reading Kafka in this sense is the very opposite to theological interpretation: it defeats the religious hope that one might pierce the surface of these autonomous words to reach a level of ultimate meaning. Not without cause does Adorno therefore call Kafka "the parabolist of impenetrability."[25]

24. Adorno, "Notes on Kafka," 247–248.
25. Adorno, "Notes on Kafka," 251.

NEGATIVE THEOLOGY OR INVERSE THEOLOGY?

For many readers, the nightmare quality of Kafka's writing has assumed an even darker hue indissociable from the history of Nazism and the death camps. It could be argued that such political associations are hardly more anchored in the actual texts than the religious themes that were imputed to Kafka by expositors such as Brod and Schoeps. Kafka himself died in 1924 and was thus spared the fate that overtook the Jewish community in Prague (including his three sisters, Ottilie, Gabriele, and Valerie, all of whom were murdered). But Adorno expresses a widespread sentiment when he observes that "it is National Socialism far more than the hidden dominion of God that [Kafka's] work cites." Scruples about historical anachronism cannot deter such associations. Precisely in its documentary style and its scrupulous recording of purposeless bureaucratic facts, a narrative such as *The Trial* can strike the reader as a "trial run of a model of dehumanization."[26]

For Adorno, then, theology in the conventional sense cannot comprehend Kafka's writing because it portrays a universe locked within itself, cut off from eternity. "This historical moment, not anything allegedly metatemporal illuminating history from above, is the crystallization of his metaphysics."[27] Precisely in its *contrast* to an absent theology, Kafka's world assumes the character of a fallen domain, where even minor gestures of transformation are robbed of significance. Josef K.'s efforts to resist the court are met less with outrage than with knowing glances and heads that shake in disappointment, as if the accused is doing something too familiar

26. Adorno, "Notes on Kafka," 255.
27. Adorno, "Notes on Kafka," 257.

to merit official censure. The governing mood is one of a fatalism that constantly undoes the meaning of effective action. Without the possibility of actually changing one's situation, Kafka's narratives lose the qualities of change—not only adventure but also mere development—that have characterized the bourgeois novel in its heroic phase. Boredom grows to anger, but anger collapses into frustration and returns to boredom. For Adorno, one of the most striking defects of Kafka's novels is their monotony. "The presentation of the ambiguous, uncertain, inaccessible, is repeated endlessly, often at the expense of the vividness that is always sought."[28] But it was Adorno who best understood this monotony as the after-effect of an inverted theology. Precisely because hope has been drained from his narratives like water from a tub, the individuals and objects that populate Kafka's stories can appear as stranded as children's toys that have lost their charm. "Made eternal, the transient is overtaken by a curse."[29] Because the events in *The Trial* occur in a truly fallen world, the theological traces that still attach themselves to our received notions of a singular and meaningful death no longer hold. When death comes to Josef K., it lacks not only the Christological significance of a unique sacrifice but also the uniqueness of an event that occurs to each individual only a single time. For Josef K., "there is no eternity" other than the indignity of a sacrifice that is "endlessly repeated."[30] His death is not even fully human: "As his sight faded, K. saw the two men leaning cheek to cheek close to his face as they observed the final verdict. 'Like a Dog!' he said." The closing lines suggest that death itself has lost the

28. "The presentation of the ambiguous, uncertain, inaccessible, is repeated endlessly." In Kafka's work, "what is perpetually the same and what is ephemeral merge." Adorno, "Notes on Kafka," 254.
29. Adorno, "Notes on Kafka," 252.
30. Adorno, "Notes on Kafka," 257.

solace of a final expiation: "It seemed as if his shame would live on after him."[31]

Such considerations suggest that Adorno was right to reject the then-fashionable readings of Kafka that associated his work with dialectical theology. For Kierkegaard as for his twentieth-century epigones, the space of merely human experience is split off by a metaphysical chasm from the "wholly other." Human history does not bear the seal of divine approval; time and eternity cannot be fused. In Kafka's world, however, the unapproachable authorities that arouse one's fear bear the names not of metaphysical powers but of purely quotidian social institutions: the castle, the court. "Dialectical theology fails in its attempt to appropriate him," Adorno writes, "not merely because of the mythical character of the powers at work, an aspect which Benjamin rightly emphasized, but also because in Kafka, unlike *Fear and Trembling*, ambiguity and obscurity are attributed not exclusively to the Other as such but to human beings and to the conditions in which they live. Precisely that 'infinite qualitative distinction' taught by Kierkegaard and Barth is leveled off."[32]

Adorno's strong and apparently irrevocable judgment against the legitimacy of received theological categories would seem to disallow any attempt to speak of Kafka and theology in the same breath. It is therefore all the more striking that Adorno recuperates these very same categories in an inverted form and with a critical intent. In their resistance to religious consolation, Adorno suggests, Kafka's novels focus our attention on this-worldly suffering without holding open the possibility for its metaphysical annulment. At the same time, however, the idea of religious perfection continues to serve a critical purpose insofar as it enhances our awareness of worldly imperfection to the greatest possible intensity. The Enlightenment-era philosopher

31. Kafka, *The Trial*, 165.
32. Adorno, "Notes on Kafka," 259.

and playwright Gotthold Lessing once distinguished between the search for divine truth (as the principle for human aspiration) and the divine truth itself: "If God were to hold all Truth concealed in his right hand, and in his left only the steady and diligent drive for Truth, albeit with the proviso that I would always and forever err in the process, and to offer me the choice, I would with all humility take the left hand."[33] Writing at a moment when the ideals of the Enlightenment had lost much of their luster, Kafka indicts even this asymptotic ideal of God's left hand for diminishing our awareness of present despair. By transforming the present into merely the starting point of a still-unrealized happiness, the Enlightenment philosophy of history converges with dialectical theology, both of whom direct their hopes toward a happiness that remains hidden from humanity. "Kafka's theology," Adorno explains, "if one can speak of such at all, is antinomian with respect to the very same God which Lessing defended against the orthodoxy, the God of the enlightenment. This God, however, is a *deus absconditus*. Kafka thus becomes not a proponent of dialectical theology, as is often asserted, but its accuser."[34]

For Adorno, then, dialectical theology remains of relevance for our understanding of Kafka's novels, but only because they offer us critical portraits in which the false doctrines of dialectical theology are transformed into social reality. Only this can explain why the Kierkegaardian and Barthian themes of radical alterity and "absolute difference" can prove so seductive for the reader of Kafka's work, in which what is in fact a social distinction assumes the guise of a metaphysical myth. In dialectical theology, Adorno explains, " 'absolute difference' converges with the mythic powers. Totally abstract, and indeterminate, purged of all anthropomorphic and mythological

33. Gotthold Lessing, *Eine Duplik* (1778), in *Gesammelte Werke*, ed. Paul Rilla (Berlin: Aufbau, 1954–58), 8: 505ff. (my translation)
34. Adorno, "Notes on Kafka," 269.

qualities, God becomes the ominously ambiguous and threatening deity who evokes nothing but dread and terror."[35] But Kafka himself does not confirm but, rather, dismantles these metaphysical fairy tales. His work "preserves the moment in which the purified faith was revealed to be impure, in which demythologizing appeared as demonology."[36] The rationalized systems of his novels invite facile comparisons to theology only because rationalized modernity itself converges with unreason. Kafka himself, however, does not accept this comparison unthinkingly but, rather, exploits it so as to develop a critique of society. Kafka's well-known fascination with Kierkegaard should not mislead us into reading his works as implicit but genuine studies in theology. For if is true that "Kafka used motifs from *Fear and Trembling*" he did so "not as heir but as critic."[37]

This critical use of theology against social injustice becomes especially obvious in *The Trial*:

He remains a rationalist . . . in his attempt to rectify the myth which thus emerges, to reopen the trial against it, as though before an appellate court. The variations of myths which were found in his unpublished writings bear witness to his efforts in search of such a corrective. The *Trial* novel is itself the trial of the trial.[38]

Kafka willfully evokes a theological atmosphere in *The Trial* only so that he can condemn more completely the social structures that masquerade as eternal. He "describes the court which sits in judgment over men in order to convict law itself."[39] Social alienation takes

35. Adorno, "Notes on Kafka," 269.
36. Adorno, "Notes on Kafka," 269.
37. Adorno, "Notes on Kafka," 269.
38. Adorno, "Notes on Kafka," 269.
39. Adorno, "Notes on Kafka," 269.

on the mythic appearance of theological alienation only in order to enhance our understanding of social despair. In *The Trial*, the equation between justice and myth becomes explicit in the strange painting that is supposed to represent both the Goddess of Justice and the Goddess of Victory but in fact looks "completely like the Goddess of the Hunt."[40] For Adorno this episode typifies Kafka's critical deployment of concepts and imagery that are borrowed knowingly from the archive of the religious imagination. "Absolute estrangement, abandoned to the existence from which it has withdrawn, is examined and revealed as the hell which it inherently was already in Kierkegaard, although unconsciously. As hell seen from the perspective of salvation."[41]

Having followed Adorno's reasoning this far, we can conclude that Kafka's "inverse theology" is not the name for a conventional theological doctrine equipped with, for example, a metaphysical distinction between God and humanity, or a cosmic map that would assign the divine and the world to separate precincts and then meditate upon the possible lines of commerce between them. On the contrary, Kafka's inverse theology, as Adorno understands it, describes not a metaphysical doctrine but a critical stance. Here, we may begin to appreciate the contrast between the traditional argumentation of "negative" (or apophantic) theology and an *inverse* theology in Adorno's sense. A negative theology (associated with, e.g., Maimonides, Al-Farabi, and Aquinas) denies the capacity of the human being to gain a properly conceptual grasp of the divine: because God is said to transcend all bounds of human representation, the divine essence is known only by means of a *via negativa*, through an indirect route that emphasizes the finitude of the human intellect and, by negative implication, enhances

40. Kafka, *The Trial*, 105.
41. Adorno, "Notes on Kafka," 269.

our awareness of God's radical transcendence. Despite its name, a negative theology in this sense still *affirms* the divine essence even if such an affirmation ends in epistemological skepticism and the doctrine of the *deus absconditus,* or divine unknowability. An *inverse* theology, by contrast, does not permit us to affirm any kind of transmundane perfection or the solace of a world to come. It abandons any affirmation of the divine even through indirection, and it devotes itself to revealing without qualification the radical imperfection of our own mundane reality. This is Adorno's crucial insight. Kafka's writing "feigns a standpoint from which creation appears as lacerated and mutilated as it itself conceives hell to be. ... The lightsource which shows the world's crevices to be infernal is the optimal one" (*Die Lichtquelle, welche die Schründe der Welt als höllisch aufglühen läßt, ist die optimale*).[42]

With this preliminary definition we can better understand why Adorno would have found the dialectical theologians' interpretations of Kafka so objectionable. Their error is not simply one of dogmatic theism (since it would be misleading to say that Kafka simply *rejects* theism and thus aligns himself with atheism). The deeper error in dialectical theology is that it tries to charge the bare concept of a theistic standpoint with an affirmative meaning the standpoint cannot sustain: it turns negation into affirmation. This may explain why Adorno characterizes Kafka's *inverse* theology as a *reversal* of negative theology. In Kafka's novels, "what for dialectical theology is light and shadow is *reversed.*"[43] For the disciples of Kierkegaard, quotidian reality when severed from its connection to God becomes as black as pitch, and it can sustain its hope across the chasm only by erecting a bridge of faith. It is in this sense that the concept of God becomes *affirmative* in its meaning even for Karl Barth and his associates. But for Kafka, the very thought of God (if God can be thought at all) can have at best

42. Adorno, "Notes on Kafka," 269.
43. Adorno, "Notes on Kafka," 269 (my emphasis).

only a *negative* meaning. It does not redeem reality; it only reveals and even enhances our understanding of the world's unredeemed condition: "The absolute does not turn its absurd side to the finite creature. . . . Rather, the world is revealed to be as absurd as it would be for the *intellectus archetypus*. The middle realm of the finite and the contingent becomes infernal to the eye of the artificial angel."[44] Here, then, is a theology of a purely negative standpoint. It should not surprise us that the inverse theology Adorno identified in Kafka's work closely resembles Adorno's often-cited statement of philosophical method presented at the conclusion of *Minima Moralia*:

> The only philosophy which would still be accountable in the face of despair, would be the attempt to consider all things, as they would be portrayed from the standpoint of redemption [*Standpunkt der Erlösung*]. Cognition has no other light than that which shines from redemption out upon the world; all else exhausts itself in post-construction and remains a piece of technics. Perspectives must be produced which set the world beside itself, alienated from itself, revealing its cracks and fissures [*ihre Risse und Schründe offenbart*], as needy and distorted as it will one day lay there in the messianic light [*im Messianischen Lichte daliegen wird*].[45]

THE DISENCHANTMENT OF THE RELIGIOUS SIGN

The concept of inverse theology—a "standpoint" that serves only a critical rather than an affirmative purpose in revealing the world's

---

44. Adorno, "Notes on Kafka," 269.
45. Theodor W. Adorno, "Finale," *Minima Moralia*, trans. E. F. N. Jephcott (New York: Verso, 2006).

distortion—may help us to understand certain features of Kafka's *Trial* that would otherwise remain obscure. The terrifying scene of the "lumber room," where the two guards, Franz and Willem, are subjected to a painful thrashing, reaches its conclusion with the solitary image of K., who meditates upon his own failure to intervene: "K. had no other choice but to close the door," he tells himself. "He couldn't help anyone any more."[46] As he ruminates over his inaction and the question of his moral complicity, he finds himself in a "small, square courtyard" surrounded by offices. "The windows were already dark, just the top ones catching a reflection of the moonlight."[47] Such scenes, which appear with remarkable frequency in Kafka's tales, convey not only the unrelieved claustrophobia of a world that lacks the hope of an exit; they also awaken if only momentarily the idea of a different world that persists only as a reflection. So faint is this scene from genuine hope that the moonlight itself seems to lack all powers of illumination. It reflects only enough light to reveal the darkness of the courtyard and the windows above.

The sense of an inverted theology that runs through the novel becomes perhaps most explicit in its penultimate chapter, "In the Cathedral," when K. carries an electric torch to examine the pictures that hang in the gloomy chapels alongside the walls. Casting his light on one picture, he finds "a standard treatment of the Entombment of Christ," an image which (as Ritchie Robertson observes in his notes) lacks any reference to the Resurrection and thus only enhances the reader's sense of hopelessness.[48] It would be too easy to interpret this image as an anticipation of K.'s own death, but the truth of the matter is that it resists interpretation altogether. The inadequacy of light in

46. Kafka, *The Trial*, 62.
47. Kafka, *The Trial*, 61.
48. Kafka, *The Trial*, 148.

the cathedral suggests that even religious imagery no longer bears an accessible meaning:

> When K. happened to turn round he saw, not far behind him, a tall, thick candle fixed to a pillar. It was also lit, but, beautiful as it was, it was insufficient to illuminate the altarpieces, which were mostly hanging in the darkness of the side altars. In fact it only served to increase the darkness.[49]

K.'s debate with the priest over the proper meaning of the doorkeeper parable suggests a world in which the Christian practice of interpreting parable has lost its power to console, not least because the very form of a parable no longer serves as a vessel for redemptive meaning. It should not surprise us that the priest himself lacks any genuine powers of interpretation. Rather than disclosing a transcendent meaning, he confines himself to citing a social opinion that replaces genuine morality with bland relativism: "Some people say that the story does not give anyone the right to judge the doorkeeper."[50] As an agent of the church and therefore an intermediary between the laity and the divine, the priest might be expected to offer an interpretation of the parable that would offer both consolation and intelligibility. Instead, he declares the inaccessibility of any meaning: "However he appears to us, he is, after all, a servant of the Law, he belongs to the Law and is, therefore, beyond human judgment."[51]

K. declares this interpretation unpersuasive, since it would make the doorkeeper the only arbiter of truth. In a situation where principles of universal rationality were permitted to reign, such an objection might be plausible, but we should not be surprised that it is an institutional authority who points out the fallacy in K.'s reasoning: " 'No,' said the priest, 'one doesn't have to take everything as the truth, one just has to accept it as necessary.' "⁵² It is then left to K. to draw the proper inference. Though he apparently lacks the conviction or the energy to challenge the veracity of the priest's statement, K. simply notes that it is "A depressing opinion," since it would mean that "lies are made into the order of the world [*Weltordnung*]."⁵³ Perhaps no other passage in the entire novel illustrates Kafka's readiness to play upon religious hope only to intensify and universalize what is essentially a condemnation of society: the original German, *Weltordnung*, sits at the boundary line between bureaucracy and metaphysics. K.'s encounter with the priest terminates abruptly on a dispiriting note, as if to suggest that the church itself has lost all relevance. In such moments one senses the pathos of religious signs that have lost their reference. As Adorno observes, Kafka's work "breaks off its meaning like broken pillars of life in nineteenth-century cemeteries, and the lines which describe the break are its hieroglyphics."⁵⁴

The inverted status of theological categories in *The Trial* becomes most apparent in the novel's final chapter, when K. finds himself taken to the quarry by two unnamed men, both of whom are "wearing frock coats and top hats that looked as if they were stuck on."⁵⁵ The last scene is a parody of ritual sacrifice: "The men laid K. on the ground, leant him against the stone, and gently placed his head on top of it." One of the men takes out a long and thin knife, but K. immediately understands he is expected to perform the murder himself. But this "final test" is beyond him: "He could not do all the authorities'

---

52. Kafka, *The Trial*, 159.
53. My own translation is given here instead of the one by Mitchell in Kafka, *The Trial*, 159. The German original reads as follows: "Trübselige Meinung," sagte K. "Die Lüge wird zur Weltordnung gemacht." Kafka, *The Trial*, 223.
54. Adorno, "Notes on Kafka," 265.
55. Kafka, *The Trial*, 161.

work for them."[56] What appears at first glance as the enactment of an archaic ritual has been turned into the final humiliation. In his refusal, K. expresses a final defiance not against the court but against its expectation that he accept his own guilt. It is therefore unsurprising that he glances upward and sees a human shape that seems to promise salvation:

> His eye fell on the top story of the house besides the quarry. Like a flash of light, the two casements of a window parted and a human figure, faint and thin from the distance and height, leant far out in one swift movement then stretched its arms out even farther. Who was it? A friend? A kind person? Someone who felt for him? Someone who wanted to help? Was it just one? Or all of them? Was help still possible? Were there still objections he'd forgotten? Of course there were. Logic may be unshakable, but it cannot hold out against a human being who wants to live.[57]

The figure that appears in the light of this distant window signals at least momentarily the possibility of K.'s release from death. At this point, however, no reader could be misled into believing that K.'s hopes are justified. The window is too far away and the apparition makes a gesture that remains indistinct and without consequence. (Prompted by this very same passage, Adorno observes that many scenes in Kafka "read as though they should have been written in imitation of expressionist paintings which should have been painted but never were."[58]) In the courtyard scene earlier in the novel, the windows reflected moonlight but remained otherwise dark. Here, the window is lit from within and the apparition prompts K.'s hopeful

56. Kafka, The Trial, 164.
57. Kafka, The Trial, 164.
58. Adorno, "Notes on Kafka," 264.

thought that somebody might come to his rescue. Although such references to light may seem to retain at least a memory trace of their old meaning as beacons of redemption, in Kafka's disenchanted universe this symbolism has dwindled to mere cliché. The obscure figure who stretches out his or her hands suggests a bid for symbolism but without symbolic content. The gesture itself is a comment on its own emptiness.

K.'s death at the novel's end does away with any thoughts of consolation. In a final indignity he dies not as a human being but instead "like a dog," a phrase that breaks the last bonds that might have associated Kafka's novel with received conventions of humanism.[59] Shakespeare's Othello ends his life with the same comparison: "I took by the throat the circumcis'd dog / And smote him, thus." But Othello retains the humanizing gift of eloquence, and even his suicide is a sign of his enduring will to determine his own fate. The conclusion of *The Trial* annuls such heroism. K. dies in a condition of silence and complete inertia that places him at the furthest remove from tragedy. His death scene carries an obvious pathos, but it is an inverted pathos that unsettles the reader precisely because it refrains from despair and withholds the expected catharsis of a meaningful death.

Allusions to dogs appear elsewhere in Kafka's oeuvre and in his correspondence as well. In a 1913 letter to Felice Bauer, Kafka interrogated his fiancée regarding her religious convictions. "Have you ever, without giving the slightest thought to anyone else, been in despair simply about yourself? Desperate enough to throw yourself on the ground and remain there beyond the Day of Judgment? How devout are you?" What may strike us as a tone of aggression in these questions is due chiefly to the fact that Kafka seemed unable to imagine what it would be like to experience religious conviction, and he was

59. Kafka, *The Trial*, 165.

accordingly prone to doubt whether Felice actually felt such conviction herself. "You go to the synagogue," Kafka notes, "but I dare say you have not been recently. And what is it that sustains you, the idea of Judaism or of God?" For Kafka even to think of such a religious consolation is virtually impossible, as it would require a mathematical hyperbole: "Are you aware, and this is the most important thing, of a continuous relationship between yourself and a reassuringly distant, if possibly infinite height or depth?" For Kafka, the person who could sustain this kind of religious feeling would not experience his quotidian life as a perpetual state of falling or self-abandonment.

> He who feels this continuously has no need to roam about like
> a lost dog, mutely gazing around with imploring eyes; he never
> need yearn to slip into a grave as if it were a warm sleeping bag
> and life a cold winter night; and when climbing the stairs to his
> office he never need imagine that he is careering down the well of
> the staircase, flickering in the uncertain light, twisting from the
> speed of his fall, shaking his head with impatience.[60]

The portrait of this "lost dog" bears a striking resemblance to Josef K. at the moment of his death. Even the nod to quotidian experience ("when climbing the stairs to his office") places us in the bureaucratic world of *The Trial*. In the letter to Felice, however, Kafka makes explicit the theme of divine absence that remains mostly unstated throughout the novel.

Here, once again, we must recall the distinction between an inverse theology and a negative theology. The former (in Adorno's sense) uses the mere idea of the divine only in order to intensify our

---

60. The letter was written presumably "during the night" of February 7–8, 1913. Quoted from Franz Kafka, *Letters to Felice*, trans. James Stern and Elisabeth Duckworth, ed. Erich Heller and Jürgen Born (New York: Schocken, 1973).

sense of the world's imperfection; it does not imply the persistent reality of a God who is elsewhere. The latter denotes a traditional religious doctrine according to which God exists but has grown inaccessible or can be approached only if one first recognizes the inadequacy of the concepts that apply within the bounds of mundane experience.[61] For Adorno, Kafka's work thus exemplifies an *inverse* rather than a negative theology; it does not keep alive the thought of a God who is elsewhere or merely inaccessible. If Adorno is right in his characterization of Kafka, this would help us to explain the novelist's difficulty in imagining the reality of Felice's religious belief. He seemed to have suspected that her belief was no more genuine than his own and that she was no different than him: a "lost dog."

The attempt to define with any precision the character of theological themes in *The Trial* raises perplexities that are unlikely to be resolved. Indeed, we may be tempted to say that the contest between negative theology and inverse theology cannot be resolved; and perhaps Kafka sustains an unresolved or dialectical tension between them. For Gershom Scholem, in disagreement with Adorno, Kafka's work never succeeded in breaking from the traditional metaphysics of negative theology. Ironically, however, according to Scholem, Kafka's continued allegiance to negative theology rendered his work *less* radical than the Hebrew Bible itself. In a commentary on the biblical theme of "God who hides his face" (e.g., in Deuteronomy 31:18), Scholem observed that "It would be too simple to understand this passage using moral categories. Rather, it expresses the idea that God leaves *without a trace*." For Scholem, Kafka's theology ultimately failed to capture this biblical idea. It sustained a bond with

61. Interestingly, Scholem suggested that Adorno's own philosophy amounted to a species of "negative theology." Upon reading Adorno's *Minima Moralia*, Scholem wrote to Adorno (on February 22, 1952) that he considered it "a remarkable document of negative theology." Quoted from Theodor W. Adorno, Gershom Scholem, *Briefwechsel, 1939–1969: "Der liebe Gott wohnt im Detail,"* ed. Asaf Angermann (Berlin: Suhrkamp Verlag, 2015), 82–84.

religious tradition, but precisely for this reason it could not awaken to the ultimate paradox of religious experience: "It is not enough to say, as in Kafka, that the master of the house has retired upstairs: no, he has left the house altogether and cannot be found. That is a state of unimaginable despair. Indeed, religion teaches us that it is here one discovers God."[62]

BIBLIOGRAPHY

Adorno, Theodor W. "Aufzeichnungen zu Kafka," originally published in *Die Neue Rundschau*, 64. Jg. 1953.
Drittes Heft. In English as Adorno, "Notes on Kafka," in *Prisms*. Translated by Samuel and Shierry Weber, 243–271. Cambridge, MA: MIT Press, 1981. Quotes from the original are from Adorno, *Gesammelte Schriften*, 10–11. *Kulturkritik und Gesellschaft* I. "Aufzeichnungen zu Kafka," 254–287.
Adorno, Theodor W. *Minima Moralia*. Translated by E. F. N. Jephcott. New York: Verso, 2006.
Adorno, Theodor W., and Walter Benjamin. *The Complete Correspondence, 1928– 1940*. Translated by Nicholas Walker, edited by Henri Lonitz. Cambridge, MA: Harvard University Press, 1994.
Beck, Evelyn Torton. *Kafka and the Yiddish Theater: Its Impact on His Work*. Madison: University of Wisconsin Press, 1971.
Benjamin, Walter. "Franz Kafka: On the Tenth Anniversary of his Death." Translated by Harry Zohn. In *Illuminations*, 111–140. New York: Schocken, 1969.
Bergman, Schmuel Hugo. *Tagebücher und Briefe*. Königstein/Taunus: Jüdischer Verlag/Athenäum, 1985.
Brod, Max. *Franz Kafka: eine Biographie*. Prague: Heinr. Mercy Sohn, 1937; in English as Brod, *Franz Kafka: A Biography*. New York: Schocken, 1947.
Brod, Max, and Hans Joachim Schoeps. "Nachwort." In Kafka, *Beim Bau der Chinesischen Mauer*. Berlin: Gustav Kiepeneuer Verlag, 1931; reprinted in Kafka, *The Great Wall of China: Stories and Reflections*. Translated by Wila and Edwin Muir. New York: Schocken, 1946.

62. Schmuel Hugo Bergman, *Tagebücher und Briefe*, vol. 1 (Königstein/Taunus: Jüdischer Verlag/Athenäum, 1985), 213. Quoted from Stéphane Moses, "Gershom Scholem's Reading of Kafka: Literary Criticism and Kabbalah," *New German Critique* 77, Special Issue on German-Jewish Religious Thought (Spring-Summer, 1999): 149–167, quoted from 154–155.

Corngold, Stanley. "Adorno's 'Notes on Kafka': A Critical Reconstruction." *Monatshefte* 94, no. 1 (2002): 24–42.

Corngold, Stanley. *Lambent Traces: Franz Kafka*. Princeton, NJ, and Oxford: Princeton University Press, 2004.

Gilman, Sander L. *Franz Kafka: The Jewish Patient*. New York: Routledge, 1995.

Kafka, Franz. *Letters to Felice*. Translated by James Stern and Elisabeth Duckworth, edited by Erich Heller and Jürgen Born. New York: Schocken, 1973.

Kafka, Franz. *The Trial*. Translated by Mike Mitchell. Oxford: Oxford University Press, 2009.

Kohlenbach, Margarete. "Kafka, Critical Theory, Dialectical Theology: Adorno's Case against Hans-Joachim Schoeps." *German Life and Letters* 63, no. 2 (2010): 146–165.

Lessing, Gotthold. *Gesammelte Werke*. Edited by Paul Rilla. Berlin: Aufbau, 1954–58.

Moses, Stéphane. "Gershom Scholem's Reading of Kafka: Literary Criticism and Kabbalah." *New German Critique* 77, Special Issue on German-Jewish Religious Thought (Summer 1999): 149–167.

Pawel, Ernst. *The Nightmare of Reason: A Life of Franz Kafka*. New York: Vintage, 1985.

Robertson, Ritchie. *Kafka: Judaism, Politics, and Literature*. Oxford: Clarendon, 1985.

Scholem, Gershom, ed. *The Correspondence of Walter Benjamin and Gershom Scholem, 1932–1940*. Edited by Gary Smith and Andre Lefevre. New York: Schocken, 1989.

Weigel, Sigrid. "Jewish Thinking in a World Without God: Benjamin's Readings of Kafka as a Critique of Christian and Jewish Theologoumena." Translated by Chadwick Truscott Smith. In *Walter Benjamin: Images, the Creaturely, and the Holy*. Stanford: Stanford University Press, 2013.

Chapter 2

Before the Law

FRED RUSH

The parable "Before the Law" ("Vor dem Gesetz") is the centerpiece of the chapter of *The Trial* (*Der Process/Der Proceß/Der
Prozeß*) to which Kafka's literary executor, Max Brod, assigned the
title "In the Cathedral" ("Im Dom").[1] The parable has some right

---

1. Citation to *The Trial* is to page and line number in what is, at present, the closest thing to a
standard German edition, *Der Proceß*, ed. Malcolm Pasley, in *Franz Kafka Kritische Ausgabe*,
ed. J Jürgen Born, Gerhard Neumann, Malcolm Pasley, et al. (Frankfurt am Main: Fisher,
1990), followed by parallel citation to page number of what is currently the most reliable
English translation, *The Trial*, trans. Breon Mitchell (New York: Schocken, 1998). I sometimes alter the translation where I think sense or emphasis demands. I have consulted a
facsimile of the autograph manuscript, the original of which is housed at the Deutsches
Literaturarchiv Marbach, in order to rectify the text of the chapter "Im Dom" in both its original German and English translation, with special attention to the parable. See Franz Kafka,
Historisch-Kritische Ausgabe sämtlicher Handschiften, Drucke und Typoskripte, ed. Roland
Reuß and Peter Staengle. Part 1: *Der Process* (Basel & Frankfurt am Main: Stroemfeld, 1995),
10, 42–46.

The *Kritische Ausgabe* hews to the *Handschrift*, much more so than did Max Brod, who
chose to insert upwards of twenty-five commas where the manuscript indicates none, to
replace the initial capitals in *Du* and *Dich* throughout the passage with lowercase initials, to
convert *ertragen* to *vertragen* (which subtly alters both sense and force), and to alter preposi-
tional phrases and associated cases (*trotz* + gen. > *trotz* + dat.; *sprechen über* + acc. > *sprechen
von* + dat.). The *Kritische Ausgabe* reverts to the manuscript in all these instances. Mitchell
generally follows the *Kritische Ausgabe* and a fortiori the manuscript. The *Kritische Ausgabe*
does follow Brod's insertion of chapter titles (Kafka indicated none), as well as the order of
chapters (there is scholarly dispute on the precise order).

to be considered the focal point of the novel, although claiming
that status is controversial, both because there are many deserving
high points that also might be so considered and because a work as
disjointed as *The Trial* beggars the very idea of a single, crystalliz-
ing episode. Yet, notwithstanding other brilliant set pieces in the
novel, the parable has an undeniable distilled force that seems to
pull the book as a whole into its vortex. Another way of putting the
point is to say that the parable has the compact power of Kafka's
best short prose. Kafka no doubt appreciated this and would own
to what would be almost apostasy to say nowadays—that is, that
his short fiction at its best is markedly superior to his novels. No
matter how taken one is with the wars of attrition fought by the
protagonists of *The Missing Person, The Trial*, and *The Castle*—all
orphaned texts—none of the extended prose work hits as hard as
"In the Penal Colony," "The Judgment," "Josephina, the Singer,"
"The Hunger Artist," or "The Metamorphosis." It is telling that
"Before the Law" is the only part of the book manuscript that
Kafka chose to publish, appearing as a self-standing tale in the collection *Ein Landarzt* (1919).

Calling "Vor dem Gesetz" a *parable* is so standard in the literature
that the ascription may not appear worthy of second thought, but it
is. After all, the priest who introduces it into the narrative of *The Trial*
does not call the story he relates a parable; rather, he presents it, in all
appropriateness given the central organizing device of the novel, as a
legal document, as one of the "introductory texts to the law" (*einlei-
tenden Schriften zum Gesetz*).[2] In the West, one most often associates

2. Kafka, *Der Proceß*, 292.18 / *The Trial*, 215. Kafka sometimes uses the word *law* to refer
to a legal system or document and at other times to designate an ontological domain.
Some commentators mark the difference by using initial capitals in cases of the second
use. I believe this introduces unnecessary complication in reading and, in any event,
sometimes Kafka means both simultaneously, so marking them orthographically is
misleading.

parables with the Abrahamic religions, but parables play significant roles in other written and oral traditions, both religious and nonreligious. Is there anything useful that one can say about their formal nature, given the diversity of cultural sources from which parables originate? Two aspects of parables seem primary. First, parables are pedagogical texts and, more specifically, didactic ones. Second, parables achieve their pedagogical effects through the presentation for interpretation of extended analogies that are intended to reveal an ethical truth. Typically the analogy is established by the use of stereotypes with easily grasped cultural significance—for example, king : vassal | god : creature. The etymological origin of the word *parable* (Gr. παραβολή) means "juxtaposition," and there is a German word, *Parabel*, that descends from the Greek. But the word Kafka deploys to denote a parable, *Gleichnis*, gives an even better indication of the centrality of the activity of comparison to the genre.

In *The Trial*, the priest who conveys the parable in the cathedral is presumably Roman Catholic; quite naturally then, one is put in mind of parables as they figure in the New Testament. But even a cursory consideration of the substance and mood of the parable here undercuts any such easy identification. The title of the parable, "Vor dem Gesetz," indicates that the parable both relates a story concerning the law and itself operates as a preamble to "the law." This conveys, as noted earlier, a legal status. Two relevant senses of the preposition *before* (*vor*) are in play in the title of the parable: (1) locative—that is, the parable is situated before the law, as the gate stands before the realm of law in the parable; and (2) precedential—that is, the parable is a condition precedent to the understanding and study of law, just as (on one understanding of the parable) an existential change in the character of the petitioner is necessary for entrance through the gate. Add to this stress on legal status the argumentative, and indeed comic, elements in the parable, and one is drawn much more powerfully to Old Testament models. Kafka was not an observant Jew, but he took a great deal of interest in two aspects of Middle European Jewish culture—Yiddish comic theater and rabbinical hermeneutics. The latter is most pertinent here, although the two are intertwined (and not just in Kafka's appropriation of them). Kafka is less concerned with specific results of rabbinical interpretative practices than he is with the argumentative labyrinth established by the deep existential devotion to argument that is central to Jewish scriptural commentary traditions—that is, to Talmudic scholarship and, even more, to Midrash.

What must have fascinated Kafka about parables is the almost ironic relation between elucidation and elusiveness that characterizes much of their employment in the rabbinical tradition with which Kafka was familiar. Parables are exegetical in that they are employed to address gaps in the surface meaning of texts. But they do so in an exceedingly indirect way. That is, parables offer themselves as ways to settle a point of textual interpretation, but understanding a parable is also a matter of interpretation. Parables are, in this hermeneutic tradition, precisely *not* ready-made moral tuition; they are both relevant and inscrutable, and often relevant *by being* inscrutable. They can take the form of riddles, providing not the sense that matters are settled relative to a text but the rather less heartening impression that settling the textual point will involve plumbing the depths of the text relative to the even greater depths of the multitude of possible further interpretations it might support. In turn, this permits an ontological extrapolation: the basis for this interpretative depth is the sheer difference in kind between divine word and human understanding, and the specific "infinity" of the task of understanding results from acknowledging that difference. In particular, the prohibition of *reference* to the divine by direct means—that is, by means of names—stands in the background. Max Brod may have gone overboard in attempting to reduce all of Kafka to religious allegory, but he was not operating out of pure fantasy.

A PARABLE ON PARABLES

In 1922, Kafka wrote a short text on parables, "Von den Gleichnissen," which Brod published posthumously in 1931 in the collection *Beim Bau der Chinesischen Mauer*.[3] It reads:

Many complained [*beklagten*] that the words of the wise are always merely parables and of no use in daily life, which is the only life we have. When the sage says: "cross over" [*gehe hinüber*], he does not mean that one should cross over to another location, which one could do anyhow if what is at the end of that path were worth it, rather he means some fabulous yonder [*sagenhaftes Drüben*], something of which we have no acquaintance [*etwas, das wir nicht kennen*] and that he cannot designate [*bezeichnen*] more precisely and that therefore cannot help us here at all. All these parables really venture to say [*wollen sagen*] merely that the incomprehensible is incomprehensible [*das Unfaßbare unfaßbar ist*], and that we know it [*das haben wir gewußt*]. But what we concern ourselves [*uns abmühen*] with every day are other matters.

Concerning this a man once said: Why do you all resist? If you all only followed the parables you yourselves would have become parables and with that be free of your daily cares [*Mühe*].

Another said: I bet that is also a parable.
The first said: You have won.
The second said: But unfortunately only in parable.
The first said: No, in reality: in parable you have lost.[4]

---

3. Perhaps the best sources from which to acquire a cumulative sense of Kafka's "parable practice" are the so-called *Blue Octavos*. Their composition for the most part coincides with an extended gap in Kafka's diaries, and some scholars suggest that Kafka was replacing his practice of working out literary ideas in his diaries with doing so in parables.
4. Franz Kafka, *Parables* (New York: Schocken, 1947), 10–11 (translation amended). I have reversed Brod's change of *beklagten* to *beklagen*. The manuscript is unpublished, but available at the Bodelian Library, Oxford. K Bod AII, 2, MS Kafka 40, fols. 27r & 28r rev.

The first thing to note is that the form of the text on parables is itself a parable, beginning, as many parables do, with a variant of the formula: "it is said," "many say"—in this case, "many complained." It consists of two parts. The first, what one might call its principal part, is a negative assessment of the everyday value of parables. The second part comprises a short dialogue between two men that is a commentary on the meaning of the principal part. The commentary opens with the first speaker challenging the contention that parables are useless for everyday life. All that parables teach, it claims, is that "the incomprehensible is incomprehensible," which is common knowledge. Why is it common knowledge? The first thing to note is that "incomprehensible" in the context of the parable does not mean "nonsensical" or "obtuse." It means, rather more literally in the German, "ungraspable." Still, one might think that the statement borders on tautology, but it appears so only on one interpretation of what the term "incomprehensible" means, and even then is not strictly speaking tautological. Although it does not come out well in a smooth English translation, the German renders the first occurrence of "the incomprehensible," with the substantive "das Unfaßbare," denoting an entity or state, and the second with the attributive adjective "unfaßbar," indicating a property. One gets hoary questions in Plato concerning whether the forms have the properties that instantiate them (e.g., is the Beautiful beautiful?); whatever one thinks about the philosophical value of such questions, such statements are not tautologies.[5] This being the case, knowledge of the truth or falsity of such statements is not common on account of their being logically trivial. It is, rather, common because theological. On some views (e.g., F. H. Jacobi), one cannot know incomprehensible things; on others (e.g., Kant, on some interpretations), one may know *that* there are such things but not *what* they are.

5. See Plato, *Phaedo* 100c3–7.

The point of this digression is that the claim on behalf of parables by those who stand by them is a bit more robust than it might seem at first and may even be close to the Kantian view, since it is description or, more specifically, "designation" (*das Bezeichnen*) that the principal part of the parable says is what marks the outer bounds of comprehensibility. This is implicitly closely allied to linguistic capacities, which yields the recognizably negative theological idea that the divine cannot (indeed, ought not) be named. There is also a hint of the relation of naming to face-to-face encounter (i.e., acquaintance) with what is named in the use of the verb *kennen*, although there is a modulation later in the passage to the more impersonal verb, *wissen*. This explicitly theological rendering of the parable is further supported by the report of the sage's exhortation to "cross over" (*hinübergehen*). The German verb, again, offers two shades of meaning. It has an everyday meaning of simply crossing from one place to the other or, slightly more abstractly, "to exceed a limit." But it also has a religious use: to cross over the threshold of death to the beyond—that is, to be transfigured. The exhortation, so understood, is to achieve a glimpse of "the unsayable," "the indescribable," or "the incomprehensible" by indirect means. The precise manner of indirection, as well as its power to convey the divine, is left unspecified, nor does the principal part of the text treat specific modes of conveyance. Parables attempt to inculcate an experience of cognitive humility and sublimity; one is overwhelmed and elevated by potential meaning. But if this is their chief lesson, so the claim goes, parables fail in principle one of the main pedagogical aims of religious instruction—to offer a reasonably determinate ethical orientation in this-worldly affairs. Accordingly, parables are failures *twice over*: they fail to say anything not already known, and lack any power to orient those to whom they are directed.

Turning to the commentary *cum* dialogue, readers might believe that they have exited the realm of parable and entered the more lucid domain of analytic deliberation. This expectation is undermined immediately. The first speaker offers a defense of parables on the surprising ground that following a parable transforms the follower into one and, in turn, that this transformation would render daily concerns beside the point. What following a parable amounts to and how such following might transform the follower into a parable is left unexplained. Whatever following a parable with such a result might turn out to be, it cannot be like following a discursive rule. There are intriguing problems with the very idea of following a rule—Wittgenstein held that, if acting in following a rule is or depends on the action being determined by a rule, then there can be no discriminate rule following because any action can be in accord with any given rule[6]—but, such concerns aside, a parable does not present an even apparently determinate rule for action. Part of the power of a parable is to require its audience to engage imaginative, interpretative powers in order to glean meaning. Any reader of the parable is, then, in the position of a commentator. Perhaps the idea that in following a parable one becomes a parable comes to just that. One follows a parable by struggling with its meaning endlessly, becoming a parable oneself because such a struggle is exemplary for others and itself a proper object of devoted interpretation.

The second speaker's response to this defense of the pedagogical function of parables is a "bet" that the defense is also a parable, the truth of which the first speaker allows. If the foregoing discussion of what it is to "follow a parable" is roughly correct, the first speaker would have to allow this. So, the bet is won. But the second speaker immediately deploys a hard-and-fast distinction between the actual world and the world toward which a parable points, discounting the win by saying that it is only a win "in parable." In so doing, he extends the scope of what counts as parable to the dialogue. The idea that *all*

6. See Ludwig Wittgenstein, *Philosophical Investigations* (London: Blackwell, 1953), §201.

is parable threatens to swallow up the distinction between actuality and the reference of the parable to something beyond the actual. The first interlocutor again turns the tables. The win is a win in the actual world (*im Wirklichkeit*), but is at the same time a loss in the parable world. This final turn reestablishes the distinction between actuality and something beyond it. But it crucially does so only by allowing in the run of commentary that the distinction is problematic to maintain determinately.[7] The second interlocutor wins, then, in the here-and-now, but the "parable value" of that win is that it is a loss relative to the beyond, for the second interlocutor discounts the win in those terms, which discounting, from the point of view of parable, is precisely to discount parables (and hence to agree with the position advanced in the principal part). Interpreting "Von den Gleichnissen" in this manner comes out on the side of a reasonably discrete outcome of the parable, one that maintains the other-worldly through this-worldly direction to the parable while also acknowledging that it is this very distinction that is everywhere at issue. One attempts to make one's way through a maze of argument that doubles back upon itself, driving home a sense of both location and dislocation. To not follow the argument alertly and rest satisfied with an obscure sense of general argumentative complexity, or a lazy ascription of "paradox," does not do justice to the precise reading Kafka demands. This is not merely an aesthetic point; it is only by means of detailed attention to argument that the reader experiences the peculiar sort of vertigo that Kafka's prose induces. The human predicament is to come to a halting acceptance that one is at base an interpreter who is at an irrevocable remove from one's utmost hope for recompense.

Tempting though it might be, it would be a mistake to see in "Von den Gleichnissen" a blueprint for approaching other parables in

---

7. "Verloren" is interesting here. The obvious meaning is losing the bet, but there are connotations as well of being in a state of helplessness.

Kafka's oeuvre, "Vor dem Gesetz" included. It is not a clutch of precepts that determines the formal and material elements of parables.
Instead, the parable on parables is a highly focused example of that
form and material. Its relation to "Vor dem Gesetz" is, rather, focal; it
is similar to how a particularly acute painting can illuminate the rest
of an artist's work.

"BEFORE THE LAW": THE PRELIMINARY
SECTIONS

The parable and the section that follows it concerning its exegesis are
so remarkable that it is easy to overlook the crucial context provided
them by the chapter at large. The chapter opens with K. preparing for
a meeting with a visiting Italian executive. K.'s supervisor has charged
K. with guiding the visitor through the city's cultural sites, on account
of K.'s knowledge of art history and his "adequate" Italian. As it turns
out, K.'s Italian, perhaps adequate for limited, scripted encounters,
is far from adequate when it comes to the businessman, who con-
verses with K.'s supervisor in swift Italian that eventually yields to a
dialect utterly incomprehensible to K.[8] The social exclusion of the
meticulous, yet under-prepared K. from the expansive and amiable
conversation not only reinforces K.'s and the reader's suspicions that
K.'s firm is out to get him (i.e., is an investigative arm of the court) but
also alerts the reader going forward that the signal form of K.'s experience of the incomprehensible will not be one in which he confronts
what is in itself incomprehensible but, rather, what is comprehensible
to others but not *to him*. K.'s everyday experience is of a domain in
which others perform as if there is ready comprehension, but one in

8. Kafka, *Der Proceß*, 274.9–19 / *The Trial*, 202.

which K.'s comprehension is compromised in a faintly insidious, yet comical way. K. apprehends that there is something comprehensible, but comprehends only that he cannot comprehend it. No matter how assiduously one thumbs through an out-of-date Italian phrase book, one will not be able to close the gap between barely serviceable Italian and accelerated Neapolitan. His being outpaced by the unforeseen strangeness of what he thought to be manageable establishes the pervading mood of the scenes that follow.

The next section of the chapter concerns K.'s arrival at the cathedral. The event that inaugurates this section is the nonappearance of the Italian visitor at the rendezvous. K. and the businessman had agreed to meet "at or around" (*etwa um*) 10 o'clock that morning.[9] In Kafka's handwritten manuscript, K. arrives at the church "punctually" at *11 o'clock*, raising a question in the reader's mind concerning whether K. has arrived late for the appointment. Matters become more complex when, well after K. has entered the cathedral (i.e., at 11 o'clock), he notes the time to be 11 o'clock.[10] This might indicate a discrepancy in the manuscript, and indeed that is how Brod sees matters, editing for consistency by substituting "ten" for the first occurrence of "11." ' The most recent German edition and most reliable English translation leave the time unaltered.[11] The decision to do so seems to have been made out of fidelity to the manuscript version, the English translator allowing that the discrepancy is likely due to a simple mistake on Kafka's part.[12] That may be, but there is another

---

9. Kafka, *Der Proceß*, 276.12 / *The Trial*, 203.
10. See Kafka, *Historisch-Kritische Ausgabe*, 10:22, 23.
11. Kafka, *Der Proceß*, 279.16 / *The Trial*, 206.
12. See Kafka, *The Trial*, xxi. Neither the *Kritische Ausgabe* nor Brod (nor the English translation) follows the autograph here in one important respect. For every pertinent mention of the time of the appointment in the chapter, Kafka employs Arabic numerals; he does not spell out the time (e.g., "10 Uhr," *not* "zehn Uhr"). See, e.g. Kafka, *Historisch-Kritische Ausgabe*, 10:16, 17. This is important because it makes it slightly more likely that he has misstated the relevant times, on the assumption that it is easier when writing longhand to falsely enter a single digit than a whole word.

possibility worth consideration. Were the novel written in the first-person, one obvious way to reconcile the inconsistency would be to see in it evidence of K.'s conflicted mental state, faulty memory or, a bit more pointedly, a suppressed wish not to face the difficulties of making himself understood in Italian. One might even find self-delusion here. After all, the action of *The Trial* to a large extent concerns K.'s defense of himself; the confusion of times—precise time being the stuff of legal proceedings—could amount to an unintended or intentional but artless attempt at self-exculpation. Kafka writes *The Trial* in the third-person, however, and that might seem to settle the point in the other direction, blunting any possible revelatory force of the reported times. But the force remains, and does so in the mode characteristic of Kafka's manifest intent that the narration conveys the weight of an authority that is both for and against K. For, while the narration is in the third-person, it does not take an omniscient point of view. With very few exceptions, only K.'s thoughts are presented directly, and the limited third-person narration in *The Trial* enforces strict focus on K., his state of mind, and the world as it is in opposition to K.'s interpretation of it. But the narrative form also allows K.'s perspective on the world to leach into the world, and the overall effect of Kafka's employment of this narrative framework is to seed objectivity with ambiguity. This goes hand in glove with another pervasive aspect of the tone of the novel—its matter-of-fact (if one were accentuating the comic element here, one might say "deadpan") presentation of the ordinary as the more-than-ordinary. In Kafka there is nothing as mysterious as facts clearly perceived. This quality of the prose constitutes the background condition for the particular type of precision that Benjamin, Borges, Calvino, Hrabal, Nabokov, and other admirers of Kafka so prize. On the one hand, it is key that the precision has an observational character, a kind of detachment bordering on disinterest. Yet, the details in question are not all on a par; there is in Kafka a verbal corollary to what Barthes, speaking of photographs, called the *punctum*—that is, a telling detail, at first glanced over, which upon continued attention becomes the organizing point of the composition.[13] Given such attention to detail, and absent clear evidence that there is a slip of the pen, it is inadvisable to shrug off the time discrepancy as unintentional. And given the narrative voice of the novel, which focuses on the projective force of K.'s understanding of events as the source of both their apparent objectivity and K.'s sense of being out of kilter, the $10.00–11.00_1$-11.00_2 schema may indicate, to the taxing reader Kafka always courts, that K.'s "evidence" that he is developing in the "proceeding" is compromised. One might suggest, moreover, that the principal role of the temporal schema is to begin to detach the events that pertain to K.'s visit to the cathedral from the externalities of everyday commerce. For, as it turns out, K. has been summoned to the cathedral by the priest, a representative of the court—in fact, the prison chaplain.[14] The business outing may have been mere pretext, which would explain the failed appearance of the businessman.

Once K. enters the vaultlike cathedral, he experiences a self-enclosed world in which, even at midday, near darkness is punctuated only by the faint glow of votive candles. Aside from an old woman praying in a side aisle and a sexton puttering about, K. seems to be its sole occupant. The darkness does not entirely hinder K., for, ever resourceful, he has brought his pocket flashlight. With it he makes his way to a side chapel, where he directs its beam onto a painting. The main point surely is that K. is attempting to make his way by his own, albeit artificial, light—a type of illumination that is unlike both the divine light that the stained glass windows allow to penetrate the stone artifice of the building and the candle glow that is the result of

13. See Roland Barthes, *La chambre eclaire: Note sur la photographie* (Paris: Gallimard, 1980), 47–49, 73–78.
14. Kafka, *Der Proceß*, 288.12 / *The Trial*, 212.

a prayerful and consecrating act. The flashlight imparts a sickly green hue to the painting, the details of which K. only makes out piece-meal owing to the limited throw of the beam. The painting in question depicts an armored knight either witnessing or standing sentry at the entombment of Christ. The treatment of its subject matter is both "conventional" and "recent," hardly an object of veneration or even sustained aesthetic reflection. In time, K. notices the sexton ges-ticulating and after a short time, follows him, sitting down in a nave near a small auxiliary pulpit. A priest mounts the pulpit, apparently to make a sermon, but K. remarks that not only is late morning an odd time for a sermon but also that he, K., seems to be the only pos-sible audience. K. wants to avoid being singled out by the priest and tries to sneak out of the cathedral, but the priest calls out to him by name, and K. is forced by civility to remain. The priest identifies him-self as the prison chaplain and gives notice that he knows of K.'s case and, moreover, understands that the litigation is proceeding poorly. K. feels the priest to be genuinely interested in his welfare, unlike other representatives of the court, and asks for the priest's advice concerning how to escape the jurisdiction of the court. This is a change in tactic; previously K. had tried to ignore the court, show up late to it, or manipulate its inner workings (through the advocate, the court painter, and his various romantic connections with women). K. asks the priest to descend from the pulpit, which he does. This is an important request. The German word *Kanzel* can mean both a pul-pit and a judicial bench, and this dual meaning inaugurates a parallel structure that is in force in the rest of the chapter, in which K.'s trial receives its penultimate expression through religious authority.

The priest deploys a parable as a corrective to what he identifies as K.'s self-deception about the nature of the court (*Im Gericht täuschst Du Dich . . .*).[15] The priest has previously clarified one aspect of the

15. Kafka, *Der Proceß*, 292.15 / *The Trial*, 215.

legal procedure. It is perhaps too obvious to mention that the word *Prozeß* can convey an ongoing *process*, not merely the completion of a process. *Trial* can also have this force, if more faintly. Noting this now is pertinent because the first "lesson" the priest teaches K. is that "[t]he judgment doesn't come all at once; the proceeding gradually crosses over into the judgment" (*[d]as Urteil kommt nicht mit einemmal, das Verfahren geht allmählich ins Urteil über*; translation modified).[16] The trial of K. is, accordingly, synonymous with the judgment of him. This might seem a trivial nuancing of a mundane truth that judges and juries are assessing purported evidence throughout a proceeding, and thus may be said to be judging the whole time. But the point goes beyond that. It is that there is no purpose to the proceeding beyond the proceeding itself. Trials merely start and stop; they do not begin and end. Were K. to credit this view, he would understand that all of his past efforts at ignoring or influencing the process were not only ineffective but also themselves objects of continuous judgment. K.'s hope that the priest will deliver "decisive . . . advice" (*entscheidenen . . . Rat*) is, therefore, fundamentally misguided.[17] It is, the priest intuits, a form of self-deception. Accordingly, the parable develops themes at the intersection of (a) deception and self-deception and (b) the nature of law.

THE PARABLE

There are two principal characters, a "man from the country" (*ein Mann vom Lande*) and a "doorkeeper" (*Türhüter*). The door in question is the entryway to the precinct of law. The near equivalence

16. Kafka, *Der Proceß*, 289.19–20 / *The Trial*, 213. Note the similarity of phrase with the slightly more theological *hinübergehen* in "Von den Gleichnissen."
17. Kafka, *Der Proceß*, 291.12 / *The Trial*, 214.

between K.'s access or lack of access to the law and his relationship to the priest, on the one hand, and the man's access to the inner sanctum and his relationship to the gatekeeper, on the other, is the centerpiece of the second half of the chapter.

The doorkeeper denies the man entry to the law, and when the man asks if it is possible for him to enter at a later time, the doorkeeper responds that "it is possible, but not now" ([e]s ist möglich ... jetzt aber nicht).[18] The gate (Tor) stands open—one can peer through it and perhaps even enter it if one is willing to disobey the doorkeeper—and the man crouches to better look inside when the doorkeeper steps to the side. At its very outset, the parable introduces a palpable ambivalence on the part of both parties: the doorkeeper does not quite seem to be someone who will physically prevent the man from entering, yet the man seems deterred, satisfied for now to steal a peek at what might lie beyond the gate. The curiosity of the man does not go unnoticed, and the doorkeeper amicably offers that the man can try to penetrate the interior if he likes, even though the doorkeeper verbally has forbidden it, warning him however that while he, the doorkeeper, is "mighty" (mächtig), he is only the "lowest" (unterste) of his cohort. The doorkeeper describes the interior as a kind of Forbidden City, in which there is hall upon hall with no apparent end, each hall having its own doorkeeper, each mightier than the last. The third doorkeeper is so frightening that the first doorkeeper cannot bear to look at him. The man, who believes the law should be "always accessible to anyone" (jedem und immer zugänglich sein), now regards the doorkeeper more closely, but reconsiders a rush on the door when he sees his "fearsome Tartar's beard." The doorkeeper then provides the man a stool and invites him to wait beside the door. And wait he does, for days and years, regularly yet rather timidly asking to be admitted.

18. Kafka, Der Proceß, 292.24 / The Trial, 215.

Often, but only "out of kindness," the doorkeeper gives the man "cursory interviews" (*kleine Verhöre*), but declines admission each time. Although there is no express indication, the implication is that such denials are not presented in a manner that precludes later admission. For the man stays on, repeatedly trying to bribe the doorman, who accepts the bribes but, we are told, only so that the man can be satisfied that he has tried everything to be admitted. The man comes to observe the doorkeeper obsessively, anthropomorphizing the fleas that live in the fur collar of his overcoat, making their acquaintance, pleading with them to intercede on his behalf. As he grows old, the man complains less outwardly, worn down by age and rebuff to mere grumbling. His sight dims, but precisely at this juncture the man encounters (*erkennt*) a radiance (*Glanz*) "streaming forth incessantly" from behind the gate. The implication is that his failing physical sight is a precondition for this extramundane perception.[19] As he nears death, the man collects all his prior experience at the gate into one question, one that he has never before thought of putting to the doorkeeper: "All strive for the law, . . . how does it happen, then, that in these many years no one but me has requested [*verlangt hat*] admittance" (translation amended).[20] *Verlangen* is difficult to render in English given the context; it carries a stronger sense of requirement than does *request* that can at the limit mean "demand" or, more subjectively, "crave." And these stronger senses are borne out by the doorkeeper's exasperated declaration that the man is "insatiable." The doorkeeper's reply to this final question—it is revealing that all of the man's "demands" have been interrogative, not imperative in form—is the punch line, as it were, of the parable: "No one else could gain admittance here, because this entrance was meant solely for you. I'm going now to shut it" (translation amended).[21]

19. Kafka, *Der Proceß*, 294.11–13 / *The Trial*, 216.
20. Kafka, *Der Proceß*, 294.21–24 / *The Trial*, 217.
21. Kafka, *Der Proceß*, 294.26–295.2 / *The Trial*, 217.

There is one additional point to mark before turning to the exegetical conversation that ensues between K. and the priest, although a fuller appreciation of the point must wait until that discussion is complete. It is important to observe the bookending of the parable with two occurrences of the adverb *now*. The first use pertains to the initial response of the doorkeeper to the man's entreaty to gain entrance: it is possible, "but not now" (*jetzt aber nicht*). Note that the notion of possibility so modified is ephemeral. Kafka is very precisely tacking away from the more conciliatory and usual "not yet" (*noch nicht*), which encourages more the "striving" in question, and steering for the more pointed and cutting "now, however, not." The conclusion of the passage brings this "now," so to speak, to fruition. *Now* the doorkeeper closes the door, in slight advance of the man's death (but not so close to death that the man cannot see the door close). It was his personal door, opened to the extent it ever was for him alone and closed now that he is about to cease to be. One may speak of past possibilities in the abstract—for example, what if Bismarck had not edited the Ems Dispatch—but as a matter of ongoing experience, there is a close relationship between modal statements like "*x* is possible" and the future tense. The second "now" is pointedly bereft of all future possibility relative to entering into the law. Part of the irony of the passage is that in retrospect, the opening "not now" seems just as final as its counterpart that closes the parable.[22]

THE EXEGESIS

K.'s immediate reaction to the parable is to claim that it is obvious the doorkeeper has deceived the man. The priest responds that such

22. J. M. Coetzee makes the interesting suggestion that Kafka "had an intuition of an alternative time, a time cutting through the quotidian." *Doubling the Point: Essays and Interviews*, ed.

an interpretation is "hasty" (*übereilt*) and directs K.'s attention back
to the precise wording of the parable, which, the priest emphasizes,
he has rendered verbatim.[23] There is no explicit mention of deception in the story, so the interpretative bar for ascribing such is high.
K. responds—his own case no doubt in mind—that the doorkeeper
only provided the man information about entry to the law when "it
could no longer help him" (*als sie dem nichts mehr helfen konnte*), the
implication being that, if provided earlier, such information may have
been of use. Crucial here is not only the soundness of this inference
concerning the usefulness of information and when it was provided,
but also the relevant sense of "helping." K.'s objection assumes that
the information may have aided the man in ordering his life, either
by turning his back on the endeavor of entering the law and going
elsewhere or, less probably, by helping him to gain access to the law.
Moreover, K. assumes that what the doorkeeper has in fact done by
disclosing the personal nature of the gate (i.e., it is only "for" the man),
taken together with the fact that the gate has always been nominally
"open," does not mean that it was "open to K. to pass through" and,
therefore, does not constitute "help." K., that is, implicitly narrows
"help" to mean "help pass through the gate or turn away from it."

The priest does not make these assumptions clear to K. in rebuttal; again, he sticks to the text: the man never asked the question that
brought the information to light until the end of his life. So, how can
one hold the doorkeeper responsible for not providing the response
earlier? There are two points here. First, the priest's observation hammers home that the information is provided in the context of *question-
ing*, a context that requires engagement on the part of both parties,

David Attwell (Cambridge, MA: Harvard University Press, 1992), 198. The consideration
of the "nows" here and the issue of the slippage in time and its reporting treated earlier
would benefit from an extended treatment of temporality in Kafka.

23. Kafka, *Der Proceß*, 295.3–7 / *The Trial*, 217.

but one in which the onus is on the one posing the questions. This complicates finding the doorkeeper blameworthy; moreover, and more important, stress on the interrogative and dialogic background should bring home to K. his own situation relative to the law and cause him to be aware that he may have received the requisite help, if "help" means something like "aid in sustaining the interrogative attitude." Second, the priest's rebuttal of the simple charge of failure to help foregrounds the integrative experience embedded in the man's final question—the question that solicits the revealing response from the doorkeeper. The implication is raised that *all* his experiences at the gate—ineffective bribery, interviews to no apparent effect, incessant waiting—were preconditions for being able to form and ask that last question. On this interpretation, the various interchanges between the man and the doorkeeper are of the essence, not a final judgment that is conceptually apart from the whole process of "life before the law." Not only is the gatekeeper not to be blamed; without him there would no revelation at all—even if the revelation in question is not tantamount to entrance "into the law."

Following this extraordinary exchange, the priest adjusts slightly to extend his approach. Besides, he says, the doorkeeper was *only* a doorkeeper, and the parable shows that he has been scrupulous in fulfilling the duties of that office.[24] K. objects flatly that the doorkeeper did not do his duty. His duty was to tell the man that the door was *his* door. He should have turned all others away and admitted the man for whom the door was meant. Again, the assumption seems to be that "my door" is shorthand for "my door to pass through," an assumption that becomes more problematic as the exegesis unfolds. This is in somewhat more concrete and plainspoken form the general precept with which K. begins his understanding of the nature of law—that is, that the law is binding on one, and to that extent is the

24. Kafka, *Der Proceß*, 295.12–15 / *The Trial*, 217.

law only if it is something to which one can have rational access and thereby ratify as binding. Again, the priest reminds K. that he lacks respect for the text and is changing the story to suit his preconceptions. There are two overt "clarifications" (*Erklärungen*) concerning entry through the gate, the priest insists, one given at the beginning of the passage and one at its end. The doorkeeper first states that "he cannot grant admission now" and, at the conclusion, he states that "the entrance was meant only for you." The priest is careful to render these propositions, again, verbatim. The priest suggests that K. would be correct in his interpretation if the two statements were contradictories. But they are not. They are clearly not logically contradictory, but even if contradiction *sensu stricto* does not enter the question but, rather, something less severe within the domain of incompatibility, the priest seems on firm ground for reasons already canvassed. But the priest extends the point in a surprising direction, suggesting that the first statement "implies" (*hindeutet auf*) the second.[25]

It is not entirely evident what the priest is suggesting. It is reasonably clear that one should not understand "implies" strictly—that is, as meaning logical implication. Something evidential like "indicates" is more apt. On this understanding, it is the property of not-yet-being-able-to-be-admitted that marks the gate as one's own. In light of this fact, the priest suggests the doorkeeper *exceeds* his duty in his first statement by representing that there is the possibility of admittance at a later time. This is evidence of compassion (*Mitleid*). Most commentators are surprised at this, the priest continues, as otherwise the parable presents the keeper as unstinting and precise. This militates against his guarding of the entrance and constitutes breaches or gaps (*Lücken*) in the character required of a true doorkeeper.[26] At this

25. Kafka, *Der Proceß*, 295.24–296.1 / *The Trial*, 218.
26. Kafka, *Der Proceß*, 297.15–17 / *The Trial*, 219. Part of the semantic play here involves the ironic modulation from "gate" to "entrance" precisely when the entrance can no

point, K. renews the conversation by repeating to the priest what he takes to be the priest's main contention—that is, that the doorkeeper does not deceive the man and, by implication, if there is any deception about entering into the law, it is self-deception on the part of the man. The priest then introduces what may be the most disconcerting interpretation for K.: that it is the doorkeeper who is deceived. The priest introduces this possibility, again, as one that commentators have pondered. Such an interpretation takes the doorkeeper to be simple-minded (*einfältig*) and conceited (*eingebildet*), exploiting a close conceptual linkage possible in German of naïveté, on the one hand, and childish haughtiness, on the other. The doorkeeper never himself dares to enter the gate, and one may feel free to disregard his word that he has ever been inside it. K. finds this to be farfetched, and it is at this point that the priest introduces two further rules of construction:

> "[T]he commentators tell us hereto: correct *interpretation* [*richtiges Auffassen*] of a matter and *misunderstanding* [*Mißverstehen*] the same matter are not completely mutually exclusive [*schließen einander nicht vollständig aus*]. . . . The text is immutable [*unveränderlich*], and the opinions [*die Meinungen*] are often only an expression of despair over it [*sind oft nur ein Ausdruck der Verzweiflung darüber*]." (translation modified; emphases added)[27]

A distinction between interpretation and understanding is crucial to the first precept. Parables attempt to represent, express, and

---

longer be—in Erich Heller's mordant gloss—"a door that is not a door." See *Kafka* (London: Fontana, 1974), 85. But it also consists in the contrast of the open "gap" or "breach" in the façade of the doorkeeper *qua* compassionate doorkeeper, on the one hand, and the closed gate, on the other.

27. Kafka, *Der Proceß*, 297.11–13, 298.20–22 / *The Trial*, 219, 220.

educate. They represent by narrative means a course of action, thereby expressing a truth, which truth is inculcated in the reader or auditor as a guide to further conduct. Moreover, in the sort of parable that interests Kafka, the cognitive and perhaps even semantic limitations of created beings (as both authors and readers of parables) are themselves subject to this representation, expression, and inculcation. We saw just this theme in "Von den Gleichnissen." Mistakes of understanding need not undermine "correct interpretation" because, while understanding aims at stable comprehension (e.g., a reasonably determinate knowledge claim that in principle is open to and can survive challenge), interpretation has as its object the ongoing provision of meaning. When interpreting, there is a presumption that no settled meaning is possible, at least not with regard to complex objects crafted for purposes of being interpreted. If one credits this distinction, canonical in philosophical and literary discussion well before Kafka, then misunderstanding in interpretation will not defeat the activity of interpretation or its products. One might press the point further and claim that misunderstanding is necessary for correct interpretation. In a way, this set of distinctions is housed *in nuce* in the adjective *richtig*, which can mean both "correct" in the sense of (1) "determinately or demonstrably true" (i.e., as of understanding) and (2) "real," "better," or "proper" (i.e., as of interpretation). This brings one to the second precept, having to do with the status of opinion. In this context, one must see opinion in light of the distinction between understanding and interpreting. Opinions are products of attempting to interpret the text, which is fixed and immutable relative to the interpretations of it (i.e., that is what makes the interpretations interpretation *of it*). The text is a criterion whose full measure cannot be taken by constructions laid upon it.

Taken together, the two precepts transform the sense in which the concept of truth plays a role in the experience afforded those who interpret parables. Parables do not communicate truths so much as they set truth as a problem, as something whose nature it is to punish conceptual overreaching. This is one explanation for why the priest later says to K. that "one does not have to consider everything true, one only has to consider it necessary."[28] If one takes truth to be a property that obtains between something like a statement or proposition, on the one hand, and something like a state of affairs or fact, on the other, one may take the priest to be suggesting that whether an interpretation is right or wrong is not the main point of "standing before" before the law. It is, rather, the implacable nature of the object to be interpreted, the law, which presents itself as both unavoidable and unapproachable. "Necessity" here is precisely *not* to be understood as conceptual invariance demonstrated by and dependent on exhaustion of possibilities—as if necessity were the extrusion of a process of making replete the logical space of possibility. The concept is much closer to that of the Greek ἀνάγκη, which denotes necessity ontologically prior to all possibility.

Let us return to the conjecture that it is the doorkeeper who is deceived, not the man. Following directly from the conversational turn to the simplicity and self-conceit of the doorkeeper is the idea that he is deceived about his elevated status relative to that of the man. The implication does not seem to be that another has deceived him but, rather, that he deceives himself. He is, after all, only a doorkeeper, the priest repeats, and thus serves the man. The man can go anywhere except through the gate; it is the doorkeeper who may not leave. Insofar as freedom is concerned, then, the man is in the superior position. Further, one may allow not only that the door is only for the man but also that the doorkeeper is in unique service to the man.[29] Moreover, one might venture that the doorkeeper is deceived about the nature of the door. The parable begins by stipulating that

28. Kafka, *Der Proceß*, 303.1–2 / *The Trial*, 223.
29. Kafka, *Der Proceß*, 300.24–27 / *The Trial*, 221.

the door *always* stands open, even if admittance cannot be granted now or ever; yet, the doorkeeper says he will shut the door, in contravention to the original statement.[30] Why does he say this—the very last words the man likely hears? The priest offers that the age-old tradition of commentators on the parable opines that the doorkeeper speaks in this way either out of compassion for the man or in order to ensure that the man's sorrow is as deeply entrenched as possible. Many commentators agree that he has no power to close the door. Finally, one might argue that the doorkeeper is epistemically subordinate to the man. The man sees the radiance from within with (or only with) his failing eyes; not only does the doorkeeper not see the light, his back is always turned to it.

K. says that he agrees with this line of reasoning, but quite properly insists that it does not follow from the doorkeeper's being deceived that the man is not deceived by him in turn. K. argues, somewhat obscurely, that one might even say that the deception of the doorkeeper is "passed on necessarily to the man" (translation modified), as perhaps a virus is communicated between hosts.[31] Ignorance can unintentionally breed deception in others. This may not amount to deceiving in a strict sense, but the effect is the same. The priest has what amounts to the last word in response. Lines of commentators have considered this possibility as well, but find it contrary to the proviso that one must not pass judgment on him (surprising, given the commentators' appetite for construing the character of the doorkeeper). The doorkeeper "belongs to the law," is thereby cloaked in the law's inviolability, and is "beyond human judgment" (*dem menschlichen Urteil entrückt*).[32] *Entrücken* has in many of its uses a strong religious dimension indicating spiritual transport—in this case, that

30. Kafka, *Der Proceß*, 301.4–7 / *The Trial*, 221.
31. Kafka, *Der Proceß*, 302.5–6 / *The Trial*, 222.
32. Kafka, *Der Proceß*, 302.15–16 / *The Trial*, 222.

the doorkeeper is not merely a finite agent whom human judgment properly could measure. To be bound to the law under this description is "incomparably better than living freely in the world" (*unvergleichlich mehr als frei in der Welt zu leben*).[33] One should not miss the spice of *unvergleichlich* here, given that part of the issue under discussion in the exegesis is the ontological commensurability of the man and the doorkeeper, and by extension the question of whether human estimates of comparability are even to the point. K. rejects this line of commentary outright; to accept it, in his view, requires one also to accept that all the doorkeeper's statements are true, which is manifestly not the case. It is this appeal to truth that occasions the priest's counter that truth is not of the essence when it comes to law; rather, necessity is.

K's response to this final, deadening proposition is that, if true, it would reveal the world to be nothing but a web of lies. On the assumption that such lies are "bad," which assumption would be one explanation for K.'s horror at the suggestion, this would constitute a reversal of the vision that, all appearances to the contrary, the world is as good as it can be. The soundness of K.'s inference from the law being necessary to the world's being a system of lies is questionable. If lying is an *action* of telling a falsehood that is *intended* to deceive, the inference is dubious given its reliance on a premise that anthropomorphizes both the law and its source.

THE PARABLE AND THE WORLD
OF *THE TRIAL*

I draw two conclusions from this interpretation of the parable, its exegesis, and its place in the overall narrative of the chapter.

33. Kafka, *Der Proceß*, 302.19 / *The Trial*, 223.

First, the world of *The Trial* systematically frustrates the protagonist's attempt to navigate it. Seeking rational structure to better understand and address his lot does not have the sought effect of putting down alternatives in order to narrow cases and reach a clarifying, discrete final result. Quite the contrary, implementation of reason yields only more reasons—reasons that as they multiply in number, lose their power to circumscribe a meaningful context for their use. In such a world, *no* conclusion of a line of reasoning quite stands as a "result" that completes and retroactively stabilizes a line of reasoning. Any purported argumentative conclusion is, rather, something on the order of a sprung trap. The deeper one reasons and the more resolutely one pursues a systematic understanding of the world, the more one finds oneself suspended over an abyss of further reasons. *Contra* Plato, comprehension is a form of descent, not ascent. It would be mistaken, therefore, to take the lesson from *The Trial* to be that reasoning is futile because the world is "chaotic," as one sometimes encounters in the secondary literature. Nowhere in Kafka is the world presented as inchoate; it is, rather, teeming with reasons, chockfull of structures where analysis cannot help but try to find a grip. It is, to adapt a phrase, "rational all-too-rational." Kafka's prose is nothing if not a lucid form of rationalism run to its point of exhaustion. Walter Benjamin is especially perceptive just here, when he declares Kafka's prose constitutes "fairy tales for dialecticians."[34] Just this realistic effect is crystallized in the hermeneutic exercise following the parable.

Second, one might hazard an answer to the *Seinsfrage* K. poses in the chapter: How can a person be guilty per se (*überhaupt schuldig sein*)? After all, we are all of us human. The priest's reply is "the guilty

---

34. Walter Benjamin, "Franz Kafka. Zur zehnten Wiederkehr seines Todestages," in *Gesammelte Schriften*, ed. Rolf Tiedemann and Hermann Schweppenhäuser (Frankfurt am Main: Suhrkamp, 1977): II.2:415.

habitually talk that way" (*so pflegen die Schuldigen zu reden;* translation modified).[35] But what might that mean? There are broadly speaking two possibilities. The first is psychological: all guilty people are disposed to deny their guilt and to do so by appealing to their humanity. A second interpretation is ontological—it presses the merely psychological point further: the guilty habitually deny their guilt because habit follows ontology. Humans are guilty in the same sense that fish are aquatic; the phrase "guilty people" is pleonastic. On this view of the matter, "guilty'" does not qualify some humans in comparison to others; it functions rather like a species name. It is clear that the priest favors the latter interpretation and that K. resists it.

Does Kafka adopt the priest's understanding, according to which guilt is a native human condition that is tempting but impossible to extirpate? Or, does he cleave to the assumption that underlies K.'s rejection of the same—that is, that a finding of guilt must be predicated on individual fault? The priest's understanding, on the interpretation of it offered here, would extend perforce to all people. K.'s preferred view—that such people are only said, or more strongly, presumed to be guilty—does not require that scope, although the view permits it. Likewise, while parables may be devices that presuppose division of knowledge into the exoteric and esoteric, required for partial communication of basic truths to the uninitiated but not to the adept,[36] "Before the Law" teaches that all humanity is by its very nature the former, not the latter.[37]

35. Kafka, *Der Proceß*, 289.8–12 / *The Trial*, 213.
36. Cf. Mark 4:1–20. Crucial for purposes of comparison is the idea in the New Testament that Jesus's disciples qualify as adepts in virtue of being personally taught by God. This qualification is impossible in Torah, related religious texts, and in Judaism generally. Kierkegaard attacks precisely this qualification from within Christianity. Joshua Landy pressed on me the importance of the formulation in Mark.
37. Many thanks go to Karl Ameriks, Paul Franks, Gregg Horowitz, and Joshua Landy for their helpful comments on a prior version of this chapter.

BIBLIOGRAPHY

Barthes, Roland. *La chambre eclaire: Note sur la photographie*. Paris: Gallimard, 1980.

Benjamin, Walter. "Franz Kafka. Zur zehnten Wiederkehr seines Todestages." In *Gesammelte Schriften*, vol. II.2, edited by Rolf Tiedemann and Hermann Schweppenhäuser, 409–437. Frankfurt am Main: Suhrkamp, 1977.

Coetzee, J. M. *Doubling the Point: Essays and Interviews*. Edited by David Attwell. Cambridge, MA: Harvard University Press, 1992.

Heller, Erich. *Kafka*. London: Fontana, 1974.

Kafka, Franz. *Der Proceß*. Edited by Malcolm Pasley. In *Franz Kafka Kritische Ausgabe*, edited by Jürgen Born, Gerhard Neumann, Malcolm Paisley, et al. Frankfurt am Main: Fisher, 1990.

Kafka, Franz. *Historisch-Kritische Ausgabe sämtlicher Handschiften, Drucke und Typoskripte*. Edited by Roland Reuß and Peter Staengle, pt. 1: *Der Process*. Basel and Frankfurt am Main: Stroemfeld, 1995.

Kafka, Franz. *Parables*. New York: Schocken, 1947.

Kafka, Franz. *The Trial*. Translated by Breon Mitchell. New York: Schocken, 1998.

Plato. *Phaedo*. In *Opera*, vol. I. Edited by J. Burnet. Oxford: Oxford Classical Texts, 1953.

Wittgenstein, Ludwig. *Philosophical Investigations*. London: Blackwell, 1953.

Chapter 3

On the Ethical Character
of Literature

JOHN GIBSON

A book must be the ax for the frozen sea in us.

—Kafka, letter from 1904[1]

INTRODUCTION

How does a distinctly ethical dimension appear in a literary work? In exactly which features of a work does this ethical dimension, when such there is, reside? And why should we be interested in moral evaluation when reading works of narrative fiction, offering as they so often do an opportunity to escape the burdens of reality, with morality often one such burden? There are surely a variety of legitimate answers to these questions, depending on the kind of literature one has in mind. My concern here is with only one way of answering them, and in respect to only one kind of literature. *The Trial* will provide my example. It shows

---

1. As quoted in Gerhard Richter, "Introduction," in *Language Without Soil: Adorno and Late Philosophical Modernity*, edited by Gerhard Richter (New York: Fordham University Press, 2010), 5.

us, I argue, something unexpected and largely overlooked about how a literary narrative can achieve ethical significance and distill it into a value—that is, a reason for ascribing a kind of worth to it that becomes essential to our ability to complement its artistic success.

My starting point is critical. I take issue with a way of understanding the ethical core of art that is widespread in contemporary philosophical aesthetics, at least as practiced in the Anglophone world. I criticize it as an insider, but my frustration with it is continuous with a general disappointment many literary theorists have with contemporary analytic philosophy of literature: its failure to reckon seriously with literary modernism and so to address fully the challenge it poses to many of our standing habits of thought regarding the nature of literature. *The Trial* offers an example of the kind of modernist work that complicates our theories and to which they must be made adequate, assuming we do not wish to run afoul of the last 100 years of literary culture. What *The Trial* brings to our attention is that the ethical dimension of literature need not consist solely or even essentially in what a work says and depicts. That is, it need not be internal to its representational content. *The Trial* pursues its fundamental ethical project obliquely, often through manipulations of nonsensical and "impossible" employments of language and imagination, and it holds out the promise of a degree of autonomy to the reader who is willing to work through its critical project. This, it turns out, is key to understanding how certain works of literature, modernist or otherwise, achieve ethical goals more radical and remarkable than those the current state of the debate is able to acknowledge.

BEYOND ATTITUDE

Philosophers who proceed without caution have a habit of speaking of the ethical and aesthetic dimensions of art as though they are easily locatable and plainly distinguishable features of works, the "ethical" as residing *here*, in their "morally repugnant" parts, and the "aesthetic" as residing *there*, in the bits that are "beautiful" or "relevant to a work's status as an artwork." Perhaps, one always wants to say; but clearly much more needs to be said if we are to achieve clarity on what a work must *do*, in properly artistic terms, to endow its form or content with ethical relevance and make it matter to its status as a work of art. In better work in the field, a certain model dominates, and while it casts helpful light on this matter, it has important limitations when we begin to look at serious art of the last 100 years.[2]

One may call the model *attitudinal*. In labeling it thus, I define the model in terms of the aspect of it that most interests me, perhaps in a manner its proponents will find exceptionable. Nonetheless, it offers a strikingly intuitive and simple—this is not to say correct—answer to the question of how an artwork comes to possess a distinctly ethical character, and this is what matters to my discussion. The core idea is straightforward.[3] In the very act of representing actions and events, a work of art inevitably "also presents a point of view on them, a perspective constituted in part by the actual feelings, emotions and desires that the reader is prescribed to have towards the

2. Following custom in this debate, I use the terms "ethical" and "moral" interchangeably. Philosophers as temperamentally diverse as Hegel and Bernard Williams will insist on distinguishing them, and I have argued elsewhere that doing so improves our conceptual resources when attempting to contribute to the debate I outline here. See my "Thick Narratives," in *Narrative, Emotion, and Insight*, edited by John Gibson et al. (University Park, PA: Pennsylvania State University Press, 2011). For the purposes of the argument I develop in this essay, there is no need to distinguish the two.

3. The question that animates the debate in contemporary analytic aesthetics is much broader than the question of in what a work's ethical character consists: it asks whether any sort of *systematic* link between the ethical and aesthetic dimensions of art obtains such that success or failure in one domain determines success or failure in the other. The extreme positions on this, *radical moralism* and *radical autonomism*, have few defenders, who strive to provide absolute answers to these questions: crudely, the ethical success (or failure) of a work of art is *always*, or *never*, relevant to just assessment of its aesthetic and artistic success (or failure).

merely imagined events."[4] A work's "point of view," then, is revealed partly through the sentiments the work manifests but also in those responses it seeks to elicit from its audience (one suspects that the two are often indistinguishable). This is effectively what delineates the basic standpoint a work has in respect to its own content: how it "feels about it," as it were. If we can speak of a literary work as manifesting a particular perspective on its content—and surely we can— then it seems a steady step from this to granting that the perspective is at times charged with moral valence. A perspective is a stance, and a great many stances are *ethical* stances: properly moral modes of expressing an *attitude*. To put it formulaically, a literary work possesses an ethical dimension by virtue of having an attitudinal structure, a basic stance of approbation or censure the work evinces in respect to the characters and events it represents. This, the idea goes, is what *constitutes* a literary work's ethical character. And once we note that it is in the very nature of attitudes to be open to questions

Varieties of moderate *ethicism* (the idea that a positive evaluative link between the ethical and aesthetic success of a work at times obtains) and *immoralism* (the claim that no general link obtains, and indeed moral flaws can at times be essential to aesthetic success) rule the roost. For helpful overviews of the major positions in the debate on the relationship between moral and aesthetic value, all of which I draw on here, see Berys Gaut, *Art, Emotion and Ethics* (Oxford: Oxford University Press, 2007); A. W. Eaton, "Literature and Morality," in *The Routledge Companion to Philosophy of Literature*, edited by Noël Carroll and John Gibson (London: Routledge, 2015); Matthew Kieran, "Art, Morality and Ethics: On the (Im)moral Character of Art Works and Inter-Relations to Artistic Value," *Philosophy Compass* 1, no. 2 (2006); and Noël Carroll, "Art and Ethical Criticism: An Overview of Recent Directions of Research," *Ethics* 110, no. 2 (2000). For a recent defense of radical moralism, see Alessandro Giovanelli, "Ethical Criticism in Perspective: A Defense of Radical Autonomism," *Journal of Aesthetics and Art Criticism* 71, no. 4 (2013). For defenses of immoralism (robust, moderate or otherwise), see A. W. Eaton "Robust Immoralism," *Journal of Aesthetics and Art Criticism* 70, no. 3 (2012); Daniel Jacobson, "Ethical Criticism and the Vice of Moderation," in *Contemporary Debates in Aesthetics and the Philosophy of Art*, edited by Matthew Kieran (Oxford: Blackwell, 2006); and Matthew Kieran "Forbidden Knowledge: The Challenge of Immoralism," in *Art and Morality*, edited by José Luis Bermúdez et al. (London: Routledge, 2003). For a broad discussion of the relationship between the aesthetics and ethics, see Elisabeth Schellekens, *Aesthetics and Morality* (London: Continuum, 2007).

4. Gaut, *Art, Emotion, and Ethics*, 231.

of appropriateness, fit, and warrant, a foundation for the ethical criticism of art begins to appear, should one be inclined to engage in it.

This often is a subtle affair, since we know the explicit narrative voice of a novel and the attitudes it expresses—think of Humbert Humbert—can diverge from the attitude the work itself seems to express in respect to its content, and it is the latter that matters here, as the idea of that general orientation in thought and feeling a work seems to bear in respect to the regions of human experience and circumstance it represents. There is debate, and obvious room for maneuver, when we ask precisely which features of the work bear these attitudes—the narrator, the implied or manifested "author," and so on—but what is crucial is that on this model these attitudes are *borne by the work*. They are ultimately part of its semantic structure, since they in part determine what the work is *about*, bound up essentially with our sense of the overall "vision" it struggles to elaborate. Now, lest someone thinks something silly, virtually no players in this debate are interested in condemning or censuring works with morally challenged attitudes. Rather, the concern is to go on to theorize the relationship, if any, between the moral success (or failure) of an artwork and its artistic or aesthetic success (or failure). Nonetheless, it makes this form of investigation into the relationship between the moral and aesthetic dimensions of art possible by virtue of how it answers the question of what literature's ethical character fundamentally consists in, and the notion of an attitudinal structure is the answer it provides.[5]

5. There is great variety in the ways in which philosophers use the notion of an attitudinal structure to ground link between the ethical and aesthetic dimensions of art, but the following offers a sense of the possibility it opens up. Works of representational art typically attempt to prompt forms of affective and cognitive *response* from the reader or viewer; they strive to get her to feel or to believe something about its content. The successful eliciting of these responses can at times be essential to a work's aesthetic success, and when it is we can begin to detect what a proper evaluative link between the ethical and aesthetic dimensions of art looks like. This is often titled a "merited response argument" since everything is made to hang on the issue of whether, from the moral point of view, the responses the work seeks from us are warranted. See Gaut, *Art, Emotion, and Ethics*, 227–250.

There are features of the attitudinal model we should wish to retain. But if read as offering an answer to the question of how literature comes to bear ethical significance, it begins to feel clumsy and insufficient when looking at works like Eliot's *The Waste Land,* Beckett's *Waiting for Godot,* Faulkner's *The Sound and The Fury,* Joyce's *Ulysses,* and, of course, *The Trial.* The reader will note that I stopped myself just shy of producing a list of literary modernism's greatest hits. This is not, or not just, because in modernism narrative voice (or the perspective of the manifested author, etc.) is often too ambiguous—or too opaque, too inconsistent, too alienating, too alien, too mendacious, or too chaotic—to seem possessed of a determinate attitudinal structure and so ethical character. These and other features of high modernist narrative technique surely complicate the idea that a novel has *a* perspective or expresses *an* attitude, at least if by these one expects to find manifested in a work something like a stable and settled state of mind. But it is also easy to make too big a deal of this, since an attitude or perspective can itself be ambiguous, inconsistent (etc.) in respect to a state of affairs, and if so, questions of moral warrant can be asked of it. The problem is otherwise. It has to do with the fact that in modernist literature the ethical ambitions of art begin to change and to demand more than attitudinal models can accommodate.

The Trial is important here because it brings into view much of what theories such as these leave out or, at any rate, much of what they must take heed of if they wish to travel to more politically engaged and *au currant* regions of artistic production. To state the concerns baldly at first mention, *The Trial* challenges the idea that a novel's ethical character is constituted by its attitudinal structure, certainly one that is manifested in features of its narrated—and thus representational—content. Content is obviously important, but, as we will see, *The Trial* brings to our attention a general truth about much narrative literature: it can bear properties—forms of meaning, aboutness, and ethical significance—that are irreducible to any feature of its narrative and its manner of elaboration, and these extra-representational features are at times what endow a work with its distinct ethical character. Moreover, and more damning, *The Trial* shows us that attitudinal models are insufficiently *critical* to be able to capture the ethical dimension of a work with more radical moral and political aspirations. *The Trial* seeks a revolution in, not an application of, ethical thought, and this requires more than questions of appropriateness and warrant of attitude can provide. And last, *The Trial* attempts to enfranchise its implied audience to a much greater degree than would seem possible on an attitudinal model. On an attitudinal model, when we evaluate a work's moral quality, we assume the traditional third-person stance of judgment and ask whether the attitudes a work manifests (or seeks to elicit from the reader) are warranted, and once we have an answer we have effectively concluded our labor. *The Trial* may demand some of this, but it chiefly seeks a change in, not a verdict from, us.

The point that is essential to my argument is that *The Trial* is far more damning of the world than are any of the attitudes given expression in its narrative, and thus the latter cannot explain how it achieves its particular ethical character: its meaning, significance, and import as a piece of ethical thinking. To be playful but not inaccurate, Kafka would expect that if Josef K. or the narrator—the two express the lion's share of moral attitude in the novel—could read *The Trial* as intended, they would find themselves vile, though of course not to same extent they would find the agents of the court vile. This is not to say that the attitudes expressed in the text are morally unwarranted. The story is right, in an obvious moral sense, to present the madness Josef. K must endure as unwarranted, as *wrong*, since indeed it is. This is the attitude expressed by the narrative voice, and it is also that of the manifested author (*The Trial* often does not distinguish the two). But here's the rub. The attitudinal structure present *in The Trial*, the

vantage points *internal* to its narrative, stands in judgment of an institution and the features of society complicit in it. Call it bureaucracy.
This is what the voice of the narrative condemns. Yet the *work*, as an
entity that is, in some still undefined sense, broader than its narrative,
stands in judgment of something much more general: an entire form
of life, one that is presumably continuous with our own, at least at the
moment of modernity Kafka found himself an author. Thus the philosophical question is how we get from one to the other, from the narrative and the attitudes expressed there to a conception of the work's
ethical interests, which I am claiming is a different thing altogether.
This is the question *The Trial* obliges us to take seriously.

TITORELLI'S MIRRORS

It would be wise to explain this problem literarily rather than
philosophically—that is, in terms of an actual problem we might
encounter in our experience of *The Trial*. What matters to my argument are the features of the story that earn it its claim to absurdism.
We have, most obviously, the nightmarish geography of the world of
The Trial, of physical spaces that seem impossibly linked.[6] And these
hold in place various other absurdist elements of the story. These geographic spaces often represent the distinct spheres of ethical life: our
personal, sexual, familial, professional, and spiritual spaces. Thus
the upending of these spatial borders is also the undoing of many of
the boundaries essential to personal and social flourishing (it is perhaps unsurprising, then, that Josef K. is unlucky with both the law

6. I am thus in agreement with Noël Carroll when he claims that, "Kafka's technique is to recall
the original wisdom and horror embedded in ordinary expressions like the labyrinth of the
law by representing the biological basis of the metaphor in terms of geographic confusion.
The narrative and stylistic themes of being lost or spatially disoriented are ideologically

and love). But the absurdist elements go beyond this. What seems most absurd, ultimately, are not the impossible spaces or unfathomable procedures of the court but the *manners*, the forms of etiquette, the officiousness, the concerns about productivity and professional advancement, the demanding of reasons, that Josef K. holds on to throughout the story, except perhaps in the very final lines. All this "culture" begins to appear incongruous, hollow, even ridiculous, against the backdrop of such an irrational and absurd world.

None of this is news, and these features of the work are well enough known that it would be tedious to elaborate them here.[7] This is just as well, since I can elaborate my argument by way of a discussion of two mere objects that Joseph K. encounters. The scene is in Titorelli's room, and the objects are the paintings he shares with Josef K. The portions of the text that describe the paintings are for us, though not for Titorelli and Josef K., ekphrastic. They are examples of ekphrasis not only in the sense that we have a case of using words to depict paintings, as poets on occasion have a habit of doing. More generally, they are ekphrastic in the wider sense that the descriptions of the paintings are themselves a painterly employment of language, one which conveys meaning not by divulging propositions but by presenting aesthetically and morally charged images. Jointly, these images embody the sense of the world that Kafka is struggling to articulate in *The Trial*, condensing into two pictures much of its essential feel and strangeness. Kafka is reputed to have told Max Brod that he saw the world as one of God's bad moods, and the paintings effectively elaborate the affective and aesthetic dimensions of a world so conceived.[8]

motivated attacks on the experience of bureaucracy." Noël Carroll, *Interpreting the Moving Image* (Cambridge: Cambridge University Press, 1998), 196.

7. For that, see Neil Cornwell, *The Absurd in Literature* (Manchester: Manchester University Press, 2006), 184–214.

8. As cited in Michael Wood, *Literature and the Taste of Knowledge* (New York: Cambridge University Press, 2005), 31.

Josef K., recall, is sent by a colleague to Titorelli's studio in the impoverished periphery of town to try one final time to influence the courts. Titorelli, who has assumed a grand and clearly foreign name, paints portraits of court officials. Like Tintoretto, whose name we hear in his, Titorelli paints those in power, if not the clergy and aristocracy of sixteenth-century Venice, then of the judiciary class of the unnamed early twentieth-century city in which he lives. The contrast is productive, even if the point it yields is now clichéd: the modern artist who works in the service of power can no longer be an artist, since an artist whose relation to culture is uncritical and affirmative—who looks upon it and attempts to produce art by reproducing what he sees—is bound to run afoul of the aesthetic and cultural standards that govern the production of art. We see Titorelli as an "artist," not an artist; and this is in part because his relationship to his society is all wrong. There is a kind of risible tension in the very idea of an artist who serves the courts in a world such as this, in a way there isn't in the idea of a fifteenth-century Venetian artist doing somewhat the same, even if corruption and general forms of nastiness are rampant in both cultures.

The first painting we find is one of Titorelli's portraits of an officer of the court. Its attempt at hagiography produces incoherence. The painting contains a depiction of a deity of challenged identity. Titorelli wishes to represent "Justice and the goddess of Victory in one,"[9] though he ultimately wants it to resolve into an image of "the goddess of the Hunt."[10] The figure is situated "atop the back of the throne,"[11] in which a judge sits, painted in gaudy pastel, per the judge's request. The figure upon the throne represents *whatever* it is that the judge, and so the courts, ultimately serve—nominally the Law and Justice, but indistinguishable from other forms of power operative

9. Kafka, *The Trial*, trans. Breon Mitchell (New York: Schocken, 1998), 145.
10. Kafka, *The Trial*, 146.
11. Kafka, *The Trial*, 145.

in the state. Justice is conjoined with Victory, thereby disrupting a mimesis of impartiality with an expression of conquest and domination; and the painting adds to this awkward tangle of divine bodies the goddess of the Hunt, and so a figure who actively seeks prey, for example, in the form of "innocent" citizens such as Josef K. So, K. remarks on the confusion of labor here. Justice has "wings on her heels," but he chides, she "must remain at rest, otherwise the scales sway and no judgment is possible."[12] Titorelli concedes the problem and adds "a few strokes to the contours of the figure, without, however, making it any clearer in the process."[13] One is left with the sense that it would be impossible for the painting to be made any clearer. It is what a metaphysician might describe as an essentially vague object—that is, an object to which added detail does not result in increased determinacy.

I take the painting of the judge to have a symbolic function twice over. In the first instance, it has a broadly synecdochical role: it is a part of the text that comes to stand for the whole of the text. Since "everything belongs to the court,"[14] including the children who throng the hallways of Titorelli's building, this is effectively an image of the force that animates and binds the various spheres of culture. It is an image of the institutional and so the social world in which Josef K. finds himself. But it also registers as a symbol, now just more abstractly, of the world beyond the work. We are expected to feel our cultural situation implicated in Titorelli's painting, at least to the extent we are expected to feel it implicated in *The Trial*, given that the former is representative of the latter. If this is so, then the painting provides a link that runs from Titorelli's studio to the world of Josef K. and then on to ours.

12. Kafka, *The Trial*, 145.
13. Kafka, *The Trial*, 145.
14. Kafka, *The Trial*, 150.

Note that this accomplishes something remarkable. It renders the nonsensical features of the painting properly mimetic—indeed, the *only* features of the painting that enjoy genuine representational success. Because they are incoherent and nonsensical, these features of the painting can sustain a mimetic relationship, since Josef K.'s world is itself incoherent and nonsensical. Our world, one assumes, is taken to be this way, too, if just figuratively. For Kafka, in other words, our world is metaphorically nonsensical in the precise respects Josef K's literally is, and in this manner the text here establishes a mimetic bond between the worlds of Josef K. and Kafka's readers. This is in part, though no small part, why we experience *The Trial* as an act of cultural critique and not just an exercise in nightmarish fantasy. It is on account of this possibility of metaphoric identification with Kafka's fiction, and the resultant mimetic link it helps establish between the nonsensical features of his world and ours, that the work is able to generate the air of moral and political seriousness, as intent on showing, even demonstrating, something.

The painting of the judge, then, doubles for the social world in which K finds himself. This world, we know, is fraught: its intuitions are corrupt and it renders ethical life, whatever it may be, impossible: no genuine relationships can be cultivated, no enduring trust established, in a world such as this. (K.'s various relationships with lovers, lawyers, and colleagues bear this out.) What makes *The Trial* so damning is that it refuses to balance the despair of this with a glimpse of an emancipating elsewhere. If Kafka had been a naïve romantic, he would have put Josef K. on a train to the countryside, or perhaps on a boat to New Zealand, to discover a space not wholly damaged by culture and so a place of potential freedom. But none of this is permitted here, and so the vision of the world it offers is thoroughly bleak and unredemptive: it shows us an execrable world and offers no compensatory vision of a possible Eden.

The second of Titorelli's paintings recasts this point from a perspective external to the culture represented in this first. Titorelli describes it as "landscape of the heath."[15] If the first painting gives us culture, the second is an attempt to represent the world beyond it, passing as it were from the normative to the natural. The landscape it depicts is scarcely an image of beautiful and animated nature. It shows only "two frail trees. Standing at a great distance from one another in the dark grass. In the background was a multicolored sunset."[16] We have here another symbol, but now of the extra-social world, and it is presented as just another absurd space. If the first painting shows an inhumane social world, the second depicts an inhuman natural world beyond it. The two wizened trees suggest not only alienation—they are separated, as though estranged people, by a great distance—but also the withering away of what once might have provided sanctuary from the reach of the institutions of the social order. The only light in the picture retires from the landscape with the sun. The sun is here, as it often is, a symbol of intelligibility, and as it sets, the extra-social world it illuminates is lost, too. Or so that is the feel of the painting, of which Titorelli's possesses many, all identical, though he is blind to the repetition. If the painting of the judge represents the social world as incoherent and mad, the heath painting represents a world beyond it as unavailable to us. It is not, of course, an indictment of the current state of the natural world but, rather, of the imagination of an artist who is at home in a world like this. The suggestion is that the existence of a vital world past the monolithic institutions of culture has become *unimaginable*, at least for one like Titorelli, who accepts this world and his place in it.

It is important to note that Titorelli's efforts fail to produce art, and this is because mere mimesis in such conditions has nothing of

15. Kafka, *The Trial*, 163.
16. Kafka, *The Trial*, 163.

value or interest to show us. Since uncritical, his paintings just reflect back to us the absurd and incomprehensible world in which Josef K. finds himself. They do nothing to overcome it or even to achieve a kind of clarity concerning its nature. And this leads to the first important point for my argument. Kafka's relationship to *The Trial* is like Titorelli's to his paintings, except that he, unlike the failed artist, will attempt to confront it and, to the extent a work of art can, overcome it. This turns out to be what distinguishes Kafka from Titorelli, as two artists who must work in a world that is either in fact or figuration of a piece with Josef K.'s. Read in this light, this section of the text functions both to reveal the conditions of artistic impoverishment in a world such as this and to draw our attention to what more *The Trial* does with its representation of absurdity such that it eludes these conditions. Put in simpler terms, we are here invited to consider what more is demanded of an artist, and to see Kafka as in part struggling to answer this.

Note that from a perspective internal to the text, the only significant difference between Titorelli's paintings and Kafka's *The Trial* is the following: while in each we find an incoherent, absurd, and senseless world, only *The Trial* expresses disapproval. The narrative of the novel, and the content it generates, yields this and nothing more. In this respect, the attitudinal model is vindicated. That is, we find in the content of *The Trial* a stance of condemnation in respect to these nonsensical features of Josef K.'s world. And this is a fine thing, revealing as it does that the work, if you will, has its head on straight. But this also is deeply unsatisfactory as an ethical response to its content, and it is false to our sense of the ethical significance of Kafka's labor. Surely it cannot be that the novel has achieved the extraordinary ethical and political significance critics and philosophers have afforded it over past ninety-two years just because it says no, in effect, to the patently immoral events and experiences it narrates. By the lights of virtually everything we know about ethics, in the face of such horror, a judgment can at best be the first step to proper moral engagement, the initial registering of a problem for which some further act provides a solution. It falls entirely short of an ethical *response*, which one would think calls for action in addition to judgment. Something that amounts to a confrontation, not merely recognition, is needed. We expect that something be challenged, changed, or overcome, and not that a mere stance or attitude be expressed. But here is the apparent problem. All we find in the representational content of *The Trial* is the narrative voice, which just expresses attitude.

So my argument hangs, then, on the idea that *The Trial* offers more than mere attitude, and thus we need to identify what this something more might be and how it is brought to view, if not *in* the work. But what could this mean?

BAD WORLDS, GOOD WORKS

Consider a series of interlocking claims about the relationship between art and society. I derive them from Raymond Geuss on Adorno, though it should be no surprise that what one says about Adorno also works for Kafka, given the great importance Kafka's writings played in the development of Adorno's moral, political, and cultural thought. Geuss's theses about art in an age of decay will help me stage the positive point I wish to make about *The Trial's* ethicality and what it means to claim that it is in some sense external to its content.

The first claim is that "if we accept for the sake of argument that our social world is evil . . . a number of interesting consequences follow for art."[17] Among these consequences is that art, to the extent it is

17. Raymond Geuss, *Outside Ethics* (Princeton, NJ: Princeton University Press, 2005), 165.

ethically serious, must confront this world in a very specific manner. It cannot, like Titorelli's paintings, simply mirror it. Nor can it earn its claim to ethical seriousness merely by expressing righteous moral attitudes in respect to it. Assuming that our world is fundamentally immoral, a great degree of representational honesty is demanded of art.

This leads to the second claim: "any form of art (or of religion or philosophy for that matter) that contributed to trying to make people affirm this world or make them think that it was worthwhile would not just be doing something unhelpful, but would be misguided in the most fundamental way possible."[18] Art must show the world to be as debased and inhospitable to human life as it in fact is, and so it follows that there is one thing art produced in the condition of an "evil" social world must never do. It must not be at home in it. In representing it, it cannot accept it, it cannot suggest that comfort can be found in it, that there are pockets of decency that make the terrible whole finally bearable, that we can escape it by becoming hipsters and moving to Brooklyn, diminish its oppression by dedicating ourselves to charity or by voting for a *really* liberal candidate, and so forth. The social world is, *ex hypothesi*, the ethically corrupt object. The problem is not with various of its institutions but with the thing itself. And so, according to this line of thought, the thing itself must change. The idea is that art's formal and imaginative powers must be used to this end, at least if we concede all that morality demands of an artist who is obliged to create in such conditions. To refuse to assume these responsibilities is to be, in effect, Titorelli.

This casts light on how Kafka wishes us to answer the question of what distinguishes his art from Titorelli's. Both attempt to produce art in the condition of "social evil," but only one succeeds. This is because only one realizes that it is by virtue of infusing the product

18. Geuss, *Outside Ethics*, 165.

of one's creative activity with a *critical* element that it can achieve a degree of distance, and so a measure of freedom, from it. It is by virtue of a critical element that we can say that a work of art comes to be "about" more than what it represents and thus that it is able to generate forms of meaning and significance that are in excess of its unrelentingly despairing content. But in what does this critical element consist? The third and final claim is that art produced in the condition of social evil—the condition, presumably, of European modernity—must "make [people] as keenly aware as possible of the discrepancy between . . . their world as potential paradise and their world as actual catastrophe."[19] It is by creating an awareness, through extra-representational means, of this contrast between our world and one worth having that an artist endows a work with a critical element.

We still need to know what these "extra-representational" means are, but the basic point is clear enough. On this model, the modern work of art must confront the world by forcing us to acknowledge the space between it and a world we should wish to inhabit—a world, say, in which *general* ethical flourishing is possible, on a cultural level and partly by virtue of its defining social and political institutions, and so a social world that is, following this line of argument, very unlike the actual one. This is one way of putting what more than mere mimesis, what more than simple depiction, is demanded of art in a world such as this. As we saw, "art" that simply pictures such a world, that just represents it as it is, will by necessity fail to generate art properly so called. And this is because it will fail to generate something worth looking upon: it will bear no aesthetic value since the object itself is empty of beauty and human meaning. It is the introduction of this critical element that marks the chief difference between a Kafka and a Titorelli.

19. Geuss, *Outside Ethics*, 165.

An otherwise counterintuitive point now becomes compelling, and it is one that runs mightily counter to the manner in which attitudinal models explain how art achieves ethical significance. Art that is produced in certain contexts—for example, in the context of profound cultural decay—partly earns it status as art by virtue of possessing an ethical project—that is, a project of creating in the subject a distance, and so a degree of freedom, from the forms of thinking, feeling, desiring, and valuing at home in our present cultural context. In other words, we cannot first have an object that we all agree to be art and then go on to wonder whether we will find something of ethical worth lurking within it. It is, rather, the other way around. It is *because* a mimetic object appears to possess a critical project that it can begin to appear as art, properly so called. It is only as such that we are welcome, on philosophical grounds, to apply the term "art" as a properly evaluative concept: one that casts an artifact as enjoying a degree of imaginative, creative, and aesthetic *success*. It is because we detect the shimmering of ethical significance in an object that we are given confidence that what we have before us is not a mere ornament, a pretty piece of propaganda, or a manipulation of the beautiful and sublime in the service of sleep and forgetting. Art, as Schiller once thought, holds out a promise of moral and political freedom, and the point on offer here is that in certain cultural conditions a serious critical project becomes a *necessary* regulative ideal in the production of objects that aspire to the status of art. Something must be done with a representation if it is to become art; and on not infrequent occasions it is the possession of a critical project that explains how an artwork transcends its rotten world in the act of representing it. *This* is what makes it possible for a story, a lyric, or a painting to bear genuine artistic value: to be art.

This is the kind of model that clearly requires the historicizing of its central claims. It is at best true of art in specific cultural contexts indexed to specific points in time. But note that it is not so narrow that it will hold true only if an artist is writing in Mitteleuropa in the wee hours before the dawn of National Socialism. The concept of a thoroughly evil social world travels, of course, to a startlingly wide array of times and places. In fact, we do not even need to explain precisely *when* it is true that a social world is evil. On purely philosophical grounds, all one needs to grant to make it *true of us* is that in our social world there is widespread suffering and alienation, and that this has something to do with the way it is organized culturally. Put differently, one just has to grant that fixing it will oblige us to create what amounts to a differently arranged form of life, at least in basic institutional and social respects. If one grants this, then one can concede the great ethical and political importance of a cultural practice that reveals to people the difference between "their world as potential paradise and their world as actual catastrophe." *Something* must happen such that we are prompted to envision the world otherwise and thus can begin to give initial content to the idea of "potential" paradise, or just of a place that is better than this. We need to come to feel that the material our social world gives us for making sense of our relationship to one another is flawed, contingent, and capable of being jettisoned, again, even if we do not quite know what the alternative shall be. Revolution starts with refusal, an initial damning expression of "no" to that which defines one's current material circumstances.

It is this inclusion of a "potential paradise," of an undiscovered and as of yet unconceptualized other-than-this, that is important here and that identifies what more than mere attitude Kafka offers us. But, again, what is it, exactly, and how does the work voice a concern with it? We have established that no such paradise is *represented* in *The Trial*. To do so, to present Josef K.'s world as possessed of a paradisiacal element, would be to lie, and *The Trial* earns part of its claim to ethical seriousness because it refuses to offer false hope. It would also, one assumes, be to introduce a didactic element into the work, which is never a good thing, in art or in life.

One might be tempted now to go on to locate this element in the work's form, thereby keeping it internal yet acknowledging that it is not an explicit feature of its narrative and so representational content. And, indeed, as literary theorists and philosophers of art (Adorno, for example) are often in the habit of telling us, *The Trial* is a case of a work of art in which form itself seems to do a lot of the thinking. This is true enough, but it will not yield what we are after. The manner in which *The Trial* presents its content—the tone, diction, and imagery it relies upon to relate it to us as a story— makes it very clear that on a formal level the work is more critical of the world than it is at the level of content. If content just yields expressed attitudes, as I have claimed, at the formal level we have a kind of *Verfremdungseffekt,* a distancing or alienating effect that establishes a felt gap between the attitudes expressed *in* the story and the more incriminatory view the work itself takes of its world. It is very likely also true that the alienating manner of formal presentation of content—and the oddness, the absurdity, it adds to a picture of life so represented—is largely what creates the sense of a critical and so, on my account, ethical project. In other words, form does much work here. But it still does not yield what we are after: a statement of what the ethical project of the work *is* or an insight into just what it means to say that it represents actual disaster to yield an awareness of possible emancipation.[20]

The answer to this is hardly mysterious, though an impoverished picture of what art is can make it very difficult to articulate it. Setting

20. In last three years there have been a number of excellent works that see the writings of Kafka and Wittgenstein as having kindred ethical projects. This is not surprising, since the *Tractatus,* published four years prior to *The Trial,* is itself a kind of masterpiece of philosophical modernism that uses nonsense, as *The Trial* itself does, to motivate its critical project. For discussions of this, see the essays collected in Michael LeMahieu and Karen Zumhagen-Yekplé, *Wittgenstein and Modernism* (Chicago: University of Chicago Press, 2016). Also see Karen Zumhagen-Yekplé, "The Everyday's Fabulous Beyond: Nonsense, Parable, and the Ethics of the Literary in Kafka and Wittgenstein," *Comparative Literature* 64, no. 4 (2012).

matters straight requires seeing that there is a subtle category error in how we tend to frame questions of how a literary work achieves its distinct ethical character. If we ask questions about a work's "meaning" or query what its story is "about," it is natural to assume that we are asking questions about a work's interior. It is natural, that is, to think that whatever can act as an answer to our question will be found in the linguistic and formal mortar that constitutes the literary work itself. But, I suggest, *The Trial* shows us that questions about ethical significance at times function very differently, not as a call to elaborate a redemptive meaning, image, or attitude to be found inside a text but something of a different kind altogether. Ethical criticism often calls on a distinct evaluative stance, one that conceptualizes the work as something other than, or at least in addition to, an object.

After all this discussion, the idea is not far from us. Everything I have said about *The Trial* links questions of ethicality to questions about what a work strives to accomplish, to create the conditions for, to bring about, *to make happen.* What is on the inside of a work is certainly crucial here, as it has been in my treatment of *The Trial.* That is, we cannot talk about what a work tries to bring about without talking about its form and content, just as we cannot talk about a revolution without elaborating the challenged form of life, and the reasons for demanding change, that give rise to it. But when we ask questions of the ethical project of a work, of how it evinces a concern with confronting and, with hope, ameliorating our present condition, the appropriate stance is to regard it as much more akin to an *action* and not, or not just, as an *object.* We must shift evaluative categories, looking away from those in which we make sense of things to those in which we make sense of events. A literary work is an action performed by means of creating an object, of course. But as with any action, it is performed for a reason, shot through with purposiveness, responsive to pressures in the world around it, and always, ultimately, an attempt to effect a change in it. This is, incidentally, one way of explaining why Titorelli's art feels so inert *as* art. It *does* nothing; it permits itself to be a mere object.

If we view a novel as a kind of doing and not simply a kind of thing, we are granted access to information and meanings that a mere object can never yield. One reason, a defining one, for writing a novel like *The Trial* is to clear the ground in the culture for which it was written for a new form of ethical life. It has absolutely nothing to *show* us about what this new form of ethical life might be. Eden, as it were, remains unavailable. It yields no propositions, it asserts nothing, it has no list of theses that specify just what is wrong with this world. But this is no loss. Its ethical significance does not consist in a declaration but, rather, in a deed. The point of *The Trial*—not the point of its story but the writing of it—is to create in the reader the capacity to give content to the idea of an elsewhere in which ethical life is, in fact, possible. The novel has no interest in specifying this content. It presumably does, however, have an interest in compelling us to become such that we might be able to do that, at least eventually and perhaps with a considerable amount of intellectual luck.

If this is so, then literary works such as *The Trial* achieve their distinct ethical character not by expressing attitude but by virtue of promising a small but essential serving of autonomy. It is not, of course, aesthetic autonomy about which *The Trial* would seem bound by character to abhor. It is not even quite political autonomy for which *The Trial* implicitly hopes but which is nonetheless too far down the road it sets before us. It is a form of autonomy that is concerned with disrupting our sense of being able to be at home in a world such as ours. It strives to prompt us to acknowledge the inaptness of this world to our basic projects of living well, and it accomplishes this in part by poisoning our hope that we can find a place of sanctuary in this "actual catastrophe." The autonomy this promises is of a humble but still vital sort: the offering of a measure of independence in thought and feeling from our world and the values that animate it. This *critical autonomy*, as we might call it, has as its goal an awaking in us of a sense that we *can* think, feel, and value otherwise than the present world conditions us to. This critical autonomy is essentially ethical, since it is implicitly *about* changing the constitution of the reader and so her ethical character. The whole point of it is to effect a change in how she hangs together as a thinking, feeling, and valuing being: to effect a change in, as it were, her *ethos*, with the hope that this will lead, with time and good fortune, to a broader change in our social and political ethos.

If we are cynics, we will doubt that better values and improved forms of life will ever be forthcoming. But if the cynic can intelligibly recite these worries, this itself will betray that she has achieved a degree, evidently nonnegligible, of critical and so ethical autonomy from this world, regardless of whether she wastes it on generating skeptical hypotheses instead of attempting to imagine an improvement. This form of autonomy is, in a formal sense, just the degree of freedom in thought that is presupposed by the notion of critical distance between a mind and its culture, not various of its institutions and practices but, again, the thing itself. In itself this form of autonomy is neither redemptive nor transformative, and so those who hear a hope-beyond-hope in talk of freedom needn't begin to worry. It is the critical act it makes possible that interests me and, if my argument is sound, is central to *The Trial*. This is the particular gift it gives to ethical thought: the capacity to imagine values and forms of personal and cultural flourishing in excess of those our culture makes available to us. Much follows from this gift of a more directly material and political sort, but it cannot follow without this initial serving of critical and so, on my account, ethical autonomy.[21] It is in this sense that *The Trial* seeks to be, as the epigraph has it, an "ax for the frozen sea in us."

---

21. In thinking through these issues, I profited immensely from Andrew Goldstone's *Fictions of Autonomy: Modernism from Wilde to de Man* (Oxford: Oxford University Press, 2013).

BIBLIOGRAPHY

Carroll, Noël. "Art and Ethical Criticism: An Overview of Recent Directions of Research." *Ethics* 110, no. 2 (2000): 350–387.

Carroll, Noël. *Interpreting the Moving Image.* Cambridge: Cambridge University Press, 1998.

Cornwell, Neil. *The Absurd in Literature.* Manchester: Manchester University Press, 2006.

Eaton, A. W. "Literature and Morality." In *The Routledge Companion to Philosophy of Literature*, edited by Noël Carroll and John Gibson, 433–450. London: Routledge, 2016.

Eaton, A. W. "Robust Immoralism." *Journal of Aesthetics and Art Criticism* 70, no. 3 (2012): 281–292.

Gaut, Berys. *Art, Emotion and Ethics.* Oxford: Oxford University Press, 2007.

Geuss, Raymond. *Outside Ethics.* Princeton, NJ: Princeton University Press, 2005.

Gibson, John. "Thick Narratives." In *Narrative, Emotion, and Insight*, edited by John Gibson and Noël Carroll, 69–91. University Park, PA: Pennsylvania State University Press, 2011.

Giovanelli, Alessandro. "Ethical Criticism in Perspective: A Defense of Radical Autonomism." *Journal of Aesthetics and Art Criticism* 71, no. 4 (2013): 335–348.

Goldstone, Andrew. *Fictions of Autonomy: Modernism From Wilde to De Man.* Oxford and New York: Oxford University Press, 2013.

Jacobson, Daniel. "Ethical Criticism and the Vice of Moderation." In *Contemporary Debates in Aesthetics and the Philosophy of Art*, edited by Matthew Kieran, 342–355. Oxford: Blackwell, 2006.

Kafka, Franz. *The Trial.* Translated by Breon Mitchell. New York: Schocken, 1998.

Kieran, Matthew. "Art, Morality and Ethics: On the (Im)moral Character of Art Works and Inter-Relations to Artistic Value." *Philosophy Compass* 1, no. 2 (2006): 129–143.

Kieran, Matthew. "Forbidden Knowledge: The Challenge of Immoralism." In *Art and Morality*, edited by José Luis Bermúdez and Sebastian Gardner, 56–73. London: Routledge, 2003.

LeMahieu, Michael, and Karen Zumhagen-Yekplé, eds. *Wittgenstein and Modernism.* Chicago: University of Chicago Press, 2016.

Richter, Gerhard. "Introduction." In *Language Without Soil: Adorno and Late Philosophical Modernity*, edited by Gerhard Richter, 1–9. New York: Fordham University Press, 2010.

Schellekens, Elisabeth. *Aesthetics and Morality.* London: Continuum, 2007.

Wood, Michael. *Literature and the Taste of Knowledge*. New York: Cambridge University Press, 2005.

Zumhagen-Yekplé, Karen. "The Everyday's Fabulous Beyond: Nonsense, Parable, and the Ethics of the Literary in Kafka and Wittgenstein." *Comparative Literature* 64, no. 4 (2012): 429–445.

Chapter 4

"A Disease of All Signification"

Kafka's The Trial *Between Adorno and Agamben*

GERHARD RICHTER

The poet W. H. Auden once memorably averred that if one had "to name the artist who comes nearest to bearing the same kind of relation to our age that Dante, Shakespeare, and Goethe bore to theirs, Kafka is the first one would think of."[1] If this assessment still rings true today, it is because Kafka's relation to our age is one not only of a certain spirit of the times, a cultural episteme, a given political configuration, or a certain *Lebensgefühl*, a feeling of life, in the experiential orbit of an alienated modernity. It also pertains with particular force to the ways in which Kafka's writing incessantly takes as one of its main categories of reflection the very question of the philosophical interpretability of what we call literature. What is one to make, on the level of the concept, of a text that begins with a protagonist named Gregor Samsa who awakens one morning to the realization that he has been inexplicably transformed into a monstrous vermin, even an un-thing (*Ungeziefer*), as in Kafka's *The Metamorphosis*? And

1. W. H. Auden, "The Wandering Jew," in *The Complete Works of W. H. Auden. Vol. 2: Prose, 1939–1948*, ed. Edward Mendelson (Princeton, NJ: Princeton University Press, 2002), 110–113, here 110.

what kinds of philosophically interpretive thoughts are elicited by a related scene of awakening, in which the character Josef K., a high-ranking bank official, finds himself unexpectedly detained by two officers waiting in his apartment? "Someone must have slandered Josef K.," Kafka famously begins *The Trial*, "for one morning, without having done anything wrong, he was arrested."[2] It is as if such scenes figuratively staged the experience of a baffled reader who awakens to a refractory text that he or she is now called upon to interpret—without a reliable key or a hermeneutically stable frame of reference. The reader, like Josef K. himself, comes to inhabit a certain narrative disruption. As the German writer Martin Walser rightly reminds us with regard to *The Trial*, the "event begins only at the moment when the disruption occurs."[3] In this state of disorientation and hesitation, the drawn-out trial of reading, as well as the exigent process of reading itself, commence—a double meaning that is encoded in the German title of Kafka's novel, *Der Proceß* which means both "trial" and "process." But to whom or what does one awaken when reading a literary text from a philosophical perspective? And is this form of awakening not also a way of dreaming—that is, of learning to follow the singular dream-logic of an artwork?

In a reflection dating from the eight intensely creative months (September 1917 through April 1918) that Kafka spent at his sister Ottla's house in the Bohemian town of Zürau, he writes:

Art flies around truth, but with the definite intention of not getting burnt. Its capacity lies in finding in the dark void a place

2. Franz Kafka, *The Trial*, trans. Mike Mitchell (Oxford: Oxford University Press, 2009), 3; *Der Proceß*, ed. Malcolm Pasley, *Kritische Ausgabe* (Frankfurt am Main: Fischer, 2002), 7. Throughout my text, I have on occasion adjusted existing English translations. Unattributed translations are my own.
3. Martin Walser, "Description of a Form," trans. James Rolleston, in *Twentieth Century Interpretation of* The Trial: *A Collection of Critical Essays*, ed. James Rolleston (Englewood Cliffs, NJ: Prentice-Hall, 1976), 21–35, here 21.

where the beam of light can be intensely caught, without this
having been perceptible before.[4]

(Die Kunst fliegt um die Wahrheit, aber mit der entschiedenen
Absicht, sich nicht zu verbrennen. Ihre Fähigkeit besteht darin, in
der dunklen Leere einen Ort zu finden, wo der Strahl des Lichts,
ohne daß dieser vorher zu erkennen gewesen wäre, kräftig aufge-
fangen werden kann.)[5]

If art swirls and circles around truth like a moth around the light
of a flame, profoundly attracted by it yet always requiring a certain
distance from it in order not to be destroyed altogether, it marks a
site upon which the relationship between the aesthetic object and
its possible illuminations, its *Schein* or appearance, first becomes
a discrete matter of inquiry. One of the central questions that here
impose themselves concerns the ways in which the elusively idiomatic artwork relates to the kind of rigorous conceptual labor that
it, in addition to the pleasure that it typically affords, also elicits. If
we can accept the premise that, as Gayatri Spivak puts it in a different context, "reading literature, we learn to learn from the singular
and unverifiable," then the relation between, on the one hand, the
singularity and unverifiability of the artwork, and, on the other hand,
the concept that seeks general validity, is itself one of the main axes
around which aesthetic production and its interpretation circle.[6] The
intricate question as to the nature and potentialities of this complex
relation inflects the way in which we may begin to understand Kafka's

4. Franz Kafka, *Dearest Father and Other Writings*, trans. Ernst Kaiser and Eithne Wilkins
   (New York: Schocken, 1954), 87.
5. Franz Kafka, *Nachgelassene Schriften und Fragmente II*, ed. Jost Schillemeit, *Kritische Ausgabe*
   (Frankfurt am Main: Fischer, 2002), 75–76.
6. Gayatri Chakravorty Spivak, *A Critique of Postcolonial Reason: Toward a History of the
   Vanishing Present* (Cambridge, MA: Harvard University Press, 1999), 145n49.

image of art as it playfully yet purposefully swirls around the flame of truth without being consumed by it entirely.

There can hardly be a conceptually subtle understanding of the work of art without the aid of philosophy. Yet if the philosophical interpretation of the work of art were entirely successful—that is, if it did not leave a remainder within the artwork that also resisted the translation of aesthetic form into this or that meaning—the artwork would, in a sense, become superfluous. What it achieves conceptually could have been achieved in another way, through discursive logic. A seminal concern that permeates Kafka's writings, including his unfinished, fragmentary novel *The Trial*, therefore, is the very way in which a literary artwork both calls for philosophical interpretation and resists such interpretation at the same time. One way of registering this aporia is to appreciate how, as Kafka puts it in another observation from the Zürau period, for "everything outside the phenomenal world, language can be used only allusively [*nur andeutungsweise*], but never even approximately in a comparative [or analogous] way [*niemals auch nur annähernd vergleichsweise*], since, corresponding as it does to the phenomenal world, it is concerned only with property and its relations."[7] If the literary work of art unfolds precisely on the far side of the phenomenal world in which language can be said to operate in a comparative, analogous, and therefore principally other-directed way, the language of the literary text inhabits an orbit of signification in which it can only ever allude, but never actually fully name, what it may be "about" on the conceptual level. Another way of putting this is to say that the language of the literary artwork requires a certain philological, theoretical, and philosophical interpretation in order to address both its allusive character as

7. Franz Kafka, *Dearest Father and Other Writings*, 40; Franz Kafka, *Nachgelassene Schriften und Fragmente II*, 59.

such and that unspoken or hidden sphere of signification to which its allusiveness seems to point, but to which it cannot ever refer in any unmediated way.

Kafka himself exhibits a keen awareness of this difficult-to-fulfill requirement throughout the entire trajectory of what he calls his *Schriftstellersein*, or constitutive "being-as-a-writer." When, for instance, he writes to his two-time fiancée Felice Bauer—whose initials, F.B., are also those of the character Fräulein Bürstner in *The Trial*, one of protagonist Josef K.'s erotic interests—to inquire about the possibility of finding any meaning in the story he wrote concurrently with *The Trial*, "The Judgment," he betrays his uneasy sense that a conceptual interpretation is both necessary and impossible: "Can you discover any meaning in the 'Judgment'—I mean some straightforward, coherent meaning that one could follow? I can't find any, nor can I explain anything in it" (*Findest Du im "Urteil" irgendeinen Sinn, ich meine irgendeinen geraden, zusammenhängenden, verfolgbaren Sinn? Ich finde ihn nicht und kann auch nichts darin erklären*).[8] As the first reader of his own text—and thus as something akin to a primordial type of reader in relation to the constellation of challenges posed by the Kafkan text to the very category of understanding—Kafka finds himself pushed by language to the limits of what can be translated into a form of recognizable meaning or sense (*Sinn*), especially if by meaning or sense is meant a hermeneutic disclosure, an effect of meaning derived from linearity, coherence, and followability. Yet Kafka the reader is unable simply to content himself with the enigma that Kafka the writer has created for him—and, by proxy, for all readers. His text refuses to be explicated according to any conventional notions of conceptual unfolding, yet it continues to provoke, in its

8. Franz Kafka, *Letters to Felice*, trans. James Stern and Elisabeth Duckworth (New York: Schocken, 1973), 265; Franz Kafka, *Briefe an Felice*, ed. Erich Heller and Jürgen Born (Frankfurt am Main: Fischer, 1983), 394.

own singular idiom and perhaps against all better judgment, ceaseless attempts to explicate.

There are few philosophical readers of Kafka more attuned to the tension between the artwork and its conceptual exposition than Theodor W. Adorno.[9] In his *Aesthetic Theory* he puts the matter in an epigrammatically condensed way when he argues that "art stands in need of philosophy that interprets it in order to say that which it cannot say, whereas art only is able to say what it says by not saying it."[10] Adorno here puts his finger on the predicament at the core of the relation between philosophical commentary and aesthetic production. On the one hand, the artwork— especially the self-consciously self-reflexive, high modernist variety of Schönberg, Alban Berg, Samuel Beckett, and, precisely, Kafka, that Adorno so often would explore— requires philosophical discourse to bring to the fore as a graspable, cognitive, and propositional structure the *Wahrheitsgehalt*—the speculative truth content, import, or substance—that, in the absence of critical commentary and conceptual elucidation, lies latent. On the other hand, the very thing that philosophy claims the artwork says, that on behalf of which philosophy acts as a kind of conceptual translator, can be said by the artwork only when it remains silent about it. If the artwork actually said what it says in a transparent cognitive proposition, shorn of the mediations and aberrations of its imaginative flourishes and its singular expression of beauty and form, then it would cease to be an artwork. It would simply be a philosophical treatise concerning a conceptual content that now no longer could claim membership in the domain of art. Yet if the artwork can be

9. I borrow the remainder of this paragraph, as well as a couple of sentences of the next, from my earlier essay "Aesthetic Theory and Nonpropositional Truth Content in Adorno," *New German Critique* 97 (Winter 2006): 119–135.

10. Theodor W. Adorno, *Aesthetic Theory*, trans. Robert Hullot-Kentor (Minneapolis: University of Minnesota Press, 1997), 72; Theodor W. Adorno, *Ästhetische Theorie: Gesammelte Schriften*, vol. 7, ed. Rolf Tiedemann (Frankfurt am Main: Suhrkamp, 1997), 113.

itself only by not saying what philosophy claims it says—that is, if the cognitive propositional content on which philosophy focuses cannot be verified in the articulations and inscriptions of the artwork itself, lest it abdicate its status as a work of art—then how can one clarify and verify philosophy's claims about the content and meaning of artworks? Why does art continue to stand in need of philosophy's translational services? And if Adorno is so acutely aware of this tension, what is it that makes him retain his conviction, even his "model," the supposition of which is "that artworks unfold in their philosophical interpretation"?[11]

Any philosophical interpretation of an artwork must confront the following paradox: If the meaning of an artwork were to remain sealed off from all logical comprehension, then no philosophy could ever truly speak to this meaning. But if the meaning of an artwork were to reveal itself readily, then no artwork would be needed—since its "content" could have been stated more easily in prosaic, discursive language that would require no philosophy to expound upon it. One lesson to be derived from this state of affairs is that what is required in engaging with a literary text such as Kafka's *The Trial* is a certain guardedness in relation to "the illusion that what is said is immediately what is meant" (*die Illusion, es wäre, was geredet wird, unmittelbar das Gemeinte*). Instead, the character of language as an elusive token (*Spielmarke*) reveals "the way that all words behave: that language imprisons its speakers one more time; that language, as the proper medium of its speakers, is a failure."[12] What a philosophical approach

11. Theodor W. Adorno, *Lectures on Negative Dialectics: Fragments of a Lecture Course 1965/ 1966*, trans. Rodney Livingstone (Cambridge: Polity, 2008), 77; Theodor W. Adorno, *Vorlesung über Negative Dialektik. Nachgelassene Schriften*, vol. 16, ed. Rolf Tiedemann (Frankfurt am Main: Suhrkamp, 2003), 115.
12. Theodor W. Adorno, "Words from Abroad." *Notes to Literature*, vol. 1, trans. Shierry Weber Nicholsen (New York: Columbia University Press, 1991), 185–199, here 189; Theodor W. Adorno, "Wörter aus der Fremde." *Noten zur Literatur: Gesammelte Schriften*, vol. 11, ed. Rolf Tiedemann (Frankfurt am Main: Suhrkamp, 1997), 216–232, here 221.

to a literary text would have to consider, then, is the relationship between, one the one hand, the tension obtaining between an aesthetic object and its conceptual content, and, on the other hand, the ways in which the aesthetic object breaks with what it appears to be saying at first sight.

The push and pull of calling forth and resisting philosophical interpretation, while shared in principle by all great literary works, is staged by a particular work in specific ways that are idiomatic and singular to the individual text. In others words, the heterogeneous ways in which literary works by Hölderlin, Goethe, Eichendorff, or Proust confront the tension between their apparent content and the philosophical interpretation of their import or substance is quite different from the variegated ways in which texts by Mann, Dickens, Wedekind, Beckett, or Heine approach the same tension—to cite the names of some of the authors to whom Adorno chooses to devote substantial essays, later collected in *Notes to Literature*. One central problem that arises out of this constellation of aesthetic form and the philosophical interpretation of its import is that of the nature of the relationship between the literal and the figurative nature of a text's rhetorical operations. Adorno's richly layered essay "Notes on Kafka" ("Aufzeichnungen zu Kafka") was begun in 1942 and first published in *Die Neue Rundschau* in 1953, and it represents—next to the many occasional references to Kafka throughout his work—his most sustained engagement with Kafka. There, he suggests that Kafka's "two great novels, *The Castle* and *The Trial*, seem to bear the mark of philosophical theorems."[13] These theorems can be approached only through an interrogation of

---

13. Theodor W. Adorno, "Notes on Kafka," in *Prisms*, trans. Samuel and Shierry Weber (Cambridge, MA: MIT Press, 1981), 243–271, here 247; Theodor W. Adorno, "Aufzeichnungen zu Kafka," in *Kulturkritik und Gesellschaft I: Gesammelte Schriften*, vol. 11, ed. Rolf Tiedemann (Frankfurt am Main: Suhrkamp, 1997), 254–287, here 256.

It is important to recall that Adorno's Kafka essay stands in permanent spectral conversation with the Kafka essays of two of his most important interlocutors and friends, Siegfried Kracauer's 1931 "Franz Kafka," first published in the *Frankfurter Zeitung*, and

the ways in which literality and figurality interact with each other in a hermeneutically unpredictable manner.[14] The "principle of literalness," in which Adorno espies "a reminiscence of the Torah exegesis of the Jewish tradition," is both upheld and undermined by Kafka's writing.[15] If Adorno is right that "Kafka's authority is textual," it is a textuality that does not reside in any mere mastery of understanding or in an ability to spawn philosophical ideas with a palatable literary packaging but, rather, in the singular ways in which "Kafka's works protected themselves against the deadly aesthetic error of equating the philosophy that an author pumps into a work with its metaphysical substance."[16] After all, if Kafka's texts were to operate in this way, "the work of art would be stillborn; it would exhaust itself in what it says and would not unfold itself in time."[17] In order to guard against a premature hermeneutic desire that "jumps directly to the significance intended by the work," two basic rules are to be followed: "take everything literally" and

Walter Benjamin's 1934 "Franz Kafka. Zur zehnten Wiederkehr seines Todestages" ("Franz Kafka: On the Tenth Anniversary of His Death"), which first appeared in the *Jüdische Rundschau*. Equally significant in this context are Adorno's extensive epistolary exchanges with Benjamin on the topic of Kafka from the time Benjamin's Kafka essay appeared in 1934 to Benjamin's death in 1940. See Theodor W. Adorno and Walter Benjamin, *Briefwechsel 1928–1940* (Frankfurt am Main: Suhrkamp, 1994). For a reading of Benjamin's Kafka essay from the perspective of an intellectual inheritance, cf. Gerhard Richter, "*Erbsünde*: A Note on Paradoxical Inheritance in Benjamin's Kafka Essay," in *Inheriting Walter Benjamin* (London: Bloomsbury, 2016), 15–33.

14. I will focus in my reading of Adorno's Kafka essay almost exclusively on the significance of this distinction between literality and figurality for the theoretical or philosophical interpretation of a (literary) work of art. For an incisive reading that focuses on other key elements of Adorno's richly textured essay, including the logic of an inverse theology that Adorno, *pace* Freud and Marx, observes at work in Kafka's writing, see Stanley Corngold, "Adorno's 'Notes on Kafka': A Critical Reconstruction," *Monatshefte* 94, no. 1 (2002), Special Issue: *Rereading Adorno*, ed. Gerhard Richter, 24–42. For a probing consideration of Adorno's Kafka essay that places the question of literality in relation to Orson Welles's film adaptation of *The Trial*, as well as to J. M. Coetzee's novel *Elizabeth Costello*, see Alexander García Düttmann, *Was weiß Kunst? Für eine Ästhetik des Widerstands* (Konstanz: Konstanz University Press, 2015), 111–125.

15. Adorno, "Notes on Kafka," 247 / "Aufzeichnungen," 257.
16. Adorno, "Notes on Kafka," 247 / "Aufzeichnungen," 257.
17. Adorno, "Notes on Kafka," 247 / "Aufzeichnungen," 257.

"cover up nothing with concepts invoked from above." To follow this double precept, a certain "fidelity to the letter" is required. Yet, at the same time, absolute fidelity to the letter, which also entails a reticence, even a refusal, to say what an artwork cannot say on its own, poses the danger that the reader will "lose all ground on which to stand."[18] A critical reading therefore "must cling to the fact that at the beginning of *The Trial*, it is said that someone must have been spreading rumors about Josef K., 'for without having done anything wrong, he was arrested one fine morning,'" a clinging that presumably is motivated by the suspicion that the literalness of the novel's sentences also are perpetually self-undermining.[19] In other words, the demand for literalness is from the outset vexed by the very fact that the tacit content of that literalness speaks of phenomena of nonliteralness, such as rumor, possible slander, or conjecture, all of which are matters precisely of interpretation rather than transparent literalness.

Kafka's own keen awareness of this tension is encoded, for instance, in the self-reflexive ways in which he introduces subtle hermeneutic doubt into the apparent matter-of-fact literalness of *The Trial*'s opening sentence. Although Adorno does not comment on this aspect of the text, it is germane to his discussion. In German, the sentence reads: "Jemand mußte Josef K. verleumdet haben, denn ohne daß er etwas Böses getan hätte, wurde er eines Morgens verhaftet."[20] Kafka's deceptively literal declarative sentence, which appears merely to report on an objective state of affairs, in fact stages an implicit call for nonliteral interpretation on an almost subterranean level. The "mußte" ("must have") not only sets the stage for a novel that, despite being told for the most part through third-person narration, will unfold from the more limited personal perspective of its central character, Josef K. Its introduction of a decidedly

18. Adorno, "Notes on Kafka," 247 / "Aufzeichnungen," 257.
19. Adorno, "Notes on Kafka," 247 / "Aufzeichnungen," 257.
20. Kafka, *Der Proceß*, 7.

interrogative and interpretive mood also serves to open the trial of reading and understanding: Josef K. "must have" been slandered, but he and we cannot be sure. Along similar lines, Kafka's ambiguous reference to "etwas Böses" far exceeds the referential confines of the English "anything wrong," for the German locution raises the interpretive stakes with respect to Josef K.'s possible guilt, alluding both to something naughty (as when a German child is scolded for having been "böse"—that is, for having been badly behaved) or, by contrast, something truly evil, *das Böse.* In addition, as has often been remarked in Kafka scholarship, the subjunctive form presented by the phrase "etwas Böses getan hätte"—which is impossible to reproduce in the English translation to the extent that it renders Josef K. as having done "nothing wrong" and thereby allows the character to appear simply as having been wrongly accused—introduces a subtle moment of interpretive doubt. This doubt is expressed merely by the umlauts that Kafka places over the *a* in "hätte"—he easily could have written "hatte," thus "ohne das er etwas Böses getan hatte," a straightforward past-perfect form indicating that Josef K. had not done anything wrong. Kafka's seemingly innocent shift from "hatte" to "hätte," from past-perfect to subjunctive, works to open the proceedings of at least three interrelated trials: the novel *The Trial* as such; the perpetually deferred trial(s) of Josef K.; and the textual trial of reading itself.[21] It is no coincidence, one might add, that Kafka bore within himself a concern with the precarious aesthetics of the umlaut, the fate of *ä*; as he writes in a 1910 diary entry, "The ä, detached from its sentence, flew away like a ball on the meadow" (*Das ä, losgelöst vom Satz, flog dahin wie ein Ball auf der Wiese*).[22]

21. To formulate it in a somewhat pointed manner: While Kafka's German sentence literally and figuratively opens the trial, its English translation is forced to close it from the start.
22. Franz Kafka, *The Diaries of Franz Kafka, 1910–1913,* trans. Joseph Kresh, ed. Max Brod (New York: Schocken, 1948), 9; Franz Kafka, *Tagebücher,* ed. Hans-Gerd Koch, Michael Müller, and Malcolm Pasley, *Kritische Ausgabe* (Frankfurt am Main: Fischer, 2002), 9.

The movement of dispersal that characterizes Kafka's recalcitrant writing even when it insists on keeping the category of literalness alive cannot be contained by the logic of symbolism and the symbol. The symbol works to gather what has been disseminated, collecting the fragments and shards of meaning into an allegedly stable relation. As Adorno emphasizes in his reading of Kafka, if "the notion of the symbol has any meaning whatsoever in aesthetics . . . it can only be that the individual moments of the work of art point beyond themselves by virtue of their interrelations, that their totality coalesces into meaning." But, he adds, while even some of Goethe's supposedly allegorical texts in the end work toward a movement of unification within the wholeness or totality promised by the symbol and symbolism, "nothing could be less true of Kafka."[23] On the contrary, in Kafka's work, "which shoots toward" the reader "like a locomotive,"[24]

each sentence is literal [*steht buchstäblich*] and each signifies [*bedeutet*]. The two moments are not merged, as the symbol would have it, but yawn apart and out of the abyss between them blinds the glaring ray of fascination. Here too, in its striving not for symbol but for allegory, Kafka's prose sides with the outcasts. . . . It expresses itself not through expression but by its repudiation, by breaking off. It is a parabolic system the key to which has been stolen: yet any effort to make this fact itself the key is bound to go astray by confounding the abstract thesis of Kafka's work, the obscurity of the existent, with its substance. Each sentence says "interpret me," and none will permit it [*Jeder Satz spricht: deute mich, und keiner will es dulden*].[25]

23. Adorno, "Notes on Kafka," 245 / "Aufzeichnungen," 255.
24. Adorno, "Notes on Kafka," 246 / "Aufzeichnungen," 256.
25. Adorno, "Notes on Kafka," 246 / "Aufzeichnungen," 255.

If Kafka's text does not belong to the order of the symbolic it is because, at odds with the correspondence-based operation of the symbol, it does not reconcile the literal and the figurative. In classical rhetorical understanding, the gathering force of the symbol is seen as superior to other modes of figuration such as allegory precisely because it unites within itself a certain literality and a figurative dimension. For instance, the crown acts as a symbol of monarchy because it depicts something that is literally part of the object for which it stands (the crown on the monarch's head) in addition to signifying its object of reference in a more abstract or indirect manner. But in Kafka's sentences, no such unification is to be found. On the contrary, the task that they impose on their interpreters is inseparable from the task of coming to terms with the multiply refracted ways in which their literal signification is at odds with anything that they may evoke on an allusive, figurative level. Indeed, the insurmountable abyss that opens up between the literal and the figurative level of Kafka's sentences is precisely what calls for philosophical intervention and interpretive exegesis in the first place.[26] It embodies, we might say, the tacit provocation of reflective engagement that Nietzsche, with whose thinking Kafka's texts are in constant spectral conversation, conjures in aphorism 146 of *Beyond Good and Evil*: "And when you look long enough into the abyss, the abyss also looks into you."[27]

---

26. The premise that any interpretation of Kafka should quite literally begin on the level of the individual sentence and linger with it is pursued by the recent collection *Kafkas Sätze*, ed. Hubert Spiegel (Frankfurt am Main: Fischer, 2009). In it, some 70 well-known critics and writers each present their single favorite sentence in Kafka and submit it, in short essays, to renewed interpretation. One of the questions that remains is whether or not the totality of sentences with a given Kafkan text can be said to amount to a literary form that invites inclusion of the text in a particular genre (and, by extension, that genre's particular histories and conceptual problems). For a structual discussion of *The Trial* from the perspective of genre, see Gerhard Neumann, "'Blinde Parabel' oder Bildungsroman? Zur Struktur von Kafkas 'Proceß'-Fragment," *Jahrbuch der deutschen Schillergesellschaft* 41 (1997): 399–427.
27. Friedrich Nietzsche, *Beyond Good and Evil*, trans. Walter Kaufmann, in *Basic Writings* (New York: Modern Library, 2000), 178–435, here 279.

If the reader's task, then, consists in looking into the abyss while also being looked at by the abyss, this task cannot be thought in isolation from the idea that a philosophically informed understanding of a literary text such as *The Trial* must remain perpetually mindful of how the literal and the figurative dimensions of the text unfold in uneasy relation to each other. For Adorno, one way of thinking the effects of this constantly shifting relation in Kafka's writing—which makes itself felt, among many other ways, in the tension between his characters' words and their enigmatic gestures—is to acknowledge the writing's "ambiguity [*Vieldeutigkeit*], which, like a disease, has eaten into all signification in Kafka" (*die wie eine Krankheit alles Bedeuten bei Kafka angefressen hat*).[28] But even this radical ambiguity, this sickness that has befallen signification in Kafka's textual world, cannot be counted on to remain self-identical. As Adorno points out, even the ambiguity is ambiguous, even the *Krankheit* that has eaten into the text will not always retain the upper hand when it comes to the assignment of meaning, as it were. After all, what is the reader to make of the apparently literalist yet simultaneously dreamlike depictions, in *The Trial*, of how "Leni's fingers are connected by a web, or that the executioners resemble tenors"?[29] How are we to tell when a passage or image in Kafka's novel is to be taken literally and when figuratively—and when, by extension, the two dimensions are inextricably intertwined with each other in a space of indeterminacy?

Adorno's insistence on confronting the elusive ways in which the literal and the figurative relate, or fail to relate, in Kafka's text raises the fundamental question as to the status of the rhetorical in any attempt

28. Adorno, "Notes on Kafka," 248 / "Aufzeichnungen," 258f. For a recent analysis of how the theatrical logic of the tension between words and gestures structures the entire opening scene of *The Trial*, see Stanley Corngold, "Medial Interventions in *The Trial*; Or, *Res in Media*," in *Lambent Traces: Franz Kafka* (Princeton, NJ: Princeton University Press, 2004), 51–66.

29. Adorno, "Notes on Kafka," 248 / "Aufzeichnungen," 258.

at providing theoretical or philosophical readings of a literary text. While Jacques Derrida's assessment, in "White Mythology: Metaphor in the Text of Philosophy," allows us to appreciate the ways in which a *philosophical* text is ultimately unable to control, even through an elaborated concept of figuration, its own metaphoric productions, Paul de Man's consideration of the divergence of figurative and literal language that can occur within one and the same utterance helps to cast the question of the rhetorical dimension of the specifically *literary* artwork into sharp relief.[30] When working (ultimately unsuccessfully) to decide whether, for instance, the final line in Yeats's poem "Among School Children" ("How can we know the dancer from the dance?") is to be understood figuratively or literally, the reader confronts the consequences of a precise insight: What is at stake is not the notion "that there are simply two meanings, one literal and the other figural, and that we have to decide which one of these meanings is the right one in this particular situation." Something else makes itself felt here. The properly rhetorical moment is reached "not when we have, on the one hand, a literal meaning and on the other hand a figural meaning, but when it is impossible to decide by grammatical or other linguistic devices which of the two meanings (that can be entirely incompatible) prevails." From the vantage point of such "vertiginous possibilities of referential aberration," de Man suggests that one should "not hesitate to equate the rhetorical, figurative potentiality of language with literature itself."[31] To the extent that literature acts as a site upon which the rhetoricity of language makes itself felt with an idiomatic and uncontainable force, the reading of a literary text is no longer directed at decoding this or that meaning. The critical task would then not be to adjudicate

30. Jacques Derrida, "White Mythology: Metaphor in the Text of Philosophy," in *Margins of Philosophy*, trans. Alan Bass (Chicago: University of Chicago Press, 1982), 207–229; Paul de Man, "Semiology and Rhetoric," in *Allegories of Reading: Figural Language in Rousseau, Nietzsche, Rilke, and Proust* (New Haven, CT: Yale University Press, 1979), 3–19.

31. De Man, "Semiology and Rhetoric," 10.

between the rhetorical prevalence of a literal and that of a figurative meaning but, rather, to trace the specific and each time singular ways in which the very idea of being able to decide between the two levels is exposed as the more or less concealed trademark of the text.

Although, unlike Adorno, de Man does not take Kafka as his touchstone, it is apparent that a concern with the relation between the literal and the figurative dimensions of the text and its interpretation inflects Kafka's sentences at every turn. *The Trial*'s pivotal doorkeeper legend, which can be said epigrammatically to condense the novel as a whole, self-consciously speaks to the problem of how to relate to the vexed relation between the literal and the figurative. Kafka first included this short text as a freestanding story under the title "Before the Law" in his 1919 collection *A Country Doctor*, six years before Max Brod published a version of it in *The Trial* from Kafka's literary estate in 1925, the year after Kafka's death. Here, the man from the country who approaches the gate, guarded by a doorkeeper, behind which he believes the law to reside, presupposes a literalist understanding of the law, according to which it is in principle possible to enter that law. In the course of the episode, the man from the country misinterprets the doorkeeper's deferral of the permission to enter as its denial. If the doorkeeper episode, like *The Trial* as a whole, rigorously demands interpretation (on the part of the man from the country, as well as from the reader) while also strenuously resisting it, the question of the text's own literalness is cast precisely into figurative terms. As Derrida points out in his reading of Kafka's parable, it "does not tell or describe anything but itself as text," which is to say that it "guards itself, maintains itself—like the law, speaking only to itself, that is to say, of its non-identity with itself. . . . It is the law, makes the law, and leaves the reader before the law."[32] In this

32. Jacques Derrida, "Before the Law," trans. Avital Ronell and Christine Roulston, in *Acts of Literature*, ed. Derek Attridge (New York: Routledge, 1992), 181–220, here 211.

sense, the man from the country fails to appreciate how "the singular crosses the universal, when the categorical engages the idiomatic, as a literature always must." As a result, the "man from the country had difficulty in grasping that an entrance was singular and unique when it should have been universal, as in truth it was. He had difficulty with literature."[33] This difficulty with literature, with the nature and implications of the specific interpretive demand issued by *The Trial*, as well as with literature as such, is the difficulty whose traumatic wound Kafka's novel will never quite allow us to close, as if it were another textual instantiation—or iteration—of the horrific wound, infested with living worms, into which Kafka dares us to stare in the story "A Country Doctor."

Learning to learn from the singular and unverifiable form of writing we call literature, then, involves learning to read a text figuratively and literally *at the same time*. To appreciate its "law," we must not repeat the error that Kafka's man from the country makes when he mistakes the literal for the figurative, as well as the singular for the universal. Yet how such learning might be accomplished is itself a matter of dispute in the logic of Kafka's writing. It is no accident that in the "Cathedral" chapter, in which the doorkeeper parable is put into the mouth of the prison chaplain, Josef K. jumps to the apparently false interpretive conclusion that the doorkeeper must have deceived the man from the country by withholding from him access to the law. " 'Don't be overly hasty,' " the chaplain reprimands Josef K., " 'don't accept someone else's opinion unchecked [*übernimm nicht die fremde Meinung ungeprüft*]. I told you the story word for word according to the text [*im Wortlaut der Schrift*]. It says nothing about being deceived.' "[34] The category of deception is disqualified from the discourse of interpretation because the text's literal level, its *Wortlaut*,

---

33. Derrida, "Before the Law," 213.
34. Kafka, *The Trial*, 155 / *Der Proceß*, 295.

does not contain it. In light of Josef K.'s hasty efforts to assign figurative meaning to the literality of what the parable presents, the chaplain issues a categorical warning: "'You don't have enough respect for the text [or for writing, *Schrift*] and are changing the story'" (*'Du hast nicht genug Achtung vor der Schrift und veränderst die Geschichte'*).[35] What Josef K. fails to appreciate in the course of the novel is that while the literalness of the text cannot be maintained in interpretation, its translation into a figural meaning harbors just as much danger, which is to say, it causes the text to change into something that it is not. Paradoxically, then, the philosopher's or critic's intervention through interpretive commentary is both necessary and superfluous, a sign of abiding faithfulness to the text and its simultaneous violation. It is also because of this aporia that the prison chaplain instructs K. that "the text [or what is written, writing, *Schrift*] is unchangeable, and opinions are often only an expression of despair over it" (*die Schrift ist unveränderlich und die Meinungen sind oft nur ein Ausdruck der Verzweiflung darüber*).[36] Writing remains identical (merely) with itself, withdraws into its own self-referentiality, yet simultaneously is exposed to its radical nonself-identity in the force field of critical attempts to provide philosophical commentary upon it.

By the same token, this special form of interpretive despair attaches to a related conclusion that Kafka's prison chaplain relays to K.: "Correct understanding of something and misunderstanding of the same thing are not entirely mutually exclusive" (*Richtiges Auffassen einer Sache und Mißverstehen der gleichen Sache schließen einander nicht vollständig aus*).[37] Presumably, if the lesson of the chaplain's sentence is correct, then that lesson applies also to the sentence itself, in which case we cannot even be sure that we have

35. Kafka, *The Trial*, 155 / *Der Proceß*, 295.
36. Kafka, *The Trial*, 157 / *Der Proceß*, 298.
37. Kafka, *The Trial*, 156 / *Der Proceß*, 297.

begun to understand the sentence correctly in the first place and thus may have to renounce the apparent lesson that it has taught us and that forms the basis, presumably, upon which it itself is to be interpreted. The particular basis of this renunciation, however, in turn only could have come into being through our attempted interpretation of the sentence. Is this merely an aberrant thought on Kafka's part? Is it a manifestation of the "disease" that Adorno suspects has befallen all meaning in Kafka's literary world? Or is such perhaps the ultimate fate of all attempts at philosophical readings of literature?

A special test case for this particular constellation of questions may be found in the Italian philosopher Giorgio Agamben's recent interpretation of *The Trial* as Kafka's commentary on the relation between law and slander. For, as we shall see, Agamben's interpretation of Kafka's novel works tacitly to place under erasure the abiding undecidability that obtains between the literal and the figurative and that is irrevocably lodged at the heart of Kafka's text. Much of the critical commentary on the novel since its appearance has focused, often in an existentially oriented perspective, on motifs of guilt, accusation, and a denied proper trial. We might think here of influential early studies by such critics as Heinz Politzer, a collaborator of Brod's in the editing and dissemination of Kafka's texts. In Politzer's view, *The Trial* mobilizes K. primarily as a figure in whom the court can anchor its problematic, even illegitimate, claims and juridical manipulations, so that the novel can be seen fundamentally as placing the court itself on trial.[38] Implicitly breaking with this exegetical tradition, Agamben, by contrast, shifts our attention to the question of slander and, in particular, self-slander. Pointing out that in the tradition of Roman law with which Kafka, as a lawyer, was well familiar, a false accuser could

---

38. Heinz Politzer, "The Trial Against the Court," in *Franz Kafka: Parable and Paradox* (Ithaca, NY: Cornell University Press, 1962), 163–217.

be punished by having the designation of "kaluminator," Latin for "slanderer," engraved upon his forehead in the form of the abbreviation "K," which also, of course, is the only initial by which the last name of the novel's main character is known and which also is the single initial-name of the protagonist in *The Castle*. Whereas critics in the wake of Brod have tended to reduce the *K.* by expanding it into "Kafka," here it becomes the mark of slander as such. Although Agamben does not mention this, it is worth noting that already Kafka himself problematizes—and thereby turns into a matter of debate and interpretation—his employment of the letter *K.* when he writes in a diary entry on May 27, 1914, the year in which he commences work on *The Trial*, that "I find the letter *K* offensive, almost disgusting, and yet I write it down, it must be very characteristic of me."[39] For Agamben, reinterpreting the letter *K* is a crucial step toward the recognition that "slander represents the key to the novel—and, perhaps, to the entire Kafkaesque universe, so potently marked by the forces of law."[40] And he goes even further when he suggests that if the letter *K* is not merely seen as referring to a false accusation, or *kalumnia*, but, rather, is thought to point to the false accuser, *kaluminator*, himself, then the protagonist of *The Trial* can be understood to conduct "a slanderous trial against himself. The someone (*jemand*) who, with his slander, has initiated the trial is Josef K. himself."[41] The novel as such can then be read as the record of a slanderous self-accusation in which the protagonist struggles to come to terms with the consequences of his illicit self-betrayal.

39. Kafka, *Diaries 1914–1923*, 33–34 / *Tagebücher*, 517.
40. Giorgio Agamben, "K.," in *Nudities*, trans. David Kishik and Stefen Pedatella (Stanford, CA: Stanford University Press, 2011), 20–36, here 20. I will bracket here the discussion of Kafka in relationship to the concept of sovereignty that Agamben undertakes in his earlier work, *Homo Sacer: Sovereign Power and Bare Life*, trans. Daniel Heller-Roazen (Stanford, CA: Stanford University Press, 1998), specifically in the chapter "Form of Law" (49ff).
41. Agamben, "K.," 21.

In order to substantiate this interpretation, Agamben reminds us that not only is Josef K. advised by a court official that he does not know whether or not he has been accused, he also is told that his having been detained is not to be construed as requiring a departure from his ordinary life. Indeed, "the judges do not seem to have any intention of initiating" a trial against K., and "the trial exists only to the extent that K. recognizes it as such," a state of affairs that "K. himself anxiously concedes to the examining magistrate during the initial inquiry."[42] As further evidence of his understanding of the text, Agamben adduces the words said to K. by the prison chaplain at the end of the "Cathedral" chapter: "The court does not want anything from you. It receives you when you come and dismisses you when you go."[43] From the perspective constructed here, the court is not the instigator of the trial but merely the site, imaginary or real, upon which the juridical and ethical negotiations between a subjective consciousness and its experience of the "lawness" of the law—the law *as* law—find a stage as well as an archive.

One of the conclusions that Agamben draws from this interpretation of *The Trial* is that Josef K.'s self-accusatory slander speaks to a certain condition within the relation between law and subject. Indeed, he argues,

> every man initiates a slanderous trial against himself. This is Kafka's point of departure. Hence his universe cannot be tragic but only comic: guilt does not exist—or rather, guilt is nothing other than self-slander, which consists in accusing oneself of a nonexistent guilt (that is, of one's very innocence, which is the comic gesture par excellence).[44]

42. Agamben, "K.," 21.
43. Kafka, *The Trial*, 160 / *Der Proceß*, 304.
44. Agamben, "K.," 21.

But this comic gesture has a rather serious purposiveness. If, as Agamben argues, humans will slander themselves, it is the task of the law to distinguish, in the cases that come into its orbit, between groundless accusations and those that are potentially legitimate. From the perspective of such a distinguishing function of the law in relation to slanderous self-accusation, it becomes possible to read "the subtlety of self-slander as a strategy to deactivate and render inoperative the accusation, the indictment that the Law addresses toward Being" because the "only way to affirm one's innocence before the law (and the powers that represent the law: for example, the father, or marriage) is, in this sense, falsely to accuse oneself."[45] The paradoxical need for self-slander to protect one's innocence when faced with the law then becomes a way for Josef K. to attempt to avoid a trial, to defer the machinations of the legal system. Such a reading opens up the sense in which "K.'s strategy can be defined more precisely as the failed attempt to render the confession, but not the trial, impossible."[46]

What are we to make, at this point, of the lingering problem that is named by the tension between literal and figurative understandings of the artwork—between, on the one hand, letting the artwork, as it were, rest in and as itself and, on the other hand, helping the artwork say what it cannot say on its own, even at the risk of thereby making it superfluous as a work of art? Could it be that *The Trial* lends itself to legal-political (re)inscription in the history of the aftermath of a particular legal system—in this case, Roman law? It is as though Agamben's interpretive strategy, for all its perceptive meritoriousness, implicitly followed the dictates of a certain displacement. It works to displace the fundamental tension between the literal and the figurative dimension of the language of the artwork onto the

45. Agamben, "K.," 24.
46. Agamben, "K.," 25.

question of how the thematic complex of the protagonist's guilt—
and, by extension, his relation to the lawness of the law as such—
engenders a certain perpetuation and simultaneous rupturing of
certain elements inherited by our tradition from Roman law. In this
sense, Agamben's reading privileges the figurative dimension of the
artwork, rendering *The Trial* in principle as an allegory of the political implications of self-slander within the framework of a certain
legal and moral-juridical inheritance. By translating the refractory
and meaning-resistant language of the novel, through an admittedly
bold new reading, into the conceptual discourse of the politics of self-
accusation, Agamben believes to have found the hermeneutic key
that Adorno tells us has been purloined. It is from this perspective,
too, that Agamben feels emboldened to assert that the politicizing
question of self-slander is lodged so deeply in the core of the artwork
that this "is precisely what an attentive reading of the novel demonstrates beyond all doubt."[47] "Beyond all doubt"—as though as readers we were free to disregard the prison chaplain's warnings to Josef
K. about the uncontainable aberrations and dangerous vicissitudes of
interpretation itself.[48]

47. Agamben, "K.," 21.
48. As readers who have spent a lifetime engaging with Kafka's work—such as the late Walter
H. Sokel, one of Kafka's most circumspect interpreters—will attest, even though Kafka's
writing represents "the ever-renewed attempt to push toward . . . an explanation," the fact
remains that a "final evaluative meaning, expressing a definite and definable intentional-
ity in his work," is "impossible." After all, the "fundamental ambivalence of Kafka's writing precludes an ultimate judgment that could be called an 'explanation.'" Walter H. Sokel,
"Beyond Self-Assertion: A Life of Reading Kafka," in *A Companion to the Works of Franz
Kafka*, ed. James Rolleston (Rochester, NY: Camden House, 2002), 33–59, here 56.
Reading Kafka's writing from a philosophical perspective would therefore have to entail an
openness to hearing a different kind of demand. Among other things, this different kind of
demand as it is mediated by the Kafkan text can be named an "imperative to write," as Jeff
Fort has recently put it, an imperative that also encompasses a persistent element of textual self-reflection in which remnants of a failed or dispersed Kantian sublimity lingers on
among the ruins of writing itself. Jeff Fort, *The Imperative to Write: Destitutions of the Sublime
in Kafka, Blanchot, and Beckett* (New York: Fordham University Press, 2014).

The wish to establish "beyond all doubt" the relations among slander, self-slander, and the law in *The Trial* presupposes the possibility of a remainderless translation between the literary text's literal and figurative dimensions, as well as their often aleatory interaction with each other. Yet this premise is complicated by the resistance of Kafka's literary language itself. When Maurice Blanchot writes that "Kafka's trial can be interpreted as a tangle of three different realms (the Law, laws, rules)," he is quick to add that this "interpretation, however, is inadequate, because to justify it one would have to assume a fourth realm not derived from the other three—the overarching realm of literature itself." "But," he reminds us, "literature rejects this dominant point of view, all the while refusing to be dependent upon, or symbolized by, any other order at all (such as pure intelligibility)."[49] If literature refuses to be derivable from other principles and realms of signification, and if it will not allow itself to be subsumed under external categories as their subspecies, its particular modes of signification also will not permit the construction of a close stretto between a text's literal and figurative levels. The reader, standing not just before the text of the law but also before the law of the text, will have to learn to do better than the man from the country. This learning, if it is to come to pass at all, would indeed have to be situated on the far side of pure intelligibility. It would have to register, along with any propaedeutic mission, something of the self-reflexive despair to which Kafka himself confesses in a diary entry from December 6, 1921, five years after he had abandoned the fragments that constitute *The Trial*: "Metaphors are one among many things which make me despair of writing" (*Die Metaphern sind eines in dem Vielen, was mich am Schreiben verzweifeln läßt*).[50]

---

49. Maurice Blanchot, *The Writing of the Disaster*, trans. Ann Smock (Lincoln: University of Nebraska Press, 1995), 144f. Blanchot pursues some of the implications of this insight in his variegated essays on Kafka collected in *De Kafka à Kafka* (Paris: Gallimard, 1981).
50. Franz Kafka, *The Diaries of Franz Kafka, 1914–1923*, trans. Martin Greenberg, with Hannah Arendt, ed. Max Brod (New York: Schocken, 1949), 200–201; *Tagebücher*, 875.

To the extent that a "disease of all signification" makes itself uncannily felt in *The Trial*, it helps us register more precisely the contours and uncontainable effects of a certain aesthetic idiomaticity: the vicissitudes of symbolic and allegorical language that bestow upon the literary text a restless and searching experience of cognition and its deferral each time these linguistic vicissitudes come to pass in a new and singular way in a different literary artwork. A philosophically motivated reading of a literary text such as *The Trial* would have to take into account the destabilizing effects of this particular mode of deferral. In other words, a philosophically oriented interpretation would need to open itself up to the far-reaching implications of the fact that a rigorous confrontation with the text cannot occur in isolation from the experience of our abiding inability to differentiate between the literal and the figurative dimensions of the aesthetic object. If Kafka's German biographer Reiner Stach worries that "Kafka's *Trial* is a monster"—regardless of whether one considers the "genesis, manuscript, form, content, or interpretation of the novel"— and that "nothing here is normal, nothing is simple," with "obscurity wherever one looks," we might say that the burden of this obscurity is both perpetuated and illuminated by the irreducibly necessary yet rigorously unmeetable demand of conceptual interpretation that

---

In a different context, it would be fruitful to investigate the implications of the fact that this passage on metaphor from Kafka's diaries also constitutes the one reference to Kafka that finds its way into Derrida's early seminal work *De la grammatologie*, where it is introduced at a crucial juncture— namely in the discussion, contained in "Deuxieme Partie: Nature, Culture, Écriture," of how the supplement and the source relate in the space of writing. Jacques Derrida, *De la grammatologie* (Paris: Les Éditions de Minuit, 1967), 383–384.

The question concerning the volatile status of metaphor as a pivotal rhetorical figure traversing Kafka's writing has received much attention in the scholarship. For an exemplary reading of how, in the test case of "The Metamorphosis," an "entire story is organized around a figure whose entire sense is to demystify and truly to deconstruct metaphor" precisely "by tampering with its normal operations" through a "chiastic movement," see Stanley Corngold and Benno Wagner, "Thirteen Ways of Looking at a Vermin (*The Metamorphosis*)," in *Franz Kafka: The Ghosts in the Machine* (Evanston, IL: Northwestern University Press, 2011), 57–73, here 73.

Kafka's novel issues with each sentence anew.[51] It is here that the artwork becomes recognizable not merely as the sensate appearance, or even embodiment, of an idea but, rather, as an aesthetic form that both elicits and resists its philosophical interpretation. And it is here, too, that the trial(s) of language will have commenced with no authoritative court and no hermeneutically stable basis for judgment in sight.[52] Before the philosophical imperative to know and to decide, the literary work of art remains an outlaw.

BIBLIOGRAPHY

Adorno, Theodor W. *Aesthetic Theory*. Translated by Robert Hullot-Kentor. Minneapolis: University of Minnesota Press, 1997.

Adorno, Theodor W. *Ästhetische Theorie. Gesammelte Schriften*. Edited by Rolf Tiedemann, vol. 7. Frankfurt am Main: Suhrkamp, 1997.

Adorno, Theodor W. "Aufzeichnungen zu Kafka." In *Kulturkritik und Gesellschaft I. Gesammelte Schriften*, edited by Rolf Tiedemann, vol. 11, 254–287. Frankfurt am Main: Suhrkamp, 1997.

Adorno, Theodor W. *Lectures on Negative Dialectics: Fragments of a Lecture Course 1965/1966*. Translated by Rodney Livingstone. Cambridge: Polity, 2008.

Adorno, Theodor W. "Notes on Kafka." In *Prisms*, translated by Samuel and Shierry Weber, 243–271. Cambridge, MA: MIT Press, 1981.

---

51. Rainer Stach, *Kafka: Die Jahre der Entscheidungen* (Frankfurt am Main: Fischer, 2004), 537.

52. One might add that the "law" of this irreducible hermeneutic lawlessness also stands in the way of any attempt to "rescue" *The Trial* and its doorkeeper episode from the threats of undecidability that have been assigned, in apparent moments of critical discomfort, designations such as "lawless reading" (*gesetzloses Lesen*), as in Hartmut Binder. Hartmut Binder, *"Vor dem Gesetz": Einführung in Kafkas Welt* (Stuttgart: Metzler, 1993), 3. And can one really speak of a redemptive "defense of writing" or a "defense of the text" if one chooses to see in *The Trial* primarily a ciphered "process of reflection" that merely requires hermeneutic unlocking and cultural retranslation in order to reveal its tacitly veiled, but in principle stable and accessible, meaning? This is the assumption made by studies such as Frank Schirrmacher, ed., *Verteidigung der Schrift: Kafkas Prozeß* (Frankfurt am Main: Suhrkamp, 1987). Yet is such an alleged defense, a *Verteidigung*, of the novel not in reality a way of making it superfluous—precisely by showing that what it says and how it says it could have been said another way as well (that is, in the language of critical commentary and explanation), without essential loss?

Adorno, Theodor W. *Vorlesung über Negative Dialektik. Nachgelassene Schriften.* Edited by Rolf Tiedemann, vol. 16. Frankfurt am Main: Suhrkamp, 2003.

Adorno, Theodor W. "Words from Abroad." In *Notes to Literature,* translated by Shierry Weber Nicholsen, vol. 1, 185–199. New York: Columbia University Press, 1991.

Adorno, Theodor W. "Wörter aus der Fremde." In *Noten zur Literatur. Gesammelte Schriften,* edited by Rolf Tiedemann, vol. 11, 216–232. Frankfurt am Main: Suhrkamp, 1997.

Adorno, Theodor W., and Walter Benjamin. *Briefwechsel 1928–1940.* Frankfurt am Main: Suhrkamp, 1994.

Agamben, Giorgio. *Homo Sacer: Sovereign Power and Bare Life.* Translated by Daniel Heller-Roazen. Stanford: Stanford University Press, 1998.

Agamben, Giorgio. "K." In *Nudities,* translated by David Kishik and Stefen Pedatella, 20–36. Stanford, CA: Stanford University Press, 2011.

Auden, W. H. "The Wandering Jew." In *The Complete Works of W. H. Auden. Vol. 2: Prose, 1939–1948,* edited by Edward Mendelson, 110–113. Princeton, NJ: Princeton University Press, 2002.

Binder, Hartmut. *"Vor dem Gesetz": Einführung in Kafkas Welt.* Stuttgart: Metzler, 1993.

Blanchot, Maurice. *De Kafka à Kafka.* Paris: Gallimard, 1981.

Blanchot, Maurice. *The Writing of the Disaster.* Translated by Ann Smock. Lincoln: University of Nebraska Press, 1995.

Corngold, Stanley. "Adorno's 'Notes on Kafka': A Critical Reconstruction." *Monatshefte* 94, no. 1 (2002): 24–42. Special Issue: *Rereading Adorno,* edited by Gerhard Richter.

Corngold, Stanley. "Medial Interventions in *The Trial*; Or, *Res* in Media." In *Lambent Traces: Franz Kafka,* 51–55. Princeton, NJ: Princeton University Press, 2004.

Corngold, Stanley, and Benno Wagner. "Thirteen Ways of Looking at a Vermin (*The Metamorphosis*)." In *Franz Kafka: The Ghosts in the Machine,* 57–73. Evanston, IL: Northwestern University Press, 2011.

de Man, Paul. "Semiology and Rhetoric." In *Allegories of Reading: Figural Language in Rousseau, Nietzsche, Rilke, and Proust,* 3–19. New Haven, CT: Yale University Press, 1979.

Derrida, Jacques. "Before the Law." Translated by Avital Ronell and Christine Roulston. In *Acts of Literature,* edited by Derek Attridge, 181–220. New York: Routledge, 1992.

Derrida, Jacques. "Deuxieme Partie: Nature, Culture, Écriture." In *De la grammatologie,* 383–384. Paris: Les Éditions de Minuit, 1967.

Derrida, Jacques. "White Mythology: Metaphor in the Text of Philosophy." Translated by Alan Bass. In *Margins of Philosophy,* 207–229. Chicago: University of Chicago Press, 1982.

Fort, Jeff. *The Imperative to Write: Destitutions of the Sublime in Kafka, Blanchot, and Beckett.* New York: Fordham University Press, 2014.

García Düttmann, Alexander. *Was weiß Kunst? Für eine Ästhetik des Widerstands.* Konstanz: Konstanz University Press, 2015.

Kafka, Franz. *Briefe an Felice.* Edited by Erich Heller and Jürgen Born. Frankfurt am Main: Fischer, 1983.

Kafka, Franz. *Dearest Father and Other Writings.* Translated by Ernst Kaiser and Eithne Wilkins. New York: Schocken, 1954.

Kafka, Franz. *The Diaries of Franz Kafka, 1910–1913.* Translated by Joseph Kresh, edited by Max Brod. New York: Schocken, 1948.

Kafka, Franz. *The Diaries of Franz Kafka, 1914–1923.* Translated by Martin Greenberg, with Hannah Arendt, edited by Max Brod. New York: Schocken, 1949.

Kafka, Franz. *Der Proceß.* Edited by Malcolm Pasley. *Kritische Ausgabe.* Frankfurt am Main: Fischer, 2002.

Kafka, Franz. *Letters to Felice.* Translated by James Stern and Elisabeth Duckworth. New York: Schocken, 1973.

Kafka, Franz. *Nachgelassene Schriften und Fragmente II.* Edited by Jost Schillemeit. *Kritische Ausgabe.* Frankfurt am Main: Fischer, 2002.

Kafka, Franz. *Tagebücher.* Edited by Hans-Gerd Koch, Michael Müller, and Malcolm Pasley. *Kritische Ausgabe.* Frankfurt am Main: Fischer, 2002.

Kafka, Franz. *The Trial.* Translated by Mike Mitchell. Oxford: Oxford University Press, 2009.

Neumann, Gerhard. "'Blinde Parabel' oder Bildungsroman? Zur Struktur von Kafkas 'Proceß'-Fragment." *Jahrbuch der deutschen Schillergesellschaft* 41 (1997): 399–427.

Nietzsche, Friedrich. *Beyond Good and Evil.* Translated by Walter Kaufmann. In *Basic Writings*, 178–435. New York: Modern Library, 2000.

Politzer, Heinz. "The Trial Against the Court." In *Franz Kafka: Parable and Paradox*, 163–217. Ithaca, NY: Cornell University Press, 1962.

Richter, Gerhard. "Aesthetic Theory and Nonpropositional Truth Content in Adorno." *New German Critique* 97 (Winter 2006): 119–135.

Richter, Gerhard. "*Erbsünde*: A Note on Paradoxical Inheritance in Benjamin's Kafka Essay." In *Inheriting Walter Benjamin*, 15–33. London: Bloomsbury, 2016.

Schirrmacher, Frank. *Verteidigung der Schrift. Kafkas Prozeß.* Frankfurt am Main: Suhrkamp, 1987.

Sokel, Walter H., "Beyond Self-Assertion: A Life of Reading Kafka." In *A Companion to the Works of Franz Kafka*, edited by James Rolleston, 33–59. Rochester, NY: Camden House, 2002.

Spiegel, Hubert. *Kafkas Sätze.* Frankfurt am Main: Fischer, 2009.

Spivak, Gayatri Chakravorty. *A Critique of Postcolonial Reason: Toward a History of the Vanishing Present.* Cambridge, MA: Harvard University Press, 1999.

Stach, Rainer. *Kafka. Die Jahre der Entscheidungen.* Frankfurt am Main: Fischer, 2004.

Walser, Martin. "Description of a Form." Translated by James Rolleston. In *Twentieth Century Interpretation of* The Trial: *A Collection of Critical Essays*, edited by James Rolleston, 21–35. Englewood Cliffs, NJ: Prentice-Hall, 1976.

Chapter 5

Unfettering the Future

Estrangement and Ambiguity in The Trial

IAIN MACDONALD

He is a free and secure citizen of the earth [*ein freier und gesicherter Bürger der Erde*] because he is bound by a chain long enough to open all earthly regions to him, and yet just long enough that nothing can drag him over the edge of the earth. At the same time, however, he is also a free and secure citizen of heaven because he is bound by another chain that is similarly arranged. Should he wish to travel earthward, the heavenly collar will tug at his throat; and likewise with the earthly collar, should he wish to travel heavenward. In spite of this, he feels that all possibilities are available to him. Indeed, he will even refuse to trace the whole situation back to an error in the original fettering.

—Kafka, Oktavheft G, 1917[1]

[Kafka] was aware of what was to come ... essentially as the *individual* upon whom it impinges.

—Benjamin to Scholem, June 12, 1938[2]

1. Franz Kafka, *Nachgelassene Schriften und Fragmente II*, ed. Jost Schillemeit (Frankfurt am Main: S. Fischer Verlag, 1992), Oktavheft G, 63. Unreferenced translations are my own. Other translations have been tacitly emended on occasion. Thanks go to W. Ross and D. Morin for editorial assistance.
2. Walter Benjamin, "Letter to Gershom Scholem on Franz Kafka," in *Selected Writings*, ed. Michael W. Jennings and Howard Eiland (Cambridge, MA: Harvard University Press, 1999–2003), 3:326; and Walter Benjamin, *Briefe* (Frankfurt am Main: Suhrkamp Verlag, 1978), 2:762.

In a diary entry from 1913, Kafka sketches an encounter between an old merchant, Messner, and a young student, Kette. Kette surprises Messner with news that he bears a message for him, which Messner shows little interest in receiving. The sketch is remarkable for at least two reasons: first, the depiction of Messner's unwillingness— or inability—to hear what Kette has to say; second, Kette's singular determination to deliver the message, lingering in the hall and banging on Messner's door even after he is told to leave. The scene's central conceit lies clearly in the unresolved tension between Messner's refusal and Kette's insistence. Moreover, and more importantly, the articulation of this conceit brings a strange distance into play between Messner and the unknown communication, of which Kette is the bearer. However, this distance between Messner's routine and the cause of its disruption, or between his present knowledge and a possible future change to that knowledge, is strangely unmeasurable. Not only is the reader given no clues as to what the content of the message might be, but Messner himself seems structurally detached from any situation in which he could actually receive the message, understand its meaning, or judge its relevance to him. In fact, Messner's apparent satisfaction with his routine and his lack of curiosity about matters unrelated to his business render him utterly indifferent. "I wouldn't know anything about receiving any such message," he says, to which he subsequently adds a more explicit refusal: "I don't want to receive any messages. Every message that I am spared is a gain, I am not curious, just go, go."[3] Yet his refusal fails, at least to the extent that he is clearly affected by the mysterious message in spite of remaining ignorant of its content: Kette's persistence disturbs his complacency.

---

3. Franz Kafka, *Diaries, 1910–1923*, trans. Joseph Kresh, Martin Greenberg, and Hannah Arendt, ed. Max Brod (New York: Schocken, 1964), 240–241; and Franz Kafka, *Tagebücher*, ed. Hans-Gerd Koch, Michael Müller, and Malcolm Pasley (Frankfurt am Main: S. Fischer Verlag, 1990), 599–600.

Messner can only react by intensifying his denial of interest in the message. In this way, he is both detached from the message through refusal and yet also bound to it through the disruption of his routine. One might say that Kette, which means "chain," is the name given to this ambiguous distancing effect.

This scene is perhaps the most concise presentation of the peculiar form of estrangement that is expressed in Kafka's works and especially in *The Trial*.[4] But what sort of estrangement is this? Who or what is estranged from what? We should not be too quick to assume that the estrangement at issue is straightforwardly assimilable to the usual philosophical or sociological uses of the term, in spite of certain similarities. Hegel's use of the term, for example, designates (among other things) a distance that can separate individual from social consciousness: the uneducated or undisciplined individual is, in this sense, estranged from the ethical life of the community. However, for Hegel, this distance can be overcome in a convergence of individual and social actualization—for example, in the dialectic of education or enculturation (*Bildung*), in which the individual ideally comes to contribute to and sustain the institutions and practices of the community. Similarly, Marx's notion of estrangement, which is tied to the capitalist treatment of labor, ultimately represents the distance between capitalist and communist forms of social organization. Estranged labor is therefore normatively charged: it names both the current state of affairs and an estrangement from the real possibility of founding a just society—that is, estrangement from a social consciousness able to transform the world for the better. Diagnosing this situation provides the theoretical impetus for its practical overcoming. Thus, estrangement in both Hegel and Marx is fundamentally a *transitional* category in the sense that the possibility of its

---

4. It may be worth noting that the words *Entfremdung, entfremden,* etc. are relatively rare in Kafka's novels and short stories.

dialectical overcoming is socially given, if only implicitly at first. Not so in Kafka, for whom the reconciliation of individual and institution seems ruled out. If anything, many of Kafka's characters seem *perpetually* estranged—that is, remote from any transformative, progressive experience. It remains to be seen what this condition consists in, but in terms of the story of Messner and Kette, the least that can be said is that Messner's refusal is not simply capricious. It reflects the practical impossibility of truly receiving any "message" that is incompatible with his familiar reality. As we shall see, this is likewise the case of Josef K. in *The Trial,* for whom the perpetual character of his estrangement negates any promise of escape, let alone any sort of reconciliation with the enigmatic authorities that persecute him.

Further variants on the theme of estrangement help to complete the picture. In some ways, the enduring distance between K. and the authorities and institutions responsible for his arrest may seem more closely related to the more visceral but at times less precisely defined forms of social anxiety that are sometimes associated with certain strands of modernist literature, whether this takes the form of isolation, existential alienation, world-weariness, or what have you. Such subjective notions have certainly provided points of reference in Kafka interpretation, and the reduction of the individual to a mere means serving abstract and incomprehensible institutional ends is not an unusual way of approaching the problem of estrangement. It is no doubt true that the individual can feel frustrated and disconnected in relation to social institutions, just as K. oscillates between defiance and bewilderment in the course of his trial. Kafka himself, as is often noted, felt "more estranged than a stranger" (*fremder als ein Fremder*)[5] within his family, not to mention the irresolvable tension

5. Franz Kafka, *Briefe 1913–März 1914,* ed. Hans-Gerd Koch (Frankfurt am Main: S. Fischer Verlag, 1999), to Carl Bauer, August 28, 1913, 272. Compare the diary entry for August 21, 1913: Kafka, *Diaries,* 231/*Tagebücher,* 580.

between his office work and his literary vocation.[6] But as he well knew, such experiences and even the most personal of biographical details are thoroughly institutionally mediated and so can only serve as an occasion for reflection, never as a principle of interpretation.

The more general problem, as Theodor W. Adorno puts it, is that under late capitalism, estrangement has become pervasive, both imposed from without and self-inflicted, such that there are few vantage points from which we can recognize estrangement *as* estrangement: "by virtue of the progressive societization [*Vergesellschaftung*] of all human interactions, [spirit] has more and more fallen prey to anonymous control by existing relations, a control that is not only experienced externally, but which has migrated into its immanent makeup."[7] Consequently, estrangement—or the suffering caused by theoretical and practical tensions between individuals and existing social institutions—has become perennial, a well-established and seemingly incontestable second nature.

As is well known, this perennial—that is, nontransitional—estrangement was severely criticized by Lukács in his interpretation of Kafka and other strands of modernist literature:

> Since the world view of these writers ... holds fast to the immutability of objective actuality ..., the possibility of human action is *a priori* rendered powerless and meaningless. .... This feeling of powerlessness—which is intensified and elevated into a world view, and which Kafka turns into a shocking vision of anxiety [*Angst*] in respect of world affairs and the complete surrender of

---

6. Reiner Stach, *Kafka: The Decisive Years*, trans. Shelley Frisch (Princeton, NJ: Princeton University Press, 2005), 426.
7. Theodor W. Adorno, "Cultural Criticism and Society," in *Prisms*, trans. Samuel Weber and Shierry Weber (Cambridge, MA: MIT Press, 1981), 21; and Theodor W. Adorno, *Gesammelte Schriften*, ed. Rolf Tiedemann, Gretel Adorno, Susan Buck-Morss, and Kalau Schultz, 20 vols. (Frankfurt am Main: Suhrkamp Verlag, 1970–97), 10.1:13.

the human being to inexplicable, inscrutable, and insurmountable [*unaufhebbaren*] horror—is what makes his life's work into a symbol for all modernist art. Tendencies that would otherwise be given form either artistically or reflectively are here gathered together into a panic-stricken, elemental Platonic wonder before an actuality that is eternally foreign and hostile to the human being. . . . Kafka's anxiety is the experience *par excellence* of all decadent modernist art.[8]

Lukács here attempts to tie Kafka's specific form of estrangement to the problem of social stagnation and resignation, and from there to a rejection of socialism and a better future for humanity:

The refusal of socialism as a perspective, whether explicit or taken for granted, . . . means that a door has been slammed shut, a curtain has dropped before the future, which in turn means that the state of the world—consisting of chaos and anxiety— becomes perennial, eternally predetermined for the subject.[9]

In this way, the subjective experience of estrangement in "decadent" modernism becomes the metonymical placeholder for a society unable to overcome its failings, thereby condemning itself to become a

8. Georg Lukács, *The Meaning of Contemporary Realism*, trans. John Mander and Necke Mander (London: Merlin Press, 1962), 36; and Georg Lukács, *Werke* (Neuwied/Berlin: Luchterhand, 1962–1986), 4:488–489. The book initially appeared in German under the title *Wider den mißverstandenen Realismus* (Hamburg: Claassen, 1958). For a discussion of Lukács's reading of Kafka, see Michael Löwy, "'Fascinating Delusive Light': Georg Lukács and Franz Kafka," in *Georg Lukács: The Fundamental Dissonance of Existence—Aesthetics, Politics, Literature,* ed. Timothy Bewes and Timothy Hall (London: Continuum, 2011). As Löwy points out, Lukács apparently tempered his critique of Kafka in later years, though perhaps in a rather more suggestive than decisive manner.

9. Lukács, *The Meaning of Contemporary Realism*, 73 / *Werke*, 4:530.

distorted picture of its own future, which is reduced to the mere repetition of the bad state of affairs that currently holds sway.

For this reason, Lukács emphasizes what he sees as a sort of modal confusion: the modernism that Kafka represents accords exclusive priority to abstract subjective possibilities over against the real, concrete possibilities of emancipation that in fact obtain within living actuality. Hopeless universal estrangement seems to *exhaust* actuality, whereas it is more like a misrepresentation or misconfiguration of its resources:

> Abstract possibility can run free only in the subject, whereas concrete possibility presupposes its interaction with objective facts and life forces. The latter always and necessarily have an objective, social-historical character. In other words, the literary presentation of concrete possibilities presupposes a concrete presentation of concrete human beings in concrete relations with the outer world. Only in a living and concrete interaction between human beings and their environment can concrete human possibility emerge from the bad infinity of abstract possibilities, and thereby prove itself to be the determining concrete possibility of just this person at just this stage of development.[10]

Thus for Lukács, the social abstractions of writers such as Kafka bring the dialectic of individual and society—that is, the dialectic of estrangement and its overcoming, as defined by Hegel and Marx—to a standstill. The fact that K. can do nothing to change his predicament is just the narrative equivalent of this modal confusion: he has essentially no real, concrete possibilities of reconciliation or overcoming available to him. The only possibility available in Kafka's world is the unique and abstract possibility of perpetual, universal estrangement.

10. Lukács, *The Meaning of Contemporary Realism*, 23–24 / *Werke*, 4:474.

The problem with this reading, as already suggested in Adorno's prompt critique[11] of it, is that it massively underestimates the critical potential proper to Kafka's peculiar notion of estrangement, which in *The Trial* takes the form of the current unavailability of a better future. The nuance is important: Kafka does not say that universal estrangement is inevitable and inescapable; rather, he says that it is a real problem that affects and afflicts us here and now, blocking the way forward. It is this blockage that fascinates him.[12] As he puts it in the parable "Before the Law":

> the doorkeeper says he cannot let the man into the Law just now. The man thinks this over and then asks whether that means he might be allowed to enter the Law later. "That is possible," the doorkeeper says, "but not now" (*Es ist möglich, . . . jetzt aber nicht*).[13]

Thus to the question as to what is estranged from what, we can provisionally say that it is the blind and everlasting continuation of the present that is estranged from the possibility of a future that would be different from it—and perhaps better than it, more just. In a word, we are estranged from something so alien and unfamiliar to us in the present that it can appear to us only negatively: in the form of abstract possibility, blockage, and bewilderment. In such a situation,

11. Theodor W. Adorno, "Extorted Reconciliation: On Georg Lukács' *Realism in our Time*," in *Notes to Literature*, trans. Shierry Weber Nicholsen (New York: Columbia University Press, 1991–1992), 1:216–240 / *Gesammelte Schriften*, 11:251–280. This text first appeared in 1958, the same year in which Lukács's *Wider den mißverstandenen Realismus* was published.
12. Kafka struggled with the problem of the future in a number of ways. In the *Diaries*, for example, he writes: "In general I lacked principally the ability to make even the slightest provisions for the real future. I thought only of things in the present and their present state." See Kafka, *Diaries*, January 2, 1912, 160 / *Tagebücher*, 335.
13. Franz Kafka, *The Trial*, trans. Mike Mitchell (Oxford: Oxford University Press, 2009), 153; and Franz Kafka, *Der Proceß* (Frankfurt am Main: S. Fischer Verlag, 1990), 292.

in which the familiar continuity of the present is the only point of reference available to us, it may be, as Adorno will put it, that "strangeness is the only antidote to estrangement."[14] Indeed, "if the strange were no longer anathema, then estrangement could scarcely exist."[15] The question then becomes one of how the apparently abstract possibility of a different future can be made more real. It is the socially conditioned inaccessibility of such a different future that is at issue, rather than its perennity or cosmological inevitability in Kafka's universe. Thus, as Adorno sometimes suggests with regard to Kafka, estrangement need not result in resignation; its artistic treatment can also transform it into the cipher of its opposite.[16] In this vein, Kafka himself remarks at one point: "To perform the negative still imposes itself upon us, the positive is already given."[17] As for Adorno, it is clear that this "negative" relation to the "positive" (i.e., given reality) is of central importance, but despite numerous hints, relatively little is said about how Kafka manages this particular feat in *The Trial*. How, then, does the critique of universal estrangement come about?

14. Theodor W. Adorno, *Minima Moralia*, trans. Edmund Jephcott (London: Verso, 1978), §58, 94 / *Gesammelte Schriften*, 4:105.

15. Theodor W. Adorno, *Negative Dialectics*, trans. E. B. Ashton (London: Routledge, 1973), 172 / *Gesammelte Schriften*, 6:174. See, too, Adorno, *Negative Dialectics*, 278 / *Gesammelte Schriften*, 6:274. Adorno manifestly refuses any notion of estrangement that would amount to self-estrangement or divergence from some essential characteristic. This is no doubt why he once said that he tried to ban it from his vocabulary. See Theodor W. Adorno, *Introduction to Sociology*, trans. Edmund Jephcott (Stanford, CA: Stanford University Press, 2000), 3 / *Einleitung in die Soziologie*, ed. Christoph Gödde (Frankfurt am Main: Suhrkamp Verlag), 12.

16. See especially Adorno, "Notes on Kafka," in *Prisms*, trans. Samuel Weber and Shierry Weber (Cambridge, MA: MIT Press, 1981), e.g., 270–271 / *Gesammelte Schriften*, 10.1:285–287. Passages from other texts express the same idea, e.g., *Aesthetic Theory*, trans. Robert Hullot-Kentor (Minneapolis: University of Minnesota Press, 1997), 230–231 / *Gesammelte Schriften*, 7:342–343.

17. Franz Kafka, "The Collected Aphorisms," in *The Great Wall of China and Other Short Works*, ed. and trans. Malcolm Pasley (London: Penguin, 1973), 83 / Adorno, *Nachgelassene Schriften und Fragmente II*, 47. Adorno cites this passage in "Notes on Kafka," in *Prisms*, 271 / *Gesammelte Schriften*, 10.1:286.

Essentially, Kafka presents us with a particular configuration of the problem of estrangement and attempts to safeguard the future possibility of its overcoming by hiding it within the intricate and claustrophobic realities that are depicted in detail in *The Trial*. The doorkeeper's response to the man from the country is but one of a number of examples that call attention to the specific quality of the distance between the present in its persistence and the current inaccessibility of a better future. In general, it is as though K. were bound by an imperceptible chain that limits his range of possibilities in the present to those which entail its apparently inevitable continuation. Through the construction of this appearance and the fettering it involves, Kafka careers along the edge of the precipice of hopelessness; and although he may seem to be at great risk of plunging into the void, he manages instead to take its measure.

As in the Messner-Kette fragment, the presence of the chain that restrains K. makes itself known not in the form of explicit knowledge of its limiting effects but, rather, through the sudden arrival of a disruptive "message" devoid of any explanatory content. The message simultaneously disturbs K.'s complacency and holds him fast—that is, arrests him—slowly revealing him to be bound to the fate that unfolds inexorably in the pages that follow and preventing him from concretely conceiving of any alternative. The message is announced in the first sentence of the novel: "Someone must have been telling tales about Josef K., for one morning, without having done anything wrong, he was arrested."[18] In the confusion that ensues, the disruption of complacency and the restriction of possibility come surging to the fore.

This disturbance manifests itself in a number of ways in the book's many episodes of misunderstanding, incomprehension, and incomprehensibility, often taking the central form of tense and apparently

18. Kafka, *The Trial*, 5 / *Der Proceß*, 7.

unproductive or aporetical ambiguities. A good number are brought out with some insistence in the first pages of the novel and others regularly emerge, determining the book's structure throughout. The first of these ambiguities lies in the nature of the "arrest," which simultaneously limits K.'s possibilities ("You are not allowed to leave, you are our prisoner"[19]) and leaves him free to go about his business ("Yes, you have been arrested, but that should not prevent you from going to work. Nor should anything prevent you from going about your usual way of life" [*Sie sollen auch in Ihrer gewöhnlichen Lebensweise nicht gehindert sein*][20]). Are the guards even guards? K. seems unsure and has to convince himself of this: "they *had* to be guards" (*es konnten ja nur Wächter sein*).[21] Perhaps most significant in the early stages of these unfolding ambiguities is the nature of the authorities before whom K. stands accused, represented by guards who seem not to belong to the usual state apparatus:

> What kind of people were they? What were they talking about? To which authority [*Behörde*] did they belong? After all, K. lived in a state of law [*Rechtsstaat*], it was a time of peace, the laws had not been suspended—who then, had the audacity to descend on him in the privacy of his own home?[22]

Indeed, it even seems that the help of a state prosecutor (*Staatsanwalt*)—that is, a representative of the law in the usual social and institutional sense of the concept—would be entirely extraneous to the proceedings ("I don't know what the point would be, unless you have some private matter to discuss with him," says the

19. Kafka, *The Trial*, 6 / *Der Proceß*, 9.
20. Kafka, *The Trial*, 14–15 / *Der Proceß*, 26.
21. Kafka, *The Trial*, 7 / *Der Proceß*, 11.
22. Kafka, *The Trial*, 7 / *Der Proceß*, 11.

supervisor[23]). In short, in the first moments of his arrest there are already strong signs that there is more than one order of law at work here. It is even uncertain that K.'s arrest has anything to do with any wrongdoing in the normal legal sense of the word: "I cannot inform you that you have been charged with anything or, rather, I do not know whether you have been or not. You have been arrested, that is a fact, and that is all I know."[24] Again, a "message" has arrived, but its content remains unknown; and although K. attempts to go about his daily business, his routine is profoundly disturbed. Things are not what they seem, but nor are they otherwise.

Such ambiguities accumulate and become ever stranger in the novel. Leni's amphibious hand, her "pretty claw,"[25] is perhaps the most succinct example. In general, conceptual confusion is frequent: for example, K. learns from the prison chaplain that the distinction between trial and judgment is blurred ("the proceedings gradually merge into the verdict"[26]). Likewise, in his first encounter with the lawyer Huld (whose name in the German language evokes notions of favor and grace, yet seems also to be a fragment of *Schuld*, "guilt" or "debt"), K. wonders about his relation to this mysterious other law to which he appears to be subject: "What he wanted to say was, 'But you work at the court in the Palace of Justice and not at the one in the attics,' but he couldn't bring himself to actually say it."[27]

In a different vein, Titorelli's striking painting of Justice, whom K. has trouble recognizing, presents us with an overtly ambiguous figure:

"Ah, now I can see," said K., "there's the blindfold over her eyes and there's the scales. But aren't those wings on her heels, and

23. Kafka, *The Trial*, 13 / *Der Proceß*, 23.
24. Kafka, *The Trial*, 12–13 / *Der Proceß*, 22.
25. Kafka, *The Trial*, 78 / *Der Proceß*, 145.
26. Kafka, *The Trial*, 152 / *Der Proceß*, 289.
27. Kafka, *The Trial*, 73 / *Der Proceß*, 136.

isn't she running?" "Yes," said the painter, "it was in the commission that I had to paint her like that, it's actually Justice and the Goddess of Victory at the same time."[28]

To make matters more complicated, K. ends up seeing the Goddess of the Hunt in the painting. How are we to understand this confusion of Dikē, Nikē, and Artemis? It is not clear, but an order of law that confuses them must also be one that sees justice as implying the threat of pursuit, defeat, submission, and slaughter.

One final example: in the "Thrasher" chapter, the difference between present and future is blurred, leaving us to wonder whether a future might one day come about that would be radically different from the past and present, along with the institutional violence that characterizes them. After witnessing the punishment of the guards Franz and Willem, K. returns the next day only to find that they are still there. His every tomorrow is modeled on his every today. Is tomorrow really tomorrow if it is always the same as today?[29]

It is in connection with these suggestive but apparently irresolvable ambiguities that we should understand the estrangement at work in *The Trial*. However, a brief detour is required in order to bring out what role such figures play in the context of the narrative. Why are they not simply idle? Why do they not lead us into the impasse of abstract universal estrangement and unalterable subjective powerlessness? Or, to phrase the question more affirmatively, might these apparently aporetical ambiguities not adumbrate a critical potential concealed within the experience of estrangement? Do they not drive us—in spite of K., if not with him—to seek a way out of broken actuality? In this respect, they recall to some extent the structure and

28. Kafka, *The Trial*, 104 / *Der Proceß*, 195–196.
29. Compare Adorno, "Notes on Kafka," in *Prisms*, 253 / *Gesammelte Schriften*, 10.1:264.

function of the ambiguities that arise in Greek tragedy. (Of course, Kafka's ambiguities are not exactly those of Sophocles or Aeschylus, but this difference itself will prove instructive.) In this regard, the work of Jean-Pierre Vernant and Pierre Vidal-Naquet offers a succinct portrait and a helpful point of departure for understanding the peculiarity of Kafka's aporetic ambiguities.[30]

Inspired in part by the polysemy of certain central concepts of Greek ethical life, the great tragedians integrated into their works conceptual ambiguities that tragic consciousness incarnates and from which its suffering derives. In this way, double or multiple meanings conveyed by words such as *nomos, dikē, kratos,* and others—frequently involving legal terminology—provide the driving tensions of classical tragedy. In terms that readily suggest a point of contact with Kafka's world, Vernant writes of law and justice:

> For [the Greeks] there are, as it were, differing degrees of law. At one pole law rests upon the authority of established fact and constraint; at the other it brings into play sacred powers such as the order of the world or the justice of Zeus. It also poses moral problems regarding human responsibility. From this point of view divine *Dikē* [Justice] herself may appear opaque and incomprehensible, in that for human beings she includes an irrational

30. Albert Camus briefly discusses Kafka's relation to Greek tragedy in "L'espoir et l'absurde dans l'œuvre de Franz Kafka," in *Le mythe de Sisyphe* (Paris: Gallimard, 1942), 173–175. Regarding the more general question of Kafka and mythology, see Beda Allemann, "Kafka und die Mythologie," *Zeitschrift für Ästhetik und allgemeine Kunstwissenschaft* 20 (1975); and Idris Parry, "Kafka's Modern Mythology," *Bulletin of the John Rylands Library* 53, no. 1 (1970). Benjamin, however, suggests that the world of myth is "incomparably younger than Kafka's world." See Walter Benjamin, "Franz Kafka: On the Tenth Anniversary of His Death," in *Selected Writings*, ed. Michael W. Jennings and Howard Eiland (Cambridge, MA: Harvard University Press, 1999–2003), 2:799; and Walter Benjamin, *Gesammelte Schriften* (Frankfurt am Main: Suhrkamp Verlag, 1972–1989), 2.2:415.

element of brute force. Thus, in the *Suppliants* we see the concept of *kratos* oscillating between two contrary meanings. Sometimes it denotes legitimate authority, legally based control [i.e., more in the sense of *kurios*], sometimes brute force in its aspect of violence, completely opposed to the law and to justice [i.e., more in the sense of *bia*]. Similarly, in *Antigone,* the word *nomos* may be used with precisely opposed connotations by different protagonists. [For Antigone, it means "religious rule," whereas for Creon it means "an edict promulgated by the head of state."] What tragedy depicts is one *dikē* in conflict with another, a law that is not fixed, shifting and changing into its opposite. To be sure, tragedy is something quite different from a legal debate. It takes as its subject the man actually living out this debate, forced to make a decisive choice, to orient his activity in a universe of ambiguous values where nothing is ever stable or unequivocal.[31]

In short, the progressive unfolding of the practical and social manifestations of such semantic tensions lead inevitably to crime, guilt, and more or less successful attempts at atonement or reconciliation. Such conceptual ambiguities are well documented. What is of interest here is not merely their presence or frequency in Greek tragedy but the various directions in which they lead us. There are three interrelated points that are worthy of mention in the present context.

First, there is the question of the tragic hero or heroine's status as guilty subject. There is, in general, no direct or unequivocal way in which guilt is ascribed to the central figures of Greek tragedy. Action and decision certainly play a role, but these aspects themselves become interwoven with another order of being that assigns

31. Jean-Pierre Vernant and Pierre Vidal-Naquet, *Myth and Tragedy in Ancient Greece,* trans. Janet Lloyd (New York: Zone Books, 1990), 26, 39, 113–114; and Jean-Pierre Vernant and Pierre Vidal-Naquet, *Mythe et tragédie en Grèce ancienne,* 2 vols. (Paris: La Découverte, 1972, 2001), 1:15–16, 1:31–32, 1:102.

guilt and metes out punishment beyond the ken of the human agent and seemingly without any possibility of acting in any way that could set things right before the hero's fate unfolds:

> The true domain of tragedy lies in that border zone where human actions are articulated alongside divine powers, from which—unknown to the agent—they derive their true meaning by becoming an integral part of an order that is beyond the human being and that eludes him.[32]

Thus the individual takes on the role of an inherently ambiguous hinge figure caught up in an actuality that exceeds all understanding, entailing a nearly undiscoverable restriction of possibilities of thought and action. This can take the form of a kind of monomaniacal blindness with respect to fate and the gods. For example:

> Oedipus is double. He is in himself a riddle, whose meaning he can only guess when he discovers himself to be in every respect the opposite of what he thought he was and appeared to be. Oedipus himself does not understand the secret speech that, without his realizing, lurks at the heart of what he says. And, except for Tiresias, no witness to the drama on stage is capable of perceiving it either. It is the gods who send Oedipus's own speech back at him, deformed or twisted around, like an echo to some of his own words.[33]

We may be reminded here of the many scenes in *The Trial* where K.'s understanding is twisted around, shown to be insufficient, and thrust back upon him, whether in his initial dealings with the guards who

---

32. Vernant and Vidal-Naquet, *Myth and Tragedy*, 47 / *Mythe et tragédie*, 1:39.
33. Vernant and Vidal-Naquet, *Myth and Tragedy*, 116 / *Mythe et tragédie*, 1:105.

inform him of his arrest or, perhaps more pointedly, in the episode in the cathedral in which the priest corrects K. on the question of his guilt. In the latter scene, K. fails to understand what is happening to him precisely because the notion of guilt at his disposal is partial, merely one fragment of a whole to which he has no cognitive or explicit experiential access—although he does frequently, if only indirectly, encounter the inadequacy of his notion of guilt: " 'But I'm not guilty,' said K., 'it's a mistake. How can a person be guilty anyway? We're all human, every single one of us.' 'That is correct,' said the priest, 'but that's the way guilty people talk.' "[34] This misunderstanding returns in K.'s defiant affirmations: "Above all, it was essential, if he was to get anywhere, to discount from the outset any suggestion that he might be guilty. Guilt did not come into it."[35] Of course, he says this to himself with the conviction of someone who has not quite grasped that he is clinging to the insufficiency of his convictions, for from the very beginning and in numerous ways it is repeatedly suggested to him that another meaning or order of guilt is at issue: "You have been arrested, true, but not the way a thief's arrested,"[36] says Frau Grubach. This conundrum, centered on the oddness of K.'s guilt, brings ambiguity to bear on his person. Like Oedipus, K. is double, a riddle.[37] Unlike Oedipus, however, K. never realizes the full extent of what he has undergone. He understands nothing. His death is therefore not self-inflicted—the performative admission and acceptance of singular responsibility—as is the case with Oedipus's blinding. Instead, K. gives up all resistance to his executioners and becomes submissive, almost "inanimate"—the ultimate proof of his inability to

34. Kafka, *The Trial*, 152 / *Der Proceß*, 289.
35. Kafka, *The Trial*, 90 / *Der Proceß*, 168.
36. Kafka, *The Trial*, 19 / *Der Proceß*, 33.
37. For another perspective on K.'s relation to Oedipus, see Walter H. Sokel, "The Programme of K.'s Court: Oedipal and Existential Meanings of *The Trial*," in *On Kafka: Semi-Centenary Perspectives*, ed. Franz Kuna (London: Elek Books; and New York: Harper and Row, 1976).

understand his predicament.[38] However, K. manages to accomplish
at least one action of interest in spite of his passivity: he passes the
enigma of his guilt onto the reader. In a way, he becomes for us what
Kette is to Messner, or what Franz and Willem are to K.: a disquieting messenger whose message may never quite reach its destination.
As such, he becomes a kind of monster that has at once "completed
its time and yet is unripe," as Benjamin says of Kafka's omnipresent
messengers.[39]

Thus, a second dimension of responsibility comes to the fore in
the depiction of K.'s guilt, with the tragic parallel again providing the
reader with important clues—not just to the meaning of K.'s guilt but
also to the reader's own implication in it. As Vernant puts it:

> By seeing the protagonists on the stage clinging exclusively to
> one meaning and thus, in their blindness, bringing about their
> own destruction or tearing each other to pieces, the spectator is
> brought to realize that in reality there are two or even more pos-
> sible meanings. The tragic message becomes intelligible to him
> to the extent that, abandoning his former certainty and limita-
> tions, he becomes aware of the ambiguity of words, of meanings,
> and of the human condition. Recognizing that it is the nature
> of the universe to be in conflict, and accepting a problematical
> view of the world, the spectator himself, through the spectacle,
> becomes a tragic consciousness.[40]

Similarly, the reader of *The Trial* is brought to an awareness of
numerous ambiguities, not the least of which concern grim and

38. Kafka, *The Trial*, 161, 164 / *Der Proceß*, 306, 311–312.
39. Benjamin, "Franz Kafka," 2:799 / *Gesammelte Schriften*, 2.2:415. There are many messengers in Kafka's writings. See, e.g., "A Message from the Emperor," in *Metamorphosis and
Other Stories*, trans. Michael Hofmann (London: Penguin, 2007); and Franz Kafka, *Drucke
zu Lebzeiten* (Frankfurt am Main: S. Fischer Verlag, 2007).
40. Vernant and Vidal-Naquet, *Myth and Tragedy*, 114 / *Mythe et tragédie*, 1:102–103.

incomprehensible social powers. For his part, K. is brought to the edge of his understanding of what it might mean to be guilty, brought face to face not with bare incomprehension (though he sometimes experiences it as such), but, rather, with a *lack* of comprehension of that which interrupts and is incompatible with his everyday understanding of guilt, to which he remains bound in spite of its insufficiency: "It was not so much finding court offices [adjoining Titorelli's studio] that had shocked K., it was mainly his own ignorance of matters concerning the court."[41] The reader, too, cannot help but struggle with the ambiguities that K.'s ordeal puts on display: we are no more knowledgeable than he is as to what is happening to him. This is not merely a problem of textual interpretation, of course, since the events are plain enough. It is a question of how we should understand the quasi-tragic ambiguities that K. struggles with.

Third, this spectatorial dimension opens onto a more explicitly social dimension, which, once again, can be brought into view through the treatment of ambiguity in Greek tragedy. For the ultimate sense of the interpellation of the spectator is to be found, not in the spectator as such, but in the society of which the spectator is a representative. In this way, we are brought full circle, back to the historical context that in the first instance provided the tragedians with the conceptual and specifically legal ambiguities that gave rise to the great B.C. tragedies. However, this context is just the starting point for the process of social reflection called for by the tragedians. Once conceptual and practical ambiguities have undergone the reworking and mediation proper to tragic art, they turn back upon the *polis* and the human being through the social enigmas that the tragedies represent:

> Although tragedy, more than any other genre of literature . . . appears rooted in social reality, that does not mean that

41. Kafka, *The Trial*, 117 / *Der Proceß*, 222.

it is a reflection of it. It does not reflect that reality but calls it into question. By depicting it as rent and divided against itself, it turns it into a problem. . . . The world of the city is called into question and its fundamental values are challenged in the ensuing debate. When exalting the civic ideal and affirming its victory over all forces from the past, even Aeschylus, the most optimistic of tragic writers, seems not to be making a positive declaration with tranquil conviction, but rather to be expressing a hope, making an appeal that remains full of anxiety even amid the joy of the final apotheosis. The questions are posed but tragic consciousness can find no fully satisfactory answers to them and so they remain open.[42]

Thus we must follow the path all the way around, from the tragedians' reception of semantic tensions that disrupt received wisdom, through their aesthetic reworking and effect upon the spectator, to their ultimate performative goal: to see the human being and society itself as profoundly enigmatic and traversed by tensions and, indeed, contradictions. What is brought into view, then, is an essentially social dialectic between citizen and society, as mediated through the tragic form, leading to reflection on the foundations of community and social existence. All of this rests upon the gradual unfolding of tragic ambiguity and its denial by a consciousness that is too unilateral in its vision of the world.

It would seem, then, that a certain parallel can be drawn between tragic ambiguity and the sorts of ambiguities at work in Kafka. In both cases, they are depicted as woven into the fabric of social relations and institutions, often emerging in surprising and perplexing ways. They also both involve deficient, unilateral interpretations of equivocal concepts, leading to suffering. More importantly, however, these

42. Vernant and Vidal-Naquet, *Myth and Tragedy*, 33 / *Mythe et tragédie*, 1:24–26.

ambiguities are, in both cases, portrayed as irresolvable within the present, established order of things. If the suffering undergone is to be overcome, a radical change of perspective is required. Ambiguity pushes us to break the spell of unilateral thinking—that is, the insistence on one branch of meaning to the exclusion of the other. *Nomos* and *dikē,* among other concepts, must be *reinvented* for their internal tensions to abate. An intervention or a decision that changes the course of history for the individual and the community is called for: new institutions or, more generally, the possibility of a future different than the contradictory present must emerge through and out of the experience of incomplete understanding. Even in cases where, in ancient tragedy, the solution comes *ex machina* or where the aporia seems to persist (as at the end of Sophocles's *Antigone,* where the chorus pleads in favor of attending to present concerns and existing rituals), the meaning of the conflict remains in the form of an implicit task for social reflection, action, and potential transformation—as Hegel knew and emphasized. For him, tragic consciousness stumbles upon such problems and "unlocks" their power through suffering and the disruption of tragic consciousness's seeming knowledge. Suffering and ambiguity are the signs of error, of what we ought to have done or understood, but they are also, for the same reason, an impetus for change, however weak:

> acting in accordance with knowledge deemed obvious, [consciousness] experienced its deceitfulness; and being inwardly devoted to *one* of the attributes of substance [i.e., one side of an ambiguous principle of the community], it violated the other and so conceded to the other attribute its right over it. [Hegel is thinking here of the two notions of law in the *Antigone* or of the two notions of justice in the *Oresteia.*] In following the "knowing god" [i.e., Apollo through the Pythia], [consciousness] seizes upon something that was not obvious, and pays the penalty for

trusting a knowledge whose ambiguity—for such is its nature—
must also have been present *to consciousness* [*für es*] in the form
of a *warning*. The ravings of the priestess, the inhuman shape of
the witches, the voices of trees and birds, dreams, and so on, are
not ways in which truth appears; they are rather the warning
signs of deception, of a lack of self-possession, of the singularity
and contingency of knowledge.[43]

With these aspects of Vernant's and Hegel's views in mind, then,
the ambiguities presented in *The Trial* should not be dismissed as the
absurd symptoms of perennial estrangement. On the contrary, they
are hints and traces of unresolved social tensions and, more specifically, should be taken to be the objective markers of the limits of K.'s
knowledge, of his inability to see beyond his everyday existence and
expectations. It is his estrangement or incompatibility with the world
that is at issue, but in a particular sense: he is the epicenter of ambiguities that reveal a world in tension with itself. It should therefore be
clear that the error in K.'s view does not stem from some idiosyncratic
shortcoming—he is far from alone in his predicament as a defendant.
Rather, the parallel with tragic ambiguity and the institutional dimension of the proceedings suggest that the error stems from antinomies
that beleaguer society itself in its inner constitution, calling attention
to the (for now) absent possibility of their overcoming. (We might
think here of the puzzling presence of "possibly" two groups at K.'s
first hearing.[44]) The nagging ambiguities in *The Trial* are, for all these
reasons, double. They are *signposts* on the path of the unfolding fate
that K. brings upon himself as punishment for the insufficiency of
his—and our—knowledge of social antinomies. At the same time,

43. G. W. F. Hegel, *Hegel's Phenomenology of Spirit*, trans. A. V. Miller (Oxford: Oxford University Press, 1977), 448; and G. W. F. Hegel, *Werke*, 20 vols. (Frankfurt am Main: Suhrkamp Verlag, 1969–1971), 3:539.
44. Kafka, *The Trial*, 32 / *Der Proceß*, 58.

however, as *warnings*, the ambiguities function as exhortations. Each and every ambiguity is an opportunity and a possibility—a goad, as it were, for seeking answers off the beaten path. But since they remain aporetical and unresolved, they take on the character of *forsaken* possibilities. They are put out of play by the priority K. gives to his "usual way of life." He concentrates his energies on present concerns and readily available possibilities, no matter how irrelevant or pointless, rather than considering the problem of why *better* possibilities are not socially available to him.

It is at this juncture, however, that we reach the limit of the parallel with Greek tragedy, for K.'s trial ends not with a judicious or even a temporary resolution of the ambiguities that hold sway in the narrative, nor with the discovery of a specific task for communal reflection, but in a death that is entirely without social explanation or even simple human meaning: "Like a dog!" are K.'s last words.[45] Thus, on the one hand, like Orestes, K. is "hounded"[46] by "vengeful officials"[47] who are "attracted by guilt."[48] Society itself, in its institutions, customs, and persecution of K., in this way calls attention to its own inner tensions and contradictions. On the other hand, however, there is no final understanding in *The Trial*, no balance struck, no transformation—the Erinyes of the court in the attics remain Erinyes, and so are never reconciled with the defective and contradiction-ridden society from which they arise. Persistent ambiguities remain the outward expression of a society riven and scarred by an enduring estrangement of individuals and institutions or, more accurately, of individuals and the *possibility* of just and transparent institutions. Thus, while aporetical ambiguities similar to those of Greek tragedy are in play, they

---

45. Kafka, *The Trial*, 165 / *Der Proceß*, 312.
46. Kafka, *The Trial*, 146 / *Der Proceß*, 278.
47. Kafka, *The Trial*, 86 / *Der Proceß*, 160.
48. Kafka, *The Trial*, 9 / *Der Proceß*, 14.

undergo a distortion in *The Trial*. For one thing, K. is no tragic hero. Leaving aside more obvious reasons, this is partly due to the fact that we have no clear purchase, no more than K. himself, on what is behind his arrest, of precisely what conflicting social orders or duties are at issue.[49] The tragic irony is incomplete—aspects of its spectatorial and social dimensions seem to be lacking or defective—and there appears to be no way to complete it from within the framework of the novel or, indeed, outside of it. In short, there is no perspective available from which the ambiguities of *The Trial* could be dispelled, no Athena to renew history through the founding of new institutions. The problem is clear, but unresolved: Why does estrangement persist? Why are better possibilities not available to us? To the extent that a solution is lacking, we remain caught in a situation of extreme estrangement from future possibilities of reconciliation.[50]

That said, the future that Kafka denies to K. is not null. Its shape can be read off his submission and the negativity that it implies. As Adorno puts it:

> If it is true that everything that happens in [Kafka's] world of constraint and compulsion [*Zwangswelt*] combines the expression of utter necessity with that of the utter contingency of its shabbiness, then it is no less true that he deciphers its heinous law in his mirror writing. Consummate untruth is the contradiction of itself; it need not, therefore, be explicitly contradicted.[51]

In other words, the apparent necessity of the miserable state of the world—its fatality—is belied by the contingency of its structure. It is

49. With Benjamin in mind, Adorno suggests that Kafka's work is more akin to allegory. See Adorno, "Notes on Kafka," in *Prisms*, 246 / *Gesammelte Schriften*, 10.1:255.
50. Compare Benjamin's claim that Kafka "postpones the future" in his writings. See Benjamin, "Franz Kafka," 2:807 / *Gesammelte Schriften*, 2.2:427.
51. Adorno, "Notes on Kafka," in *Prisms*, 257 / *Gesammelte Schriften*, 10.1:269.

K.'s ignorance that indirectly conveys this to the reader: not only does he not take his ignorance very seriously, nor the possibility that society has perhaps not given him the means to acquire sufficient knowledge, but he also neglects the fact that this world and its implacable institutions, in all their shabbiness, are the historical products of human activity and so might yet be refashioned. A presentation, however caricatural or indirect, of the dysfunctional arbitrariness of apparently necessary (or at least unavoidable) social structures is enough to reveal their contingency and therefore the possibility of their being otherwise. As such, Kafka need not and does not

> sketch, in some unmediated manner, the image of an emergent society—for in his as in all great art, an asceticism reigns with regard to the future—but rather depicts it as a montage composed of waste products that the new, in taking shape, expels in the perishing of the present.[52]

In effect, Kafka describes society as a world composed of lumber rooms and debris—a decomposing world that, in its irrationality, ought not to exist. He does this not in order to trap us in this world but, rather, in order to show us that its ambiguities, while aporetical, are an expression of failure. They are, in essence, the symptoms of a deeper tension: that of a society whose principles no longer hold—while still being held onto. (Think of the court usher's emblem, consisting of "two gilt buttons that seemed to have been removed from an old officer's coat."[53])

For want of better knowledge, K. cannot perceive ambiguity as a warning sign; and for want of a better society, he must capitulate. As

---

52. Adorno, "Notes on Kafka," in *Prisms*, 251–252 / *Gesammelte Schriften*, 10.1:262. This is also the lesson of Benjamin's *The Origin of German Tragic Drama*, trans. John Osborne (London: Verso, 1998) / *Gesammelte Schriften*, 1.1.
53. Kafka, *The Trial*, 48 / *Der Proceß*, 89.

an unassuming and in every way typical representative of his society and social standing, he is constitutively unable (i.e., due to the social realities of his upbringing, education, social standing, and so on) to solve the riddles that rain down upon him. Meanwhile, Kafka, who has no answers to offer us, does the best he can with his readers by pointing, like the sexton in the cathedral, "in an indeterminate direction."[54] Yet, however slight this gesture may seem, it is not insignificant. There is something to see, but coming to see it would require overcoming the initial incomprehension and refusal that attends its announcement. This is perhaps the simplest and most direct indicator of K.'s failing, his particular *hamartia:* in spite of the sexton's insistence, he refuses to turn around and look in the direction of the pointing.

This is not the first scene in which we encounter K.'s obstinacy or his refusal to engage with the law in any way that would run counter to his existing perspective and expectations. "You're too intransigent [*unnachgiebig*], that's what I've heard," says Leni at one point.[55] At another key juncture, Huld rebukes K. for his gross and persistent misunderstandings of the proceedings and of the lawyer's role in them.[56] Moreover, at the end of his conversation with the priest in the cathedral, he is said to be "too tired" to understand the consequences of the priest's parable.[57] Indeed, to the priest's remark that "one doesn't have to take everything as the truth, one just has to accept it as necessary," K. says that this would imply "that the whole world is founded on lies." No truer word is spoken in *The Trial,* but he cannot go further than this vague impression because he immediately turns away from the "unusual trains of thought [*ungewohnte*

54. Kafka, *The Trial*, 148 / *Der Proceß*, 282.
55. Kafka, *The Trial*, 76 / *Der Proceß*, 143.
56. Kafka, *The Trial*, 135 / *Der Proceß*, 257.
57. Compare Block's description of the fatigue that plagues defendants. See Kafka, *The Trial*, 125 / *Der Proceß*, 236.

Gedankengänge]" and "unreal things [*unwirkliche Dinge]*" that the conversation stirs up in him.[58] In these passages, we see K. pushed to the limit of his understanding. Ultimately, he fails to draw the correct conclusion from the situation: if actuality appears as necessary without being true, and if the alternative consists of "unreal things"—that is, possibilities—that are too remote from his everyday existence to bring clearly into view, then this can only be because he is *artificially bound* to the merely apparent necessity of the existing order of things. If such is the case, of course, then the necessity of the present state of affairs would be a *sham* necessity and actuality would cry out for possibilities other than those of K.'s "usual way of life." K. grapples with this idea, however briefly and inadequately, when he thinks to himself that there must be some way to "break out of" the trial, to "circumvent it," or "live outside it": "That possibility must exist, K. had thought about it quite often recently."[59] At the same time, his frustration should come as no surprise to him: Titorelli had already suggested that such possibilities are "legends,"[60] which is to say that they hover uncomfortably and equivocally between reality and unreality. It is in such moments of frustrated possibility that he comes to feel the full force of the law, as predicted by the guard Willem in the opening scene (*Sie werden es zu fühlen bekommen*).[61]

It is in such moments that he feels the tug of the chain at his throat, while yet being unable to turn around in order to see what is holding him fast—and no amount of gesturing on the part of the sexton or anyone else is enough to change K.'s mind because, as "a free and secure citizen of the earth . . . he feels that all possibilities

---

58. Kafka, *The Trial*, 159 / *Der Proceß*, 302–303.
59. Kafka, *The Trial*, 153 / *Der Proceß*, 291.
60. Kafka, *The Trial*, 110 / *Der Proceß*, 208.
61. Kafka, *The Trial*, 9 / *Der Proceß*, 15.

are available to him."[62] His error, in short, is that he believes that reality must exhaust possibility, that existing knowledge and resources should suffice—his own knowledge, certainly, but also that sound common knowledge that circulates within society, never deviating from the familiar and the reassuring—whereas it is his very attachment to this belief that is at issue. As Kafka once remarked of the Chukchi people and their attachment to their icy and inhospitable homeland: "Why don't the Chukchi simply leave their awful country; considering their present life and desires they would be better off anywhere else. But they cannot; all things possible do indeed happen—but only what happens is possible (*möglich ist nur das, was geschieht*)."[63] (Not that the Chukchi people should really move elsewhere. Rather, Kafka's point is socially and modally charged: what is of interest is that they *take it to be* impossible.)

In this way, then, K. is estranged from possibilities other than those which belong to the fate that plays itself out through him. For what is fate but an inscrutable restriction of possibilities that would not be so restricted in slightly different circumstances? Kafka calls attention to this restriction of possibility in a number of scenes—for example, in Titorelli's affirmation regarding the three possible outcomes of such trials, of which only two are *really* possible.[64] Similarly, K. makes a bold claim in the cathedral: "There are still certain possibilities I've not made use of."[65] He is no doubt right in this assumption, although not in the way he thinks. Hence the prison chaplain

62. Kafka, *Nachgelassene Schriften und Fragmente II*, Oktavheft G, 63.
63. Kafka, *Diaries*, January 5, 1914, 251 / *Tagebücher*, 621. In a similar vein, Bernard Lahire writes that Kafka is preoccupied by the "restriction on the horizon of possibilities due to its being forged in given cultural circumstances. It is the interiorization of the normality or self-evidence of their situation that explains why, for human beings, they think it necessary to live in the manner in which they live." See Bernard Lahire, "Kafka et le travail de la domination," *Actuel Marx* 49 (2011): 52.
64. Kafka, *The Trial*, 110 / *Der Proceß*, 208.
65. Kafka, *The Trial*, 152 / *Der Proceß*, 289.

is quick to correct him, essentially suggesting that he is looking in all the wrong places for such possibilities of escape: "Can you not see further than the end of your nose?"[66] Likewise, in one of the novel's chapter fragments, K. says to himself that his deputy manager "had to be made aware as often as possible that K. was alive and that, however harmless he might appear at the moment, he could one day, like everything alive, surprise everyone with new abilities (*eines Tages mit neuen Fähigkeiten überraschen konnte*)."[67] And yet this surprising discovery of new abilities or potentialities is precisely what K. proves himself, time and again, to be incapable of. He is not "learned" enough to understand the proceedings against him precisely to the extent that he is too ignorant to believe that they are meaningful independently of the familiarity of his "usual way of life." Consequently, their meaning remains veiled. Frau Grubach makes the point clearly, if inadvertently: at issue is "something learned that I can't understand, but which one doesn't have to understand."[68] This is precisely K.'s predicament: he experiences but does not affirm the need to alter his understanding. As he says at the outset: "I am not familiar with this law."[69] He never sees that he is being called toward that which is profoundly *unfamiliar* and *estranged* from his existing standard of familiarity.

This reflexive but socially mediated denial of unfamiliar yet perhaps liberating possibilities goes some way toward explain the monomaniacal character of K.'s behavior. In order to go further, he would first have to acknowledge that the court in the attics is making demands on him that are incompatible with ordinary beliefs and customs, and that these demands require an answer that is socially

66. Kafka, *The Trial*, 152 / *Der Proceß*, 290.
67. Kafka, *The Trial*, 180 / *Der Proceß*, 341.
68. Kafka, *The Trial*, 19 / *Der Proceß*, 33.
69. Kafka, *The Trial*, 9 / *Der Proceß*, 14.

unavailable to him. Of course, if he is unable to give it, then, once again, this is not due to a personal failing. He is the product and victim of irrational institutions and the ways of life they promote. However, as a locus of this social suffering, he is also *responsible* for interpreting the ambiguous signs that point out this irrationality and thereby the possibility of a more rational form of social organization. "The one who acts must suffer,"[70] but the one who suffers is also called upon to act, to solve the riddle of suffering. To be guilty, *schuldig,* is not merely to be the object of a founded accusation; it is also to be responsible, in the manner of a debt, toward oneself, others and, by extension, toward society itself, if not in its present form then in a future form that would rid it of its most vicious defects.

Are we then trapped in an impasse of universal estrangement? Is there no future other than the "shame" that may "live on" after K.'s death?[71] The outlook may not seem bright, but we should consider that *The Trial* attempts to awaken us to knowledge of the weird predicament in which K. finds himself, thereby pushing us—if not K. himself—toward a reflection on the structure and sense of social institutions in relation to the individuals they shape. What is it about society that postpones its own better future? Why is the real possibility of liberation (or "real acquittal" [*wirkliche Freisprechung*][72]) blocked—that is, not a "real" possibility at all? In bringing us to pose these questions, the spectatorial and social dimensions of Greek tragedy are reconfigured by Kafka. The novel implicitly calls attention to the current lack of a social future worthy of the name to the extent that K.'s half-understanding and complacency—as well as his blind acceptance of ambiguity and estrangement as brute social

---

70. Aeschylus, "Agamemnon," in *The Oresteia*, trans. Robert Fagles (New York: Viking, 1975), 165; and Aeschylus, "Agamemnon," in *Aeschylus II*, trans. Herbert Weir Smyth (London: William Heinemann, 1926), line 1564.

71. Kafka, *The Trial*, 165 / *Der Proceß*, 312.

72. Kafka, *The Trial*, 109–110, see, too, 46, 55 / *Der Proceß*, 205–208, 85, 102.

facts—impede reflection on the possibility of things being otherwise. As Huld puts it: "it is often better to be in chains than free"[73]—"better," that is, at least in the sense that chains show that the freedom on offer is an illusion.

The key to defusing the threat of so-called universal estrangement thereby lies in the idea that *The Trial* shows us another side of the problem, provided we understand it not merely as a social but also as a modal and temporal phenomenon. In other words, we have to approach it in terms of the future possibility of social development beyond existing actuality's façade of necessity, as accentuated by the aporetical ambiguities that signal social antinomies and dysfunction. The estrangement in question is thus twofold. It resides in the tension between: (i) the restriction of possibilities—that is, the fate to which K. submits in his failed attempts to reestablish his normal life; and (ii) the pressing need for new possibilities, as adumbrated by the many ambiguities whose irrationality calls for solutions, even if that remains impossible at the present time. What *The Trial* shows us, in this regard, is that this impossibility is institutionally mediated and perpetuated by everyday existence. It is not absolute—though it may appear as absolute to the subject unwilling to question the alleged axioms of existing actuality and to reflect upon the reciprocal dependence of individuals and institutions.

As such, K.'s predicament and his fettered subjectivity are perhaps best understood along the lines of the Messner-Kette fragment. Like Messner, K. is sent a message that he believes he does not have to understand on its own terms. Yet he cannot simply carry on as before once the message arrives. For both Messner and K., denial is fused with disruption, forming an ambiguous unit of distress. This situation has as its first consequence the discovery that the status quo is incompatible with the task at hand. For Messner, this emerges when he

73. Kafka, *The Trial*, 136 / *Der Proceß*, 258.

demands that Kette deliver the message immediately on the landing outside his flat, to which Kette replies: "No, . . . it is impossible for me to say it here."[74] Why is "here" not good enough? *The Trial* may provide us with the answer: the message that disturbs K.'s complacency has more to do with the "here" of his socially conditioned outlook and expectations than with the abstract impossibility of overcoming estrangement. In this way, Kafka's interest lies in exploring a form of subjectivity unable, for social reasons, to see a way forward. Above all, Kafka understands that it is a deep and disquieting problem that we believe all possibilities to be available to us when, in fact, this belief stems from not perceiving the chains that bind us. As he once wrote in a letter to Felice Bauer, the future is closed off to those who remain chained to the present—and especially to its deficiencies:

> I cannot step into the future; I can crash into the future, grind into the future, stumble into the future, this I can do; but best of all I can lie still. Plans and prospects, however—honestly, I have none; when things go well, I am entirely absorbed by the present; when things go badly, I curse even the present, let alone the future![75]

BIBLIOGRAPHY

Adorno, Theodor W. *Aesthetic Theory*. Translated by Robert Hullot-Kentor. Minneapolis: University of Minnesota Press, 1997.

Adorno, Theodor W. "Cultural Criticism and Society." In *Prisms*. Translated by Samuel Weber and Shierry Weber. Cambridge, MA: MIT Press, 1981.

74. Kafka, *Diaries*, 240 / *Tagebücher*, 599.

75. Franz Kafka, *Letters to Felice*, ed. Erich Heller and Jürgen Born, trans. James Stern and Elisabeth Duckworth (New York: Schocken, 1973), February 28–March 1, 1913, 209 / *Briefe 1913–März 1914*, 115.

Adorno, Theodor W. *Einleitung in die Soziologie*. Edited by Christoph Gödde. Frankfurt am Main: Suhrkamp Verlag, 2003.

Adorno, Theodor W. "Extorted Reconciliation: On Georg Lukács' *Realism in our Time*." In *Notes to Literature*. Translated by Shierry Weber Nicholsen. New York: Columbia University Press, 1991–1992.

Adorno, Theodor W. *Gesammelte Schriften*. Edited by Rolf Tiedemann, Gretel Adorno, Susan Buck-Morss, and Klaus Schultz. 20 vols. Frankfurt am Main: Suhrkamp Verlag, 1970–1997.

Adorno, Theodor W. *Introduction to Sociology*. Translated by Edmund Jephcott. Stanford, CA: Stanford University Press, 2000.

Adorno, Theodor W. *Minima Moralia*. Translated by Edmund Jephcott. London: Verso, 1978.

Adorno, Theodor W. *Negative Dialectics*. Translated by E. B. Ashton. London: Routledge, 1973.

Adorno, Theodor W. "Notes on Kafka." In *Prisms*. Translated by Samuel Weber and Shierry Weber. Cambridge, MA: MIT Press, 1981.

Aeschylus. "Agamemnon." In *Aeschylus II*. Translated by Herbert Weir Smyth. London: William Heinemann, 1926.

Aeschylus. "Agamemnon." In *The Oresteia*. Translated by Robert Fagles. New York: Viking, 1975.

Allemann, Beda. "Kafka und die Mythologie." *Zeitschrift für Ästhetik und allgemeine Kunstwissenschaft* 20 (1975): 129–144.

Benjamin, Walter. *Briefe*. Frankfurt am Main: Suhrkamp Verlag, 1978.

Benjamin, Walter. "Franz Kafka: On the Tenth Anniversary of His Death." In *Selected Writings*, edited by Michael W. Jennings and Howard Eiland. Cambridge, MA: Harvard University Press, 1999–2003.

Benjamin, Walter. *Gesammelte Schriften*. Frankfurt am Main: Suhrkamp Verlag, 1972–1989.

Benjamin, Walter. "Letter to Gershom Scholem on Franz Kafka." In *Selected Writings*, edited by Michael W. Jennings and Howard Eiland. Cambridge, MA: Harvard University Press, 1999–2003.

Benjamin, Walter. *The Origin of German Tragic Drama*. Translated by John Osborne. London: Verso, 1998.

Camus, Albert. "L'espoir et l'absurde dans l'œuvre de Franz Kafka." In *Le mythe de Sisyphe*. Paris: Gallimard, 1942.

Hegel, G. W. F. *Hegel's Phenomenology of Spirit*. Translated by A. V. Miller. Oxford: Oxford University Press, 1977.

Hegel, G. W. F. *Werke*. 20 vols. Frankfurt am Main: Suhrkamp Verlag, 1969–1971.

Kafka, Franz. *Briefe 1913–März 1914*. Edited by Hans-Gerd Koch. Frankfurt am Main: S. Fischer Verlag, 1999.

Kafka, Franz. "The Collected Aphorisms." In *The Great Wall of China and Other Short Works*. Translated by Malcolm Pasley, edited by Malcolm Pasley. London: Penguin, 1973.

Kafka, Franz. *Der Proceß*. Frankfurt am Main: S. Fischer Verlag, 1990.

Kafka, Franz. *Diaries, 1910–1923*. Translated by Joseph Kresh, Martin Greenberg, and Hannah Arendt. Edited by Max Brod. New York: Schocken, 1964.

Kafka, Franz. *Drucke zu Lebzeiten*. Frankfurt am Main: S. Fischer Verlag, 2007.

Kafka, Franz. *Letters to Felice*. Translated by James Stern and Elisabeth Duckworth. Edited by Erich Heller and Jürgen Born. New York: Schocken, 1973.

Kafka, Franz. "A Message from the Emperor." In *Metamorphosis and Other Stories*. Translated by Michael Hofmann. London: Penguin, 2007.

Kafka, Franz. *Nachgelassene Schriften und Fragmente II*. Edited by Jost Schillemeit. Frankfurt am Main: S. Fischer Verlag, 1992.

Kafka, Franz. *Tagebücher*. Edited by Hans-Gerd Koch, Michael Müller and Malcolm Pasley. Frankfurt am Main: S. Fischer Verlag, 1990.

Kafka, Franz. *The Trial*. Translated by Mike Mitchell. Oxford: Oxford University Press, 2009.

Lahire, Bernard. "Kafka et le travail de la domination." *Actuel Marx* 49 (2011): 46–59.

Löwy, Michael. "'Fascinating Delusive Light': Georg Lukács and Franz Kafka." In *Georg Lukács: The Fundamental Dissonance of Existence—Aesthetics, Politics, Literature*, edited by Timothy Bewes and Timothy Hall. London: Continuum, 2011.

Lukács, Georg. *The Meaning of Contemporary Realism*. Translated by John Mander and Necke Mander. London: Merlin Press, 1962.

Lukács, Georg. *Werke*. Neuwied/Berlin: Luchterhand, 1962–1986.

Lukács, Georg. *Wider den mißverstandenen Realismus*. Hamburg: Claassen, 1958.

Parry, Idris. "Kafka's Modern Mythology." *Bulletin of the John Rylands Library* 53, no. 1 (1970): 210–226.

Sokel, Walter H. "The Programme of K.'s Court: Oedipal and Existential Meanings of *The Trial*." In *On Kafka: Semi-Centenary Perspectives*, edited by Franz Kuna. London: Elek Books; and New York: Harper and Row, 1976.

Stach, Reiner. *Kafka: The Decisive Years*. Translated by Shelley Frisch. Princeton, NJ: Princeton University Press, 2005.

Vernant, Jean-Pierre, and Pierre Vidal-Naquet. *Myth and Tragedy in Ancient Greece*. Translated by Janet Lloyd. New York: Zone Books, 1990.

Vernant, Jean-Pierre, and Pierre Vidal-Naquet. *Mythe et tragédie en Grèce ancienne*. 2 vols. Paris: La Découverte, 1972, 2001.

Chapter 6

The Trouble with Time

Kafka's Der Proceß

ANNE FUCHS

KAFKA'S DYSCHRONIA

Kafka started writing *Der Proceß* (*The Trial*) on August 11, 1914, approximately seven weeks after his meeting with Felice Bauer and Grete Bloch in the Askanischer Hof in Berlin had ended his engagement to Felice on July 12. The immediate period after a bruising encounter that Kafka called "Gerichtshof im Hotel" (court sitting in the hotel) was at first productive.[1] Kafka notes on August 15, "mein regelmäßiges, leeres, irrsinniges junggesellenmäßiges Leben hat eine Rechtfertigung. Ich kann wieder ein Zwiegespräch mit mir führen und starre nicht so in vollständige Leere. Nur auf diesem Wege gibt es für mich Besserung" (my monotonous, empty, mad bachelor life has some justification. I can once more carry a conversation with myself, and don't stare so into complete emptiness. Only in this way is there

---

1. Franz Kafka, *Tagebücher. Bd. 3: 1914–1923 in der Fassung der Handschrift*, ed. Hans-Georg Koch, Michael Müller, and Malcolm Pasley (Frankfurt am Main: Fischer, 2008), 24. Franz Kafka, *Diaries 1910–1923*, ed. Max Brod (New York: Schocken, 1976), 293. Occasionally I deviate from this translation in favor of a more literal translation.

any possibility of improvement for me).[2] However, the writing process soon began to falter: on October 5, Kafka took a week's holiday to advance the novel but noted just two days later that he had made little progress: "ich habe wenig und schwächlich geschrieben" (I have written little and feebly).[3] A further extension of his vacation by one week seems to have reenergized the writing process: Kafka could now look back over fourteen days of "gute Arbeit zum Teil" (partially good work),[4] before observing ten days later that his work had come to an almost complete standstill: "Fast vollständiges Stocken der Arbeit. Das was geschrieben wird scheint nichts selbständiges, sondern der Widerschein guter früherer Arbeit" (My work almost completely at a standstill. What I write seems to lack independence, seems only the pale reflection of earlier work).[5] On the first of November, Kafka recorded some progress before reflecting once more on his failure to advance his work:

> Und jetzt vollständiges Versagen bei der Arbeit. Und es ist nicht einmal Versagen, ich sehe die Aufgabe und den Weg zu ihr, ich müßte nur irgendwelche dünne Hindernisse durchstoßen und kann es nicht. (And now a complete failure at my work. And it isn't failure even, I see the task and the way to it, I should only have to overcome some paltry obstacles and cannot do it.)[6]

Kafka's chronotope of a pathway merely obstructed by paltry obstacles is striking:[7] it evokes the determined, linear process of writing

2. Franz Kafka, *Tagebücher. Bd. 2: 1912–1914 in der Fassung der Handschrift*, ed. Hans-Georg Koch, Michael Müller, and Malcolm Pasley (Frankfurt am Main: Fischer, 2008), 169. Franz Kafka, *Diaries 1910–1923*, 303.

3. Kafka, *Tagebücher. Bd. 3*, 39 / *Diaries*, 314.

4. Kafka, *Tagebücher. Bd. 3*, 39 (my translation).

5. Kafka, *Tagebücher. Bd. 3*, 42 / *Diaries*, 316.

6. Kafka, *Tagebücher. Bd. 3*, 42 (my translation).

7. In his famous 1930 essay, the Russian formalist Mikhail Bakhtin defined the chronotope as follows: "In the literary artistic chronotope, spatial and temporal indicators are fused

which Kafka discovered in the night of September 22 to 23, 1912, when he wrote *Das Urteil* (*The Judgement*) from beginning to end in one uninterrupted sitting. "Nur so kann geschrieben werden," Kafka commented, "nur in einem solchen Zusammenhang, mit solcher vollständigen Öffnung des Leibes und der Seele" (Only in this way can writing be done, only with such coherence, with such a complete opening out of the body and the soul).[8] Because the epic length of the novel made such sustained and concentrated absorption impossible, Kafka attempted to ensure the completion of *Der Proceß* by writing the opening and concluding chapters first, thus preventing his story from going astray as had happened with his first novel *Der Verschollene*. Although the narrative frame of beginning and end of *Der Proceß* was intended to impede the dispersal of the novel, Kafka did not develop the plot in linear fashion. As Malcolm Pasley has documented, he worked on diverse chapters nonchronologically, adopting precisely the simultaneous system of partial construction described in his later story *Beim Bau der chinesischen Mauer* (*The Great Wall of China*).[9] On December 26, 1914, he then lamented his inability to complete yet another story—the "Dorfschullehrer" ("Village Teacher")—even

into one carefully thought-out, concrete whole. Time, as it were, thickens, takes on flesh, becomes artistically visible; likewise, space becomes charged and responsive to the movements of time, plot and history. The intersection of axes and fusion of indicators characterizes the artistic chronotope." See Mikhail Bakhtin, "Forms of Time and of the Chronotope in the Novel: Notes toward a Historical Poetics," in *The Dialogic Imagination: Four Essays*, ed. Michael Holquist (Austin: University of Texas Press, 1981), 84.

8. Kafka, *Tagebücher. Bd. 2*, 101 / *Diaries*, 213.

9. Malcolm Pasley, "Wie der Roman entstand," in *Nach erneuter Lektüre: Franz Kafkas Der Proceß*, ed. Hans Dieter Zimmermann (Würzburg: Königshausen & Neumann 1992), 1. On the genesis of the novel, also see Manfred Engel, *Der Process*, in *Kafka-Handbuch: Leben— Werk—Wirkung*, ed. Manfred Engel and Bernd Auerochs (Stuttgart: J. B. Metzler, 2010), 192–193. On Kafka's perennial problems with narrative openings and progressions, see Beatrice Sandberg, "Starting in the Middle? Complications of Narrative Beginnings and Progression in Kafka," in *Franz Kafka: Narration, Rhetoric & Reading*, ed. Jakob Lothe, Beatrice Sandberg, and Ronald Speirs (Columbus: Ohio State University Press, 2011), 123–145.

though he had four free days that he spent in the company of his friend Max Brod and his wife in Kuttenberg. Kafka's hope that he could make good use of his holidays was short-lived because he did not manage to convert the four free days into three free nights. The diarist therefore admonishes himself: "Neue Tageseinteilung von jetzt ab! Noch besser die Zeit ausnützen!" (New schedule! Use the time even better!).[10] But the pursuit of a temporal economy that aimed to convert mundane daytime into creative night time remained an unrealized dream. Instead of "chasing" his stories through the night,[11] Kafka deplores the "jämmerliches Vorwärtskriechen der Arbeit, vielleicht an ihrer wichtigsten Stelle dort wo eine gute Nacht notwendig wäre" (wretched crawling forward of the writing, maybe at the most important point where a good night would be needed).[12] On January 20, 1915, he concedes the end of writing, asking "Wann wird es mich wieder aufnehmen?" (When will it receive me again?).[13] According to this entry, then, the process of writing is not something that can be driven forward by sheer willpower and time planning as suggested in the earlier diary entry. For Kafka writing is a mode of open-ended receptiveness of mind and body that is incompatible with both dogged determination and with a life regulated by mechanical clock time. Kafka's urgent question when and if writing would receive him again also resonates with the nonchronological and unpredictable workings of the court in *Der Proceß*, where the accused is received and discharged in an incalculable fashion.

And so it is that Kafka's diaries dramatize the regulation of his life by two opposing temporal orders: while his daytime was ruled by common clock time, work, and family commitments, Kafka

---

10. Kafka, *Tagebücher. Bd. 3*, 67 / *Diaries*, 323.
11. Kafka, *Tagebücher. Bd. 3*, 68. I prefer the more active verb "chase" to Martin Greenberg's "pursue," *Diaries*, 324.
12. Kafka, *Tagebücher. Bd. 3*, 64 (my translation).
13. Kafka, *Tagebücher. Bd. 3*, 73 (my translation).

envisaged night time as a time of writerly creativity that, in this process, also engenders subjective time. Kafka's diaries document his determination to free up more creative time by means of a carefully planned schedule that designated the afternoons for sleeping and night time for writing. He often describes how he was lying on his daybed in idle fashion to prepare for his night's work. As Hans-Gerd Koch has shown, Kafka's daybed is a place of transition where he could surrender himself to his phantasies and daydreams at a remove from the world of daily drudgery.[14] However, his plan to work late into the night often fell apart because he had not factored in a third temporal order, namely that of his biological clock. Kafka found that if he worked later than one o'clock at night, he could not sleep at all and felt shattered the next day. "Ich bin also nachmittag zu lange gelegen," observes Kafka, "habe in der Nacht aber selten über 1 Uhr gearbeitet, immer aber frühestens um 11 Uhr angefangen. Das war falsch. Ich muß um 8 oder 9 anfangen, die Nacht ist gewiss die beste Zeit (Urlaub!) aber sie ist mir unzugänglich" (I was lying down for too long in the afternoon but rarely worked beyond 1 o'clock at night while starting not earlier than 11. This was wrong. I have to start at 8 or 9, the night is surely the best time [holidays!] but it is not within my reach).[15] Clock time invaded Kafka's precious night time, stifling precisely the conditions for the type of creative receptiveness that he had discovered when writing *Das Urteil*.

Kafka's battle with time as a scarce resource thus produced a state of permanent dyschronia that also became a source of conflict with Felice. In his famous letter to Felice dated November 1, 1912, he had detailed his daily schedule to prepare her for a life that left little room for anything but his current commitments and his writerly

14. Hans-Gerd Koch, "Kafkas Kanapee," in *Nach erneuter Lektüre: Franz Kafkas Der Proceß*, ed. Hans Dieter Zimmermann (Würzburg: Königshausen & Neumann, 1992), 86.
15. Kafka, *Tagebücher. Bd. 3*, 69–70.

ANNE FUCHS

existence.[16] When they met again after splitting up, they argued once more over their incompatible interpretations of what constitutes the good life. Kafka's diary chronicles how he insisted on dedicating his entire life to his work, while—in his view—Felice merely wanted to settle for "das Mittelmaß" (mediocrity), as expressed in her expectation of a conventional family life in a comfortable flat with heated rooms and a normal social timetable. According to Kafka, she demonstratively underlined her demand for a bourgeois time regime by resetting his watch, which—as Kafka notes—he had deliberately set to run fast by one and a half hours to cheat clock time.[17] But Kafka's various attempts to beat the clock in order to make space for more creative time only aggravated his perpetual dyschronia as manifest in a range of somatic symptoms, including sleeplessness, recurring headaches, and "Zerstreutheit," a state of distractedness that—as we will see—also characterizes Kafka's protagonist Josef K.

Kafka's interminable fear of wasting time thus reflects the modern rationalization and commodification of time that, by enforcing a collective script of temporal efficiency, fueled and accelerated the rise of capitalism.[18] The introduction of the mechanical clock in the thirteenth century led to a new organization of human time. In the early modern period the quantification of the day into twenty-four hours then prepared the ground for a competition between commercial time and liturgical time.[19] The clock spread quickly from the

16. Franz Kafka, *Briefe an Felice und andere Korrespondenz aus der Verlobungszeit*, ed. Erich Heller and Jürgen Born (Frankfurt am Main: Fischer, 1983), 67.
17. Kafka, *Tagebücher. Bd. 3*, 74 / *Diaries*, 328.
18. On the nexus between speed and capitalism, see Enda Duffy, *The Speed Handbook: Velocity, Pleasure, Modernism* (Durham, NC, and London: Duke University Press 2009), 35. Marshall Berman, *All that Is Solid Melts into the Air: The Experience of Modernity* (London and New York: Verso, 2010); Stephen Kern, *The Culture of Time and Space 1880–1918* (with a new preface) (Cambridge, MA: Harvard University Press, 2003), 109–131.
19. See Leofranc Holford-Strevens, *The History of Time: A Very Short Introduction* (Oxford: Oxford University Press, 2005).

church tower to the town hall, and from there into the living rooms of wealthy tradesmen and merchants before it made its way into the watch pockets of the bourgeoisie. While in the sixteenth century the clock could indicate minutes, by the seventeenth century its hand showed seconds. It prompted "a disciplining and rationalizing of the human world of work and its latitude for action."[20] Modern time consciousness thus emerges as a "practically determinate, reflective, and agent-related stance towards time" that provides social actors with "temporal orientation, structure and meaning."[21] Paradoxically, time efficiency is indicative of the sovereign and authoritative subject: the more able one is to handle time efficiently, the more authority and status the subject gains.

A further facet of the modern time regime is the division of life into a public and a private sphere, the latter where the modern subject could cultivate a degree of temporal sovereignty. Helga Nowotny has shown how the modern era gave rise to a specific temporal order that polarized the public time of work and the self's private time of leisure, so-called *Eigenzeit*.[22] *Eigenzeit* is, however, not simply "selfish" time: as the subject's own time, it is the time of creativity, reflection, and care for the other—in other words, a nonutilitarian time where subjectivity, intimacy, and self-reflexivity can unfold. It was precisely this division of human temporality into two opposing time regimes that helped to legitimate yet at the same time to curb modern subjectivity, because the self's *Eigenzeit* is merely a defined segment of "the objective spatio-temporal reality."[23] But such authorization of limited

20. Reinhart Koselleck, "Time and History," in *The Practice of Conceptual History: Timing History, Spacing Concepts*, trans. Todd Samuel Presner, foreword by Hayden White. (Stanford, CA: Stanford University Press, 2002), 104.
21. Espen Hammer, *Philosophy and Temporality from Kant to Critical Theory* (Cambridge: Cambridge University Press, 2011), 19.
22. Helga Nowotny, *Time: The Modern and Postmodern Experience*, trans. Neville Plaice (Cambridge: Polity Press, 1994), 13.
23. Nowotny, *Time*, 28.

Eigenzeit also entailed the option of viewing it as "a form of resistance to those impersonally exercised constraints of time" that facilitated capitalism. *Eigenzeit* thus emerges as a fundamentally ambivalent category: on the one hand, it is an integral part of the capitalist temporal economy that subjugates all aspects of human temporality under the rule of the mechanical clock. *Eigenzeit* is only permissible to the extent that it does not threaten the modern valorization of temporal efficiency in the pursuit of profit. This was precisely Kafka's dilemma: he could only create more *Eigenzeit* by carefully calculating his daily schedule down to the minute. On the other hand, the very notion of the subject's own time entails the possibility of temporal resistance to modernity's regimented time regime. Arguably, the potential of *Eigenzeit* to disrupt, resist, and query the dominance of rationalized public time was then delegated to a different arena: as technological innovation, accelerated social change, and the increased tempo of everyday life became key strategies in the service of progress, a modern aesthetic discourse turned into a domain that took care of the subject's desire for *Eigenzeit*.

THE DISRUPTION OF SCHEDULES IN *DER PROCESS*

Prior to *Der Proceß*, Kafka explicitly thematized the detrimental effects of modern time consciousness in *Der Verschollene* (*The Man Who Disappeared*, better known as *Amerika*; 1912, published in 1927) and in *Die Verwandlung* (*The Metamorphosis*, 1912).[24] The

---

24. Kafka engages with the modern revolution of time and a radically new experience of temporality throughout his oeuvre. For an analysis of time in Kafka's early prose see Elizabeth Boa, "Observations on Time and Motion: Kafka's *Betrachtung* and the Visual Arts around 1912," in *Time in German Literature and Culture, 1900–2015*, ed. Anne Fuchs and J. J.

America of Kafka's first novel is the place of modernity par excellence where the temporal slackness that still marks Europe has been harnessed by Taylorist time efficiencies.[25] The protagonist Karl Roßmann is a young European immigrant who, upon his arrival in New York, meets an unknown uncle, the living embodiment of the rags-to-riches myth, who takes him under his wing. Uncle Jakob is driven by modern chrono-mania: he has not only introduced the Taylorist time practices in his business but also applies them to his nephew, who becomes the victim of his disciplinary time regime.[26] Accordingly, he withdraws his guardianship when the young Karl offends the uncle's rigid timetable by accepting an invitation to spend a leisurely weekend in the countryside. In *Die Verwandlung*, Gregor Samsa wakes up from troubled dreams to find himself transformed into a giant beetle who, instead of responding to his amazing new bodily existence, bemoans his rushed life as a traveling salesman, the job that forces

Long, (Basingstoke, Houndmills: Palgrave Macmillan, 2016), 93–112; for a comprehensive analysis of time and historical experience in Kafka's oeuvre, see Beda Allemann, *Zeit und Geschichte im Werk Franz Kafkas*, ed. Diethelm Kaiser and Nikolaus Lohse (Göttingen: Wallstein, 1998).

25. For more details on Taylorism and "Psychotechnik," a branch of applied psychology encompassing methods of testing and training which in the early twentieth century were widely used across society, see Carolin Duttlinger, "Syncope, Pause, Caesura: Robert Musil and the Psychotechnics of Acceleration," in *Time in German Literature and Culture, 1900–2015*, ed. Anne Fuchs and J. J. Long (Basingstoke, Houndmills: Palgrave Macmillan, 2016), 154–169.

26. Franz Kafka, *Der Verschollene. Roman in der Fassung der Handschrift* (Frankfurt am Main: Fischer, 1994). All quotations refer to this edition. On the representation of America in this novel, see Mark Harman, "Wie Kafka sich Amerika vorstellte," *Sinn und Form* 60 (2008): 794–804; Dieter Heimböckel, ' "Amerika im Kopf": Franz Kafkas Roman *Der Verschollene* und der Amerika-Diskurs seiner Zeit," *Deutsche Vierteljahrsschrift für Literaturwissenschaft und Geistesgeschichte* 77 (2003): 130–147; on patriarchal power, see Elizabeth Boa, "Karl Rossmann, or the Boy Who Wouldn't Grow Up: The Flight from Manhood in Franz Kafka's *Der Verschollene*," in *From Goethe to Gide: Feminism, Aesthetics and the French and German Literary Canon 1770–1936*, ed. Mary Orr and Lesley Sharpe (Exeter: University of Exeter Press 2005), 168–183; Anne Fuchs, "A Psychoanalytic Reading of *The Man Who Disappeared*," in *The Cambridge Companion to Kafka*, ed. Julian Preece (Cambridge: Cambridge University Press, 2002), 25–41.

him to get up early, to make train connections, to settle for irregular meals and bad food, and to put up with the continual dealings with strangers. Alarmed at having missed the five o'clock train, Gregor is anxiously worrying about the repercussions of running late when his parents and sister begin to knock on the three doors of his room. Such prompt social enforcement of the rule of the clock is heightened by the layout of the apartment, which turns Gregor's room from a private refuge into a prison cell. With this famous opening, Kafka emphasizes the conflict between social time and the self's unfulfilled desire for *Eigenzeit*. Even though Gregor has been liberated from his human body, he cannot embrace his new existence. Instead of adapting to the creaturely needs of a beetle, he anxiously attempts to uphold his role as the disciplined and obedient son in the service of social time. Rare moments of joy, as exemplified in his crawling freely across the ceiling, are bracketed off as escapades that have little to do with his identity as a functioning cog in the machine.

In *Der Proceß*, Kafka considerably complicates his engagement with modernity's time regime. Here, the protagonist's trouble with time no longer concerns merely its crippling effects on the self but, also, the ethical ramifications of a time consciousness that is oblivious to any meaningful notion of care for the other. Josef K. is the proverbial modern Western man whose routinized time schedule underlines the functionalization of all human relations. His weekly schedule revolves around work in the bank until nine o'clock, followed by a short walk that takes him to a public house where he spends the evening in the company of older and professionally important men until eleven o'clock at night. This habitualized schedule is complemented by a weekly visit to Elsa, a waitress who also works as a prostitute, and on weekends he accepts the odd invitation by his boss.[27] The striking

27. Franz Kafka, *Der Proceß: Roman in der Fassung der Handschrift* (Frankfurt am Main: Fischer, 1995), 26. Franz Kafka, *The Trial*, trans. Breon Mitchell (New York: Schocken, 1998).

THE TROUBLE WITH TIME

absence of proper friends, family, and intimate relations in K.'s life accentuates the lack of nonutilitarian time in his life; even his leisure time is dominated by calculated considerations and exploitative relations. In the pursuit of his case, Josef K. is then confronted with a dyschronic and ultimately metaphysical schedule that paradoxically makes use of clock time to only invalidate its rule. And so it is that even though Kafka equipped the narrative with a clear timeline—it begins on Josef K.'s thirtieth birthday and ends one year later on the eve of his thirty-first birthday—the novel enacts temporal dyschronia to stage the crisis of modern time consciousness.

As in *Die Verwandlung*, the narrative opens with an incident that overturns the routinized time structures of the protagonist's everyday life: on the morning of his thirtieth birthday, Josef K. wakes up only to be arrested in his bedroom. As Elizabeth Boa comments,[28]

> [t]he opening of the trial conveys a public intrusion into the private sphere of men, who seem to be state officials but turn out to be also associated with his place of work, penetrate a citizen's bedroom and arrest him. These public, yet secret, yet strangely familiar emissaries immediately bring a frightening vulnerability into the so-called private sphere where men sought refuge from the strains of public life.[29]

Even though the threat comes from men, it is K.'s relations with women that ultimately signal the erosion of his accustomed rights and status. Josef K. immediately attempts to rectify this disruption by asking authoritatively for his breakfast, which is normally served before

28. On the riskiness of waking up in Kafka's world, see Gerhard Neumann, "Ritualität und Theatralität—der Anfang des Proceß-Romans," in *Verfehlte Anfänge und offenes Ende: Franz Kafkas poetische Anthropologie* (Munich: Carl Friedrich von Siemens Stiftung, 2009), 51–60.
29. Elizabeth Boa, *Kafka: Gender, Class, and Race in the Letters and Fictions* (Oxford: Oxford University Press, 1996), 188.

eight o'clock by the servant girl Anna. But on his thirtieth birthday his request is merely met by a sniggering response that appears to emanate from the room next door. K.'s authority as a male bourgeois subject is thus challenged by the invasion of his privacy, the discontinuation of his daily routine, and the erosion of his authority as a man.[30] When K. wants to demand an explanation from his landlady Frau Grubach, he is told that he is arrested and that he must return to his room and wait: "Das Verfahren ist nun einmal eingeleitet und Sie werden alles zur richtigen Zeit erfahren" (Proceedings are underway and you'll learn everything in due course), explains one of the wardens.[31] The trial, so it seems, is a process that will unfold according to a radically alternative notion of time that has nothing to do with the type of chronological imagination that defines bourgeois male identity. K.'s fast advancement in the bank to the position of Prokurist shows that he has internalized a biographical script of self-determination alongside the capitalist notion that time is money. He is therefore unable to accept that the "right time" is beyond his influence. In his exchange with the wardens, K. therefore tries to seize back his authority as a male subject by producing various identification papers, ranging ludicrously from his bicycle permit to his birth certificate. The warden Willem tells him that he is behaving worse than a child because he wrongly believes that he can bring his trial to a quick end by talking about identification papers and arrest warrants.[32] In the course of the novel, K. then aims to reclaim his damaged sense of autonomy either by attempting to accelerate proceedings or, alternatively, by letting others wait.

In chapter 1, K. continues to query the reason for and legitimacy of his arrest: he attempts to establish which office is conducting the

30. "Domestic arrangements," comments Boa, "are intrinsically trivial; part of the unchanging, natural order of things, they are beneath notice. But by the same token, they belong to the very basis of patriarchy." Boa, *Kafka: Gender, Class, and Race*, 189.
31. Kafka, *Der Proceß*, 11 / *The Trial*, 5.
32. Kafka, *Der Proceß*, 14 / *The Trial*, 8.

trial and whether the arresting officers are proper state employees. His questions assert the institutional makeup of the modern state, which requires clearly defined governance structures, a well-functioning bureaucracy, a civil service, and the rule of law. Even though the supervisor tells him all these considerations are entirely peripheral to his case, the chapter seemingly ends with the reinstatement of the normal temporal order: K. is informed that he can and should now resume his accustomed duties and lifestyle. Three junior bank employees— Rabensteiner, Kullich, and Kaminer—have been rallied round to accompany K. to the bank. Too preoccupied by his arrest, K. had not noticed their earlier presence at the window in Fräulein Bürstner's room where he was interviewed by the supervisor. Departing with his watch in his hand, K. decides to take a taxi to make up for the loss of time incurred by his arrest. As Kaminer summons a taxi, Kullich points to the doorway of the house on the other side of the street where a man with a blond goatee beard appears who had been gawking at the proceedings together with an old couple from the window across the road. Setting off in the taxi, K. realizes that he was too distracted to notice the supervisor's and the wardens' departure: "der Aufseher hatte ihm die drei Beamten verdeckt und nun wieder die Beamten den Aufseher. Viel Geistesgegenwart bewieß das nicht und K. nahm sich vor, in dieser Hinsicht genauer zu beobachten" (the supervisor had diverted his attention from the three clerks and now the clerks had done the same for the inspector. That didn't show much presence of mind, and K resolved to pay greater attention to such things).[33]

I have paraphrased the ending of the first chapter in some detail to demonstrate how Kafka stages the crisis of K.s worldview as a crisis of timing. The trial unfolds as a battle between opposing time regimes: with its rational division into a public time and a harnessed private time, the linearity of modern time is cut through by

33. Kafka, *Der Proceß*, 25 / *The Trial*, 19.

a nonchronological and ultimately metaphysical time that invalidates the type of functionalized human agency K. represents. While the dyschronic nature of the world of the court is a constant theme, it is given its fullest expression in two paradigmatic episodes. One day, K. opens the door of a junk room at his workplace, the bank, and finds the wardens Franz and Willem being flogged because he had made a complaint about them. When K. passes the junk room the next day, he opens the door again and, to his horror, finds the same scenario as on the previous evening: the whipper is still there with his cane and the two wardens, still undressed, who beg him for help as on the previous day.[34]

The second dyschronic episode is the legend of the Doorkeeper, which the prison Chaplain relates to illustrate how deluded K. has been about the court.[35] This famous parable is shot through with temporal adverbs that evoke expectations steeped in linear time. By telling the man from the country that he cannot let him into the law right now, the Doorkeeper gestures to the future as a time when the law might be reached. Accordingly, the man from the country inquires whether he may gain access later, to which the Doorkeeper responds that it is possible, but not now. The illocutionary and temporal logic of "now"— "not now"—"later" misleads the man from the country to waste his life waiting for permission to enter the law. While these adverbs gesture to the modern concept of linear time, in reality they set in motion a

34. On the temporal structure of the novel and the whipper scene in particular, see Beda Allemann, "Noch einmal Kafkas *Process*," in *Zeit und Geschichte im Werk Kafkas* (Göttingen: Wallstein, 1998), 104–105.
35. On this much-interpreted parable, see Hartmut Binder, *Vor dem Gesetz: Einführung in Kafkas Welt* (Stuttgart: Metzler 1993); Aage Hansen-Löve, "Vor dem Gesetz," in *Interpretationen— Franz Kafka: Romane und Erzählungen*, ed. Michael Müller (Stuttgart: Reclam, 1994), 146– 158; Bernd Auerochs, "Innehalten vor der Schwelle. Kafkas 'Vor dem Gesetz' im Kontext der traditionellen Parabel," in *Grenzsituationen: Wahrnehmung, Bedeutung und Gestaltung in der neueren Literatur*, ed. Dorothea Lauterbach, Uwe Spörl, and Ulrich Wunderlich (Göttingen: Vandenhoeck & Ruprecht 2002), 131–150; Wolf Kittler, "Burial Without Resurrection: On Kafka's Legend 'Before the Law,'" *MLN* 121, no. 3 (2006): 647–678.

dyschronic mode of deferral that, in the end, fails to reward the man from the country and leaves the reader too unsatisfied. After long-winded attempts at exegesis, the chapter concludes with the Chaplain pointing to the nonchronological temporality of the court: "Es nimmt dich auf, wenn du kommst und es entläßt dich wenn du gehst" (It receives you when you come and it dismisses you when you leave).[36]

Kafka employs three temporal tropes that map K.'s growing inability to time his life: when it really matters, Josef K. is either tired, late, or too distracted to pay attention. On the one hand, these temporal disorders indicate that Josef K. is falling out of step with modernity's time regime as he is increasingly consumed by his case; on the other, they symptomatically disclose the lack of proper *Eigenzeit* in his life. Josef K.'s rigid schedule, as sketched earlier, leaves no room for a nonfunctional experience of time. From a temporal perspective, then, it is the lack of *Eigenzeit* in K.'s life that makes him increasingly desynchronized with all aspects of time, including his daily life and the timing of the court. Precisely because K. never took time to properly care for nonutilitarian relations between the Self and the Other, he ends up as a time-troubled man who is out of sync with all modes of temporality. Next, I analyze those instances where lateness, lack of attention, and tiredness play a crucial role in Kafka's narrative.

TIREDNESS, LATENESS, AND THE LACK OF *GEISTESGEGENWART*

Time only gained a historical quality when history no longer "occurred *in* but *through* time."[37] As a consequence of the modern

36. Kafka, *Der Proceß*, 235 / *The Trial*, 224.
37. Reinhart Koselleck, "'Neuzeit': Remarks on the Semantics of Modern Concepts of Movement," in his *Futures Past: On the Semantics of Historical Time* (New York: Columbia University Press, 2004), 236.

ANNE FUCHS

agency of time, modernity then evaluated historical change quali-
tatively in terms of progress or lateness: those who were deemed to
have been left behind became the focus of attention for enlightenment educators who viewed lateness a moral stigma necessitating
disciplinary action. Lateness can thus be viewed as an epiphenom-
enon of the modern drive toward total synchronization of time and
the superimposition of a universal time grid.[38] If lateness designates
the perceived failure to fulfill a social or economic obligation to arrive
on time, then it is produced by slowness, which in turn can be defined
as the perceived inability to keep up with the social, economic, and
cultural speed of the modern age.

As two complementary modes of desynchronization, the
outcome-oriented notion of lateness and the procedural term slowness emerged in the cultural discourse around 1900 as symptomatic
tropes giving expression to various fears about the *mal du siècle,*
including the anxiety that the accelerated pace of social change would
challenge male dominance and overturn the gender hierarchy. A salient example in this regard is K.'s conversation with Frau Grubach
about Fräulein Bürstner in chapter 2, where he observes that the
young woman often comes home late at night. When the landlady
responds by suggesting that Fräulein Bürstner ought to have more
pride and be a bit less forthcoming with men, Josef K. reacts angrily,
slamming the door in his landlady's face, seemingly defending the
young woman's independence. But he then decides to stay up to find
out at what time Fräulein Bürstner arrives home and to have a few
words with her. Smoking a cigar to pass time, he lies down on his bed
until about eleven o'clock. Unable to wait any longer, he steps into
the hallway as if in that way he could make Fräulein Bürstner arrive

38. On lateness as a key trope in modernist temporal discourse, see Anne Fuchs, "Defending
   Lateness: Deliberations on Acceleration, Attention, and Lateness, 1900–2000," *New
   German Critique* 125 (2015): 31–48.

sooner. Even though he cannot even remember what she looks like, he is deeply irritated by her late arrival, as this means that his day will have been full of unease and disorder right to its very end. He also blames Fräulein Bürstner for his missing dinner that evening and for not having been able to visit Elsa and satisfy his sexual desire.[39] When Fräulein Bürstner eventually turns up shortly after half past eleven at night, he reproaches her by claiming that he had been waiting for her since nine o'clock. His moral indignation at her perceived lateness underlines not only the loss of control over his scheduled life but also his authoritarian approach to others, especially women.

At the beginning of chapter 3, Josef K. is informed by telephone that there will be a small hearing concerning his case the following Sunday. He is made aware that these cross examinations will follow one another regularly, perhaps not every week but quite frequently. Upon hanging up the telephone receiver, K. realizes that he has not been given a precise time for the hearing and decides to get there by nine o'clock. However, on the Sunday in question he nearly oversleeps because he had stayed out drinking until late in the night. Rushing out without breakfast to make up for lost time, he comes across Rabensteiner and Kullich, who are traveling in a tram that crosses K.'s route, while Kaminer is sitting on the terrace of a café. All of them seem to be surprised at seeing their superior now running on foot. Josef K.'s interior thought process then reveals that he only decided to walk to the hearing out of a sense of pride: the idea of accepting any help from strangers, however slight, is repulsive to him. He does not wish to humiliate himself before the committee by being too punctual, but he ends up running the last stretch so that he will get there by nine o'clock.[40] As he reaches his destination, he slows down again, "als hätte er nun schon Zeit oder als sähe ihn der

39. Kafka, Der Proceß, 32/ The Trial, 26.
40. Kafka, Der Proceß, 43/ The Trial, 38.

ANNE FUCHS

Untersuchungsrichter aus irgendeinem Fenster und wisse also daß sich K. eingefunden habe. Es war kurz nach neun" (as if he had plenty of time now, or as if the examining magistrate had seen him from some window and therefore knew that K. had arrived. It was shortly after nine).[41]

My summary of K's contradictory thought process points to a clash between the modern subject's assertion of autonomy and a higher order that challenges such sovereignty. When the sitting magistrate tells K. on his arrival that he is precisely one hour and five minutes late, K. therefore demonstratively refuses to apologize: "Mag ich zu spät gekommen sein, jetzt bin ich hier" (I may have arrived late, but I'm here now).[42] And when he delivers his grand accusatory speech, he has the audacity to admonish the magistrate to listen to him because he has no time to waste and will leave soon.[43] K.'s deliberate lateness and his supposed time scarcity are complementary modes of behavior meant to make manifest his sense of authority and control over his life. In the course of the novel, he becomes a time gambler whose games with time are always misguided; for example, when his concerned uncle takes him to Advokat Huld for a first consultation, instead of availing himself of the opportunity to discuss his case with Huld and the Kanzleidirektor who happens to be present, K. is distracted by Leni, who takes him to the kitchen where he loses his sense of time in an eerie scene of rising sexual tension. When he finally leaves Huld's house, his uncle leaps out of the car, reproaching him for his inconsiderate conduct toward the lawyer and the office director who were waiting in vain for K. to return and discuss his case. The aggrieved uncle concludes: "Und mich deinen Onkel läßt Du hier im Regen, fühle nur, ich bin ganz durchnäßt, stundenlang

41. Kafka, Der Proceß, 44 / The Trial, 39.
42. Kafka, Der Proceß, 49 / The Trial, 43.
43. Kafka, Der Proceß, 55–56 / The Trial, 49–50.

190

warten" (And you leave me, your uncle, waiting here in the rain for hours: just feel, I'm soaked clear through).[44] In his conversation with Kaufmann Block the topic of waiting comes up once more when K. discovers that he had already met Block among the waiting clients in the corridor of the court rooms where he had gotten so violently sick. When K. says that it seemed pointless for them to be waiting in that way, Block responds: "das Warten ist nicht nutzlos . . . , nutzlos ist nur das selbständige Eingreifen" (Waiting is not pointless . . . , the only thing that's pointless is independent action").[45] Later on in the chapter, K. demonstrates once more that, as the proverbial modern man, he feels entitled to capitalize on the time of others without any regard for timeliness. Leni rightly observes that he does not seem in the slightest surprised that the lawyer, despite being ill, is willing to receive him at eleven o'clock at night: "Du nimmst das, was deine Freunde für dich tun, doch als zu selbstverständlich an" (You take what your friends do for you too much for granted).[46] And when Huld tells him that he has been waiting for him for a long time, instead of apologizing he withdraws representation of his case from Huld, with immediate effect. When Huld admonishes K. not to rush things, he responds with an affirmation of his rational decision making: "Es ist nichts übereilt . . . , es ist gut überlegt und vielleicht sogar zu lange. Der Entschluß ist entgiltig" (There is nothing hasty about it . . . it's been carefully considered, perhaps at even too great a length. The decision is final).[47]

K.'s ownership of time as modern man's resource is a prominent theme of the Elsa fragment in which the court summons him once more by phone. Setting aside all warnings that this is his last chance, K. decides to visit Elsa instead of obeying the court. Chuffed that his

---

44. Kafka, *Der Proceß*, 117 / *The Trial*, 110.
45. Kafka, *Der Proceß*, 185 / *The Trial*, 176.
46. Kafka, *Der Proceß*, 190 / *The Trial*, 181.
47. Kafka, *Der Proceß*, 195 / *The Trial*, 186.

decision might cause difficulties for the sitting court, he indulges in fantasies about the waiting judge, thus feeding his false sense of self-determination: "der Richter wartete also, vielleicht wartete sogar die ganze Versammlung, nur K. würde zur besonderen Enttäuschung aller nicht erscheinen" (the judge was waiting, perhaps the entire assembly was waiting; K. alone would fail to appear to the particular disappointment of the gallery).[48] Both K.'s ill-judged choice to let others wait and his inability to wait for others (as in the case of Fräulein Bürstner) underline his poor timing: as Willem already observed in chapter 1, he has no sense for the "richtigen Zeitpunkt," the right time. Prior to the trial, his life was ruled by a rigid and utterly functional timetable that left no room for nonalienated relations and meaningful human interactions. In the course of the trial, K.'s modern belief in self-determination is then gradually eroded by his inability to control time: he turns from a temporal control freak into an untimely man who is out of sync with the timing of the court, as well as the modern time regime that produced his type.

A conspicuous symptom of K.'s growing dyschronia is his lack of "Geistesgegenwart," a condition that indicates far more than momentary absent-mindedness. As art historian Jonathan Crary demonstrates, by the 1880s a discourse on attention had emerged that dealt with a precarious subjectivity, which appeared to be threatened by the force of modernity's dazzling visual sensations.[49] By the end of the nineteenth century, the collapse of classical models of vision, and of the stable subjects these models had presupposed, motivated an empirical-scientific approach to the notion of human sensation, which was now produced, controlled, and observed in the laboratory environment. For psychologists such as Wilhelm Wundt or Alfred

48. Kafka, Der Proceß, 262 / The Trial, 252.
49. Jonathan Crary, Suspensions of Perception: Attention, Spectacle, and Modern Culture (Cambridge, MA: Harvard University Press, 2001). A foundational essay that dwells on the

Binet, attention became the single most important category deemed to guarantee unity of consciousness and perception.[50] The disintegration of perception through distraction posed a threat to the social order, which required containment by way of attention as a regulatory tool.[51] It is worth noting that in *fin de siècle* discourse, attention had no clear empirical definition, but was used to explain the mind's capacity for perceptual synthesis in the wake of the collapse of classical models of vision and epistemology. At the same time, attention came to be seen as something controllable in terms of both industrial production and spectacle. Attention was meant to contain the danger of too much distraction and ultimately of psychic disintegration. However, it also allowed for the rapid switching of attention from one object to the next.[52] It thus performed a disciplinary function that managed the perpetual production of the new as one of modernity's striking hallmarks.

problem of distraction and attention is Georg Simmel's essay of 1903, "Die Großstädte und das Geistesleben," in *Gesamtausgabe*, ed. Rüdiger Kramme (Frankfurt am Main: Suhrkamp 1995), 7:227–242. For an English translation, see Georg Simmel, "The Metropolis and Mental Life," in *Simmel on Culture*, ed. David Frisby and Mike Featherstone (London and New Delhi: Sage, 1997), 174–185.

50. Crary, *Suspensions of Perception*, 38. The perceived threat to the unity of consciousness was given further expression by the Viennese philosopher Ernst Mach, who captured the modern self in the impressionistic metaphor of the "Elementenkomplex," a complex of elements. Mach dissolved the subject's unity as well as the external world, which in his analysis was nothing but an effect of floating perceptions that were no longer integrated by Kant's transcendental unity of apperception. Ernst Mach, *Analyse der Empfindungen und das Verhältnis des Physischen zum Psychischen* (Darmstadt: Wissenschaftliche Buchgesellschaft, 1991), reprint of the 9th ed. (Jena: Fischer, 1922).

51. Siegfried Kracauer addresses the problem of distraction and attention in "Der Kult der Zerstreuung" (1926), in *Das Ornament der Masse. Essays* (Frankfurt am Main: Suhrkamp, 1977), 311–317; and Kracauer, "The Cult of Distraction: On Berlin's Picture Palaces," in *The Mass Ornament: Weimar Essays*, ed. and trans. Thomas Y. Levin (Cambridge, MA: Harvard University Press, 1995), 323–328.

52. See also Georg Franck, *Ökonomie der Aufmerksamkeit: Ein Entwurf* (Munich: Hanser, 1998); Georg Franck, *Mentaler Kapitalismus: Eine politische Ökonomie des Geistes* (Munich: Hanser, 2005).

And so it is that in Kafka's novel, K.'s lack of *Geistesgegenwart* sym-
bolizes his loss of authority and a growing sense of alienation from
his habitual world. A salient example in this regard is his visit to the
court offices in the company of the court usher the Sunday after his
first hearing. As he is being led though the corridor of the attic rooms
of the court, K. is overcome by an overwhelming sense of tiredness
that makes him implore the court usher to take him immediately
back to the exit. Astonished that K. has already lost his sense of orientation, the court usher explains that he will have to wait until he
has delivered a message. But we already know that K. is notoriously
unable to wait for others. As a young woman fetches an armchair for
K., she is joined by another court employee who turns out to be the
information man. Even though the young woman points out that the
information man has an answer to all questions, K. is too overcome
by dizziness to inquire about his case. Kafka employs the metaphor
of a ship during a violent storm to give expression to K.'s crisis of orientation: he feels as if he were suffering seasickness in a rough sea and
as if water was hitting against the wooden walls with thunder swell-
ing up from the depths of the corridor caused by crashing waves.[53]
Having been led to the exit propped up by the young woman and the
information man, K. is deprived of his sense of autonomy and violently made aware of his bodily reality, which appears to cause him a
second trial.[54]

While in this scene K.'s lack of presence occurs in the domain of
the court, it soon affects all aspects of his life, including the world
of work where, instead of looking after his waiting bank clients, he
now spends hours planning the petition he intends to write.[55] When
his great rival, the Deputy Director, admonishes K. and takes over

53. Kafka, *Der Proceß*, 84 / *The Trial*, 78.
54. Kafka, *Der Proceß*, 85 / *The Trial*, 79.
55. Kafka, *Der Proceß*, 134 / *The Trial*, 127.

one of K.'s oldest clients, the factory owner, K. realizes that the trial is not a contained affair but an open-ended process, the duration of which is unpredictable.[56] In this dreamlike scene, K.'s lack of presence of mind at the workplace indicates a state of dyschronia that corrodes the seeming rationality of linear time. On the one hand, dyschronia gives expression to the crisis of the modern time regime, which in Kafka's world can no longer guarantee control over the future. On the other hand, K.'s lack of presence of mind indicates a new temporal modality that, in the end, attunes him to the alternative unfolding of his trial.[57] And so it is that in the "Cathedral" chapter, K. begins to recognize the reciprocity of time: while up until know he always expected others to be immediately available and see to his needs, in his encounter with the Chaplain he enquires politely whether the latter has a little time for him, to which the Chaplain responds: "Soviel Zeit als du brauchst" (as much time as you need).[58] Time as a utilitarian resource has been superseded here by a subjective temporality that makes room for the type of careful reflection and dialogue that K. has been incapable of up until now. As I have already argued, the legend of the Doorkeeper then paradigmatically enacts the overturning of the linearity of time. Our expectation that we might gain access to the law some time in the future is dislodged by a profoundly frustrating mode of deferral that destroys the logic

56. Kafka, Der Proceß, 139 / The Trial, 132.
57. This also explains why the novel no longer unfolds in the paradigm of the Bildungsroman with its teleological biographical script but, rather, as a "Folge von Probeläufen" (a sequence of trial runs) that, as Gerhard Neumann observes, continually rewrite the opening scene. Gerhard Neumann, "Der Zauber des Anfangs und das 'Zögern vor der Geburt'—Kafkas Poetologie des 'riskantesten Augenblicks'," in Nach erneuter Lecktüre: Franz Kafkas Der Proceß, ed. Hans Dieter Zimmermann (Würburg: Königshausen & Neumann, 1992), 128. Also Gerhard Neumann, "'Blinde Parabel' oder Bildungsroman? Zur Struktur von Franz Kafkas Proceß-Fragment," in Franz Kafka: Experte der Macht (Munich: Hanser 2012), 101–136.
58. Kafka, Der Proceß, 225 / The Trial, 215.

ANNE FUCHS

of modern time: the future is no longer the time where man's hopes will be realized.

It is important to note, however, that the narrative contains one episode in which K. appears to briefly embrace *Eigenzeit* through playfulness. In chapter 2, he theatrically reenacts the scene of his arrest in front of Fräulein Bürstner by creating a stage set and then playing the part of the supervisor who loudly calls out Josef K.'s name. Fräulein Bürstner's laughter suggests that, with this theatrical and comical reenactment of his earlier arrest, K. has momentarily entered the domain of playful performance, thus suspending his habitualized and utilitarian time practice. But even in this scene, K.'s playfulness remains opportunistic because instead of producing pleasure in his audience, his miming is meant to recruit Fräulein Bürstner's support. This means that K. remains incapable of experiencing a mode of *Eigenzeit* that could make room for nonprofitable human interaction.

Significantly, Kafka employs the theatrical metaphor once more in the final chapter when K. is taken away by two manhandlers who lead him to his execution. By sharp contrast to the opening scene in which K. was surprised by his arrest, at the very end he awaits his executioners who arrive on the evening of his thirty-first birthday about nine o'clock. Even though K.'s timing at the end indicates his submission to a higher force, he attempts to reclaim a moment of independence by asking his executioners at which theatre they are engaged. The interpretation of his coming end in terms of a stage play thus repeats the earlier theatrical scene in Fräulein Bürstner's room—only this time it is a bad comedy that leads to K.'s gruesome death. This synchronization of clock time and metaphysical time which culminates in K.'s horrifying execution "like a dog" (as he himself describes it) stands for a brutal new order in which modern efficiency services archaic practice.

BIBLIOGRAPHY

Allemann, Beda. *Zeit und Geschichte im Werk Franz Kafkas.* Edited by Diethelm Kaiser and Nikolaus Lohse. Göttingen: Wallstein, 1998.

Auerochs, Bernd, "Innehalten vor der Schwelle. Kafkas 'Vor dem Gesetz' im Kontext der traditionellen Parabel." In *Grenzsituationen: Wahrnehmung, Bedeutung und Gestaltung in der neueren Literatur,* edited by Dorothea Lauterbach, Uwe Spörl, and Ulrich Wunderlich, 131–150. Göttungen: Vandenhoeck & Ruprecht, 2002.

Bakhtin, Mikhail, "Forms of Time and of the Chronotope in the Novel: Notes toward a Historical Poetics." In *The Dialogic Imagination. Four Essays,* edited by Michael Holquist, 84–258. Austin: University of Texas Press, 1981.

Berman, Marshall. *All that Is Solid Melts into the Air: The Experience of Modernity.* London and New York: Verso, 2010.

Binder, Hartmut. *Vor dem Gesetz: Einführung in Kafkas Welt.* Stuttgart: Metzler, 1993.

Boa, Elizabeth. *Kafka: Gender, Class and Race in the Letters and Fictions.* Oxford: Oxford University Press, 1996.

Boa, Elizabeth. "Karl Rossmann, or the Boy Who Wouldn't Grow Up: The Flight from Manhood in Franz Kafka's *Der Verschollene.*" In *From Goethe to Gide: Feminism, Aesthetics and the French and German Literary Canon 1770–1936,* edited by Mary Orr and Lesley Sharpe, 168–183. Exeter: University of Exeter Press, 2005.

Boa, Elizabeth. "Observations on Time and Motion: Kafka's *Betrachtung* and the Visual Arts around 1912." In *Time in German Literature and Culture, 1900–2015,* edited by Anne Fuchs and J. J. Long, 93–112. Basingstoke, Houndmills: Palgrave Macmillan, 2016.

Crary, Jonathan. *Suspensions of Perception: Attention, Spectacle, and Modern Culture.* Cambridge, MA: Harvard University Press, 2001.

Duffy, Enda, *The Speed Handbook: Velocity, Pleasure, Modernism.* Durham, NC, and London: Duke University Press, 2009.

Duttlinger, Carolin. "Syncope, Pause, Caesura: Robert Musil and the Psychotechnics of Acceleration." In *Time in German Literature and Culture, 1900–2015,* edited by Anne Fuchs and J. J. Long, 154–169. Basingstoke, Houndmills: Palgrave Macmillan, 2016.

Engel, Manfred, and Auerochs, Bernd, ed. *Kafka-Handbuch: Leben—Werk— Wirkung.* Stuttgart: J. B. Metzler, 2010.

Franck, Georg. *Mentaler Kapitalismus: Eine politische Ökonomie des Geistes.* Munich: Hanser, 2005.

Franck, Georg. *Ökonomie der Aufmerksamkeit: Ein Entwurf.* Munich: Hanser, 1998.

Fuchs, Anne. "Defending Lateness: Deliberations on Acceleration, Attention, and Lateness, 1900–2000." *New German Critique* 125 (2015): 31–48.

Fuchs, Anne. "A Psychoanalytic Reading of *The Man Who Disappeared.*" In *The Cambridge Companion to Kafka,* edited by Julian Preece, 25–41. Cambridge: Cambridge University Press, 2002.

ANNE FUCHS

Hammer, Espen. *Philosophy and Temporality from Kant to Critical Theory*. Cambridge: Cambridge University Press, 2011.

Hansen-Löve, Aage, "Vor dem Gesetz." In *Interpretationen –Franz Kafka: Romane und Erzählungen*, edited by Michael Müller, 146–158. Stuttgart: Reclam, 1994.

Harman, Mark. "Wie Kafka sich Amerika vorstellte." *Sinn und Form* 60 (2008): 794–804.

Heimböckel, Dieter. ' "Amerika im Kopf': Franz Kafkas Roman Der Verschollene und der Amerika-Diskurs seiner Zeit." *Deutsche Vierteljahresschrift für Literaturwissenschaft und Geistesgeschichte* 77 (2003): 130–147.

Holford-Strevens, Leofranc. *The History of Time: A Very Short Introduction*. Oxford: Oxford University Press, 2005.

Kafka, Franz. *Briefe an Felice und andere Korrespondenz aus der Verlobungszeit*. Edited by Erich Heller and Jürgen Born. Frankfurt am Main: Fischer, 1983.

Kafka, Franz. *Diaries 1910–1923*. Edited by Max Brod. New York: Schocken, 1976.

Kafka, Franz. *Der Verschollene: Roman in der Fassung der Handschrift*. Frankfurt am Main: Fischer, 1994.

Kafka, Franz. *Der Proceß: Roman in der Fassung der Handschrift*. Frankfurt am Main: Fischer, 1995.

Kafka, Franz. *Tagebücher. Bd. 2: 1912–1914 in der Fassung der Handschrift*. Edited by Hans-Georg Koch, Michael Müller, and Malcolm Pasley. Frankfurt am Main: Fischer, 2008.

Kafka, Franz. *Tagebücher. Bd. 3: 1914–1923 in der Fassung der Handschrift*. Edited by Hans-Georg Koch, Michael Müller, and Malcolm Pasley. Frankfurt am Main: Fischer, 2008.

Kafka, Franz. *The Trial*. Translated by Breon Mitchell. New York: Schocken, 1998.

Kern, Stephen. *The Culture of Time and Space 1880–1918* (with a new preface). Cambridge, MA: Harvard University Press, 2003.

Kittler, Wolf. "Burial Without Resurrection: On Kafka's Legend 'Before the Law.'" *MLN* 121, no. 3 (2006): 647–678.

Koch, Hans-Gerd. "Kafkas Kanapee." In *Nach erneuter Lektüre: Franz Kafkas Der Proceß*, edited by Hans Dieter Zimmermann, 85–94. Würzburg: Königshausen & Neumann, 1992.

Koselleck, Reinhart. *Futures Past: On the Semantics of Historical Time*. New York: Columbia University Press, 2004.

Koselleck, Reinhart. "Time and History." In *The Practice of Conceptual History: Timing History, Spacing Concepts*, translated by Todd Samuel Presner, foreword by Hayden White, 100–114. Stanford, CA: Stanford University Press, 2002.

Kracauer, Siegfried. "The Cult of Distraction: On Berlin's Picture Palaces." In *The Mass Ornament: Weimar Essays*, edited and translated by Thomas Y. Levin, 323–328. Cambridge, MA: Harvard University Press, 1995.

Kracauer, Siegfried. "Der Kult der Zerstreuung' (1926)." In *Das Ornament der Masse: Essays*, 311–317. Frankfurt am Main: Suhrkamp, 1977.

Mach, Ernst. *Analyse der Empfindungen und das Verhältnis des Physischen zum Psychischen*. Darmstadt: Wissenschaftliche Buchgesellschaft, 1991.

Neumann, Gerhard. "Blinde Parabel' oder Bildungsroman? Zur Struktur von Franz Kafkas *Proceß*-Fragment." In *Franz Kafka. Experte der Macht*, 101–136. Munich: Hanser, 2012.

Neumann, Gerhard. "Der Zauber des Anfangs und das 'Zögern vor der Geburt'—Kafkas Poetologie des 'riskantesten Augenblicks." In *Nach erneuter Lektüre: Franz Kafkas Der Proceß*, edited by Hans Dieter Zimmermann, 121–142. Würzburg: Königshausen & Neumann, 1992.

Neumann, Gerhard. "Ritualität und Theatralität—der Anfang des Proceß-Romans." In *Verfehlte Anfänge und offense Ende: Franz Kafkas poetische Anthropologie*, 51–60. Munich: Carl Friedrich von Siemens Stiftung, 2009.

Nowotny, Helga. *Time. The Modern and Postmodern Experience*. Translated by Neville Plaice. Cambridge: Polity Press, 1994.

Pasley, Malcolm, "Wie der Roman entstand." In *Nach erneuter Lektüre: Franz Kafkas Der Proceß*, edited by Hans Dieter Zimmermann, 11–34. Würzburg: Königshausen & Neumann, 1992.

Sandberg, Beatrice, "Starting in the Middle? Complications of Narrative Beginnings and Progression in Kafka." In *Franz Kafka: Narration, Rhetoric & Reading*, edited by Jakob Lothe, Beatrice Sandberg, and Ronald Speirs, 123–145. Columbus: Ohio State University Press, 2011.

Simmel, Georg. "Die Großstädte und das Geistesleben." In *Gesamtausgabe*, edited by Rüdiger Kramme, 7:227–242. Frankfurt am Main: Suhrkamp, 1995.

Simmel, Georg. "The Metropolis and Mental Life." In *Simmel on Culture*, edited by David Frisby and Mike Featherstone, 174–185. London and New Delhi: Sage, 1997.

Chapter 7

Judges, Heathscapes, and Hazardous Quarries

Kafka and the Repetitive Image-Series

HOWARD CAYGILL

The meeting between Josef K. and the painter Titorelli in *The Trial* presents us with two views of art practice, one highly codified and ostensibly devoted to the official portrayal of judges, the other consisting in the repetitious working of an identical heathscape. Both approach what Roberto Calasso has aptly called the *arcanum imperii*, or secret place of power and rule dominating the court that is pursuing the accused Josef K. The Painter and later the Chaplain are para-legal figures who urgently advise Josef K. to give up his pursuit of truth and justice and finally to compromise with necessity. Both are deeply implicated in the work of the court, but their council is not "legal" in the same way as the advice of the Advocate. Walter Benjamin would have described the distinction between the advice given by the Painter and Chaplain and that by the Advocate in terms of the Talmudic distinction between *Haggada* and *Halakah*, the first telling stories around and about the law and the second engaging

HOWARD CAYGILL

in direct legal reasoning. Titorelli's indirect advice is rendered first through a reflection on the work in progress of an official portrait commission, and then by his forced sale or gift of a series of identical paintings of "A Heathscape," while the Chaplain narrates the parable "Before the Law" before entering into a discussion of its meaning with the hapless Josef K.

The identical image-series of "A Heathscape" is contemporary with the repetitive photographic series of dangerous quarries that appeared in Kafka's office work "Accident Prevention in Quarries," written at the same time as *The Trial* and published in the Yearbook of the Workers' Accident Insurance Institute. Kafka's interest in the image-series testifies to an understanding of the relationships between mimesis, truth, justice, and necessity indebted to Nietzsche and providing an implicit reply to Plato's arguments in *The Republic* that culminated in the expulsion of the artists.[1] In the image-series, Kafka was able to suspend precise definitions of identity and difference, leaving a degree of undecidability surrounding identification and reference that made possible an account of truth and justice oriented toward the models of artistic production and reception.

Philosophical readers of Kafka have been fascinated by the repetitive sequence and especially its appearance in the Heathscapes of *The Trial*. In his "Notes on Kafka," Adorno saw the episode as confirming his view that repetition or the "eternal return of the same" mimicked the operation of reification or the translation of real differences into

1. Kafka possessed a collection of the works of Plato, mainly in Rudolf Kassner's translations into German and published in cheap editions by the Diederich's publishing house in Jena. From very early on, he owned editions of *Phaedrus* (1904), *Phaedo* (1906), and *The Republic* (1909), as well as later editions of *Symposium* (1920) and *Ion, Lysis,* and *Charmides* (1920) (see Herbert Blank, *In Kafkas Bibliothek* [Praha: Nakladatelstvi Franz Kafka, 2004]). The significance of his close acquaintance with the works of Nietzsche, especially *Also Sprach Zarathustra*, has been convincingly shown by the work of Benno Wagner; see Stanley Corngold and Benno Wagner, eds., *Franz Kafka: The Ghosts in the Machine* (Evanston, IL: Northwestern University Press, 2011).

the identical measure of exchange value that constituted commodity exchange. In the Heathscape episode, "what is perpetually the same and what is ephemeral merge,"[2] implying that the paintings purchased from Titorelli as commodities first by the figure of the Manufacturer and later by Josef K. were rendered identical by their exchange value. For Adorno, Kafka extracts comedy from this identification by insisting the artworks are *literally* the same and so producing an allegory of the condition of the artwork under capitalism. The scene is thus crucial evidence for Adorno's understanding of Kafka's allegorical exploration of the inclusions and exclusions of reified life under conditions of commodity production developed at length in his notes on Kafka and later extended into Wilhelm Emrich's comprehensive investigation of Kafka's work.[3]

Carolin Duttlinger's approach in *Kafka and Photography* proposes a technological complement to Adorno's analysis, one indebted to Walter Benjamin's essay "The Work of Art in the Era of Its Technical Reproducibility." She views the image-series, and specifically the identical paintings in the Titorelli episode, as displaying a "quasi-photographic seriality" that testifies to paintings' approximation (or reduction) to the condition of photography. The image-series is understood by Duttlinger according to the analogy of the photographic print: "In the age of the technical media, traditional art emulates the effect of mechanical reproduction, even if the artist himself does not seem to realize the extent to which his paintings are determined by the principle."[4] The artist in *The Trial* thus artisanally mimics a form of mechanical reproduction analogous to the photographic print that issues in the image-series, one adding up to a technological

2. Theodor Adorno, *Prisms*, trans. Samuel and Shierry Weber (Cambridge, MA: MIT Press, 1967), 253.

3. Wilhelm Emrich, *Franz Kafka: A Critical Study of his Writings*, trans. Sheema Z. Buehne (New York: Frederick Ungar, 1958).

4. Caroline Duttlinger, *Kafka and Photography* (Oxford: Oxford University Press, 2007), 195.

view of the image-series that easily complements Adorno's under-standing of its commodity character in terms of the equivalence of exchange value.

The image-series also plays an important role in Deleuze and Guattari's understanding of the assemblage, as is evident in their discussion of Titorelli and his identical paintings in the transition between the chapters "Immanence and Desire" and "Proliferation of Series," in their *Kafka: Towards a Minor Literature*. The crucial dis-tinction between "An unlimited field of immanence" and an "infi-nite transcendence," or between the "abstract machine" of the law characterized by hierarchy and the "machinic assemblage," of justice is illustrated by a reference to Titorelli—"a special character of the novel."[5] They see Titorelli's advice to Josef K., and especially the third option he describes of infinite postponement of the sentence, as an anticipatory critique within the text of the Neoplatonic readings of Kafka in terms of "hierarchised hypostases that are capable of halt-ing and repressing desire."[6] The undoing of the hierarchical machine of law is succeeded by "composition of the assemblage, always one piece next to another. It is the process itself, the tracing of the field of immanence."[7] And of course, one of the key examples of the com-posed machinic assemblage is the case of Titorelli, who "produces a series of completely identical paintings"[8] in an episode they present as a fractal of the repetitive procedures at work throughout the novel.

Each of these readings of the repetitive image-series moves quickly to situate it according to an external logic, whether of com-modity exchange, of mechanical reproducibility, or of the tracing of a field of immanence. But its precise structure, function, and context in

5. Gilles Deleuze and Felix Guattari, *Kafka: Towards a Minor Literature*, trans. Dana Polan (Minneapolis and London: University of Minnesota Press, 1968), 51.
6. Deleuze and Guattari, *Kafka: Towards a Minor Literature*, 51.
7. Deleuze and Guattari, *Kafka: Towards a Minor Literature*, 52.
8. Deleuze and Guattari, *Kafka: Towards a Minor Literature*, 53.

which it appears in Kafka's work is rarely subject to close analysis. In the case of the Titorelli episode, the focus of attention falls on the spatially distinct series of "A Heathscape," occluding the accompanying temporal image-series constituting the representation of the court's presiding goddesses in the same episode. The latter offers important insight not only into Kafka's views on power and representation but also into the problem of the referent for a visual image in his work. This is also significant for understanding the complex photographic image-series that Kafka assembled at the same time as writing *The Trial* for the article "Accident Prevention in Quarries," in which the time, space, and character of the referent in the image-series remains very much in question.

JUDGES AND HEATHSCAPES

We first hear of the painter Titorelli during a confidential conversation between Josef K. and a *Fabrikant*, or "Manufacturer," who visits the bank on business. The Manufacturer says he learned of K.'s case through "a certain Titorelli," a painter, quickly adding that this, however, is not his real name.[9] From the outset the artist is identified in terms of dissemblance—he is not who he claims to be. The Manufacturer explains—none too convincingly—that Titorelli has for many years been visiting his office bringing little paintings "for which I always give him a kind of offering—he is almost a beggar."[10] Anticipating Adorno, he takes care to situate his commerce with the

---

9. A similar claim will accompany the episode of the identical series of the landlady's dresses in *The Castle*, where K. claims to tell by her clothes that she is a dissembler.
10. Franz Kafka, *The Trial*, trans. Willa and Edwin Muir, in *Franz Kafka: The Complete Novels* (London: Vintage, 2008), 117; *Der Proceß: Historisch-kritische Ausgabe sämtlicher Handschriften, Drucke und Typoskripte*, eds. Roland Reuss and Peter Staengle (Frankfurt am Main: Stroemfeld Verlag, 1997), 61.

artist outside the commodity exchange by insisting that the money he exchanges for the paintings is charitable donations, not payments. The Painter comes to him as a supplicant, bringing paintings. There follows the first description of Titorelli's unofficial work—"What is more they are pretty pictures—heathland scenes and suchlike."[11] Kafka thus opens the repetitive series of the identical heathland paintings with these "gifts" to the Manufacturer, but also gives the first hint of the repetitive character of this production in the latter's impatience with the artist's insistence on producing and supplying them. The "purchases," he relates, at first went smoothly—"we had already got used to them"—until the frequency of the artist's visits began to escalate. In a first manuscript version the Manufacturer complains: "But once he didn't keep the pause between visits we had tacitly agreed and came twice."[12] Kafka intensified this reference to the occasion of a once repeated visit into a general reflection on the repetitive character of the artist's visits: "Once however these visits repeated themselves too often and I reproached him."[13] The artist's bid to change the terms of exchange from an asymmetrical charitable donation to an exchange of commodities between "equals" is inter-rupted by the Manufacturer's reproach and the disturbance in the delivery of the series. The exchange of paintings for money between Manufacturer and Painter is succeeded by an exchange of gossip as the painter reveals that his main source of income comes from work-ing for the court as a portrait painter and then sharing with the reluc-tant Manufacturer his knowledge of the court and the doings of its judges and accused.

The Manufacturer advises K. to visit the Painter for advice, for even if the latter has little direct influence, he at least would be able to advise K. on how to get into contact with more influential people

11. Kafka, *The Trial*, 117 / *Der Proceß*, 61.
12. Kafka, *The Trial*, 117 / *Der Proceß*, 61.
13. Kafka, *The Trial*, 117 / *Der Proceß*, 61.

in the court. The Manufacturer's first assurance that the artist on his recommendation would do everything possible for K. and his casual plea—"Why don't you go"—is deleted in the manuscript and replaced by his view that although K. was almost a lawyer himself and with no fear for the outcome of his case, he might nevertheless find Titorelli's advice to be of "great significance."[14] He then makes his move "Why don't you go then to . . ."[15] followed by what seems like a strange large floating cursive *A* in the manuscript that editors have forcibly (and implausibly) interpreted as a *T* for Titorelli. However, this singular graphic figure, not repeated at any other point in the manuscript, seems to denote something else—perhaps the artist's real name? It serves to intensify the growing sense of mystery surrounding the Manufacturer's scarcely concealed desire for Josef K. to visit the artist, especially when it is revealed that he has already prepared a letter of introduction for him which, with all due precaution, he hands over. To K.'s distracted acknowledgment that he will call Titorelli to visit him at the bank or write him a letter, the Manufacturer fervently warns him never to receive Titorelli nor expose himself by writing to him. This seems strange advice coming from someone who had himself regularly received Titorelli and had just written him a letter introducing Josef K. However, in a deleted passage just before this warning, he advises K.—quite to the contrary of his and Kafka's second thoughts—to write to Titorelli and say that he wants "to buy a painting and for him to come here the next day."[16] Leading the Manufacturer to the door, K. wonders at his own judgment in thinking of writing to, or even inviting, Titorelli, but nevertheless he is driven to prepare to leave at once to visit the Painter, surrendering three waiting clients to his hated rival, the Assistant Director.

14. Kafka, *The Trial,* 118 / *Der Proceß,* 61.
15. Kafka, *The Trial,* 118 / *Der Proceß,* 61.
16. Kafka, *The Trial,* 118 / *Der Proceß,* 61.

The next paragraph begins with a deleted "The painter lived . . ." that is replaced by a reiteration of K.'s immediate departure to visit the Painter, who lived, it is now carefully specified, "in a suburb on almost the opposite side of town to the Court house."[17] This change is significant, since K.'s later rushed exit from the artist's room would issue directly into the court, which seems to spread like an archipelago across the entire city. His arrival at the artist's squalid tenement is met by an audiovisual assault—steaming yellow fluid oozes out of a hole under the door and a rat flees to an adjoining canal. A baby's screams are drowned out by the noise of three apprentices beating an object with their hammers in the reflected light of a sheet of tin. Fleeing this scene of artisanal mayhem, K. climbs the stairs, only to be assaulted by a gang of precocious girls overtaking and swarming him. Hoping to gain some information about Titorelli, K. tells one of them that he wants to have his portrait painted by the artist, provoking the child's irate incredulity. After escaping the girls, taking refuge in the artist's tiny studio, and handing over the Manufacturer's letter, he learns that the artist not only paints portraits and heathland landscapes but has also painted the portrait of one of the girls, as well as a lady whom "he wanted to paint." And contrary to the assumption of the young informant on the staircase, he even seems ready to paint K.'s portrait: "Do you want to buy pictures or have yourself painted?"[18] K. evades the question by pointing to a shirt covering a canvas, and playing the disinterested connoisseur, asks "You're working on a painting just now?," which prompts Titorelli to reveal the unfinished work that "strikingly resembled the portrait hanging in the advocate's office."[19] Although it depicts a different judge in a different medium (pastels instead of oil), "everything else showed a

17. Kafka, The Trial, 121 / Der Proceß, 70.
18. Kafka, The Trial, 125 / Der Proceß, 78.
19. Kafka, The Trial, 126 / Der Proceß, 78.

close resemblance, for here too the judge seemed to be on the point of starting menacingly from his throne, bracing himself firmly on the arms of it."[20]

K. senses that this painting is part of a wider series of such images, but is troubled by a large figure in the painting looming behind the throne of the judge. This reference to a single figure in the final version significantly replaces a reference from one to *two* figures on the corners of the throne in the corrected manuscript, indicating the beginning of a series in the first version. The *sie*, or third-person plural, referring to the two painted figures "not completely finished" in the first manuscript version, metamorphoses into the polite second-person address to the artist in the corrected version, who is now advised by K. to do a bit more work to finish the painting. The Painter approaches it with his crayons and begins instead to address an allegorical lesson to K. on the nature of the court: he "fetched a crayon from a table, armed with which he worked a little at the outline of the figure but without making it anymore recognisable to Josef K. It is justice [*Gerechtigkeit*], said the painter."[21] The explanation permits K. to think that he has recognized the image and so he confirms "Here's the blindfold over the eyes, and here the scales . . . " but he also detects that something is not quite right: "But aren't there wings on the figure's heels, and isn't it flying?"[22] The artist says he was commissioned to paint it like that because "actually it is justice and the goddess of Victory [*Siegesgöttin*] in one."[23] Josef K. aptly if flippantly observes, "Not a good combination [*Verbindung*], surely," adding "Justice must stand still, or else the scales will waver, making a just verdict impossible."[24] The Painter repeats that he is just making an

20. Kafka, *The Trial*, 126 / *Der Proceß*, 78.
21. Kafka, *The Trial*, 126 / *Der Proceß*, 81.
22. Kafka, *The Trial*, 126 / *Der Proceß*, 81.
23. Kafka, *The Trial*, 126 / *Der Proceß*, 81.
24. Kafka, *The Trial*, 126 / *Der Proceß*, 81.

image to order: "I had to adapt myself to my client."[25] He then turns again to work on the painting, trying silently to warn K. of his predicament. This time "the figure of justice was left bright except for an almost imperceptible touch of shadow; that brightness brought the figure sweeping right into the foreground and it no longer suggested the goddess of Justice, or even the Goddess of Victory, but looked exactly like a Goddess of the Hunt [*Göttin des Jagd*]."[26] Absorbed by the Painter's activities, K. not only forgets the real reason for his visit but also fails to heed the warnings he is being offered about the character of the court that accuses him and the danger that he is now facing.

Roberto Calasso's reading of this episode is characteristically sensitive and insightful, situating the Painter's portrait work within the tradition of Reynolds, adding the caveat that Titorelli's painting remains an enigma: "A blindfolded woman running: that's what Titorelli is painting. More than a goddess, she's a riddle whose solution isn't clear. Is she solemn? Derisive? This is all we know for sure: the Goddess of Justice is visible at once, and the Goddess of the Hunt is the last to reveal herself. Does this, perhaps, foretell the court's ultimate, esoteric meaning?"[27] For Calasso, K. is clearly being warned that the court he still thinks is dedicated, despite its manifest failings, to the pursuit of justice is in reality dedicated first of all to victory—and surely not *his* victory—and then ultimately to the hunt. K., in other words, is not a plaintiff but an adversary, and more gravely, he is an adversary in the process of metamorphosing into prey and being hunted down and exterminated. The "ultimate,

25. Kafka, *The Trial*, 126 / *Der Proceß*, 81.
26. Kafka, *The Trial*, 127 / *Der Proceß*, 82. Kafka's first draft emphasizes the brightness of the figure more emphatically, using the words *Hell* and *helles* twice instead of only once in the final version.
27. Roberto Calasso, *K.*, trans. Geoffrey Brock (London: Vintage, 2006), 231.

esoteric meaning" Calasso refers to is that the court is not, as it may appear, engaged in the pursuit of justice but, rather, in war, and ultimately not even that but a cruel manhunt that will end only when the quarry is brought to bay, as we shall see, in a suburban quarry at the end of the novel.[28]

What is important and perhaps underestimated by Calasso in K.'s encounter with the image-maker is that K.'s lesson is presented in the form of a serial painting. Early in the composition, Kafka decided in a textual *pentimento* to reduce the proto-series of two allegorical figures into one. This becomes the basis of an image-series that unfolds over time with the first painting of the Goddess of Justice being succeeded by a second of the Goddess of War and then a third of the Goddess of the Hunt. Each goddess emerges to fill the space in the painting above the enthroned judge as the artist works through his visual warning to K. about the character of the institution he is confronting. Yet the fact that it is a series also leaves a thin wedge of hope for K., because the figures, although differing in their significant attributes, are the same. This means that reversing the series also makes it possible that the relentless Goddess of the Hunt before whom the victim/prey can only flee for cover can become first an adversary with whom one can hope to do battle and finally even the Goddess of Justice from whom one can expect a fair and balanced trial. The image-series has the property of suspending judgments about both identity and difference, casting the responsibility for such decisions back onto the viewer. In one case, a viewer might despondently see the Goddess of the Hunt in the figure of justice, while in another hopefully see the Goddess of Justice in the figure of the hunt. The image-series leaves

---

28. In his recent *Il cacciatore celeste* (Milan: Adelphi, 2016), Calasso intensifies his theoretical reflection on the hunt, which sheds much light on his insistence of the centrality of the motif in Kafka. It may be supplemented by Chamayou's diptych. As with Calasso, Chamayou sees the hunt as the *truth* of law and politics rather than an aspect of it that is reversible—that is to say, the truth of the *hunt* can also be legal and/or political.

the decision suspended, the ultimate esoteric meaning of the *Gericht* being not that justice is a hunt but that the hunt also is as much justice as both are war, and that the decision and, in a sense, the judgment and sentence rest with the accused and the way in which he contemplates the image-series.

Calasso underestimates the reversibility of the image-series and the play of identity *and* difference that it makes possible. For him, and fully consistent with his work on the ubiquity of the hunt, "Josef K. has lucidly perceived that the Court is the place where the Goddess of Justice and the Goddess of the Hunt blur into a single figure. Titorelli suggests that the Goddess of Victory can be seen in the same figure. But that's a superfluous addendum. Victory, for the court, is a given for every moment of the world's existence."[29] The implication to be drawn from Calasso's bleak reading (citing K.'s own scarcely "lucid" understanding—in fact, his self-condemnation) is that "A single executioner could take the place of the entire court."[30] Yet this requires that the image-series "blur" into a single figure, that K.'s "lucidity" concerning his ineluctable fate be the outcome of a blurring of irrelevant differences into a single catastrophic figure. Fortunately, K. is spared this lucidity, but this is not to say that he achieves a fully nuanced understanding of the interchangeability of the elements of justice, war, and the hunt that make up the image-series.

Once it is revealed that K. is really pursuing information about the court, Titorelli makes this lesson even clearer by presenting K. with three legal options with respect to the court that parallels the image-series of the three goddesses. However, before doing so the painter reflects on the limits of his expression that are set by the power of the court. Just before the metamorphoses of the Goddess

---

29. Calasso, *K.*, 233.
30. Kafka, *The Trial*, 133 / *Der Proceß*, 97, cited in Calasso, *K.*, 233.

of Justice into those of Victory and the Hunt, K. asks if the allegorical figure has a referent—had the painter portrayed the throne and the allegorical figure behind it as it really existed somewhere in the court? "'Of course,' says K., who had not wished to give any offence by his remark. 'You have painted the figure as it actually stands above the throne.'"[31] Titorelli quickly counters this naïve representational assumption about his painting, saying he does not portray what exists but only what he is ordered to paint by those in power: "'No,' said the painter, 'I have neither seen the figure nor the throne, that is all invention, but I am told what to paint and I paint it.'"[32] He also makes clear that this is not *his* invention but that of his commissioning client, and that he is fully prepared to paint images that he knows to be false—indeed, such is for him the very art of painting.

K. points to the painting again, saying "It is surely a Judge sitting on his throne of Justice?," to which the Painter replies, "Yes, ... but it is by no means a high Judge and he has never sat on such a throne in his life."[33] The portraits pander to the vanity of their clients, but within carefully codified limits: "'Yes, my lords are vain,' said the painter, 'but they have superior permission to have themselves painted like that. Each one of them gets precise instructions how he may have himself painted.'"[34] The instructions bind not only the client but also the Painter, and yet this does not exclude a certain degree of latitude: the painting in question, for example, is in pastel, not oil, and was intended "for a lady."[35] Later, Titorelli goes into more detail about the control of representation exerted by the court and his decreasing degree of freedom within these rules, his waning "elan." Titorelli professes that the representation of power and his constant

31. Kafka, *The Trial*, 126 / *Der Proceß*, 81.
32. Kafka, *The Trial*, 126–127 / *Der Proceß*, 81.
33. Kafka, *The Trial*, 127 / *Der Proceß*, 81.
34. Kafka, *The Trial*, 127 / *Der Proceß*, 81–82.
35. Kafka, *The Trial*, 131 / *Der Proceß*, 82.

acquaintance with the judges is compromising his artistic drive, but both this confession and the existence of such elan remains itself very much in question. This becomes immediately clear when Titorelli explains the conditions of his artistic production that involve secret rules and models bequeathed by his father.

Painting in the court rests on a dynastic principle focused on an *arcanum*, or body of secret rules for the representation of the varying grades of power:

> My father was the Court painter before me. It's the only post that is always hereditary. New people are of no use for it. There are so many complicated and various and above all secret rules laid down for the painting of the different grades of functionaries that a knowledge of them must be confined to certain families. Over there in that chest, for instance, I keep all my father's drawings, which I never show to anyone. And only a man who has studied them can possibly paint the Judges. Yet even if I were to lose them, I have enough private knowledge tucked away in my head to make my post secure against all comers. For every Judge insists on being painted as the great old Judges were painted and nobody can do that but me.[36]

This complicated reflection reveals the aspiration that painting be without novelty, that each work be a precisely codified repetition of the appropriate but secret rules of representation and their traditional execution. His art consists in producing images according to these rules; he represents a rule rather than an object or an idea. But his practice is not only governed by secret rules but also by the arcane drawings bequeathed by his father—the rules have already been schematized into secret drawings kept in an *arcanum*,

36. Kafka, *The Trial*, 132 / *Der Proceß*, 93.

or chest of secrets.[37] The artist does not so much represent the judges who commission him as repeat the drawings and rules he has been bequeathed and that he is bound to observe when representing a particular bureaucratic grade.

The arcane nature of the rules and their accompanying secret drawings also lends a degree of freedom to the artist, for he is in a privileged position to judge whether he has obeyed the rules that are, after all, known only to him. This allows him some discretion to deviate from the rules, as in the case of painting the judge in pastels instead of oils for a lady, or more significantly in the serial changes of the Goddess of Justice he performs for benefit of Mr. K. And yet he remains an ambivalent figure, since the degree and extent of his obedience is never wholly disclosed. It may be that he has been expressly instructed to represent the Goddess of the Hunt to K. as part of a temporal series, and that his seemingly spontaneous and apparently subversive superimposition of the successive goddesses is, in fact, an already highly codified visual sequence. In any case, the image-series of the three Goddesses of the Court corresponds to the three forms of acquittal the Painter describes as the only possible favorable outcomes or lines of flight for the case of Josef K.

The Painter's advice to K. comes after the aesthetic discussions when the "truth" about the reason for Josef K's visit is revealed. However, Titorelli knew all along from the Manufacturer's letter why Josef K. has come and has already given the most important advice. Now he starkly presents Josef K. with the aporia or "greatest difficulty" that confronts him, provoking Josef K. to respond by declaring himself "completely innocent" and to begin to lose patience with the Painter's

---

37. A similar mis-en-scene of inherited authoritative drawings can be found in the contemporary "In the Penal Colony," where the Officer possesses the Old Commandant's arcane diagrams that allow him to program the Apparat to perform the punishment by inscription of the arcane law.

insistent, ironic repetition of "But you're innocent. . . ." The reason for
the Painter's feigned perplexity is that, for the court, the accused are
always guilty: "Never in any case can the Court be dislodged from
that conviction,"[38] but adding as if to underline his powerlessness and
that of his art in such a case, "If I were to paint all the Judges in a row
on one canvas and you were to plead your case before it, you would
have no more hope of success than before the actual Court."[39] Titorelli
then presents K. with the three grades of "acquittal": definite, ostensible, and indefinite postponement. He knows no cases of the former,
only beautiful legends which, he reveals, he too has painted: "I myself
have painted several pictures founded on such legends."[40] The truth of
such legends is that justice has been done and the innocent acquitted,
corresponding to the first of the goddesses presiding over the court.
The second option, "ostensible acquittal," is a form of peace treaty
between the accused and the court mediated by the diplomacy of a
third party—in this case, the Painter who visits the judges with an affi-
davit guaranteeing K.'s innocence. This only means that hostilities are
provisionally suspended, and the possibility of victory has been indefinitely deferred for both parties, although hostilities may be resumed
at any time and the case reopened; this is the option corresponding
to the Goddess of Victory. The third acquittal, postponement, consists in indefinitely deferring the case and the arrival of the moment
of judgment and of execution. To achieve this, the accused must go
to ground, acting evasively like prey in order not to draw the hunter's
attention, keeping the case moving slowly enough and in circles suffi-
ciently restricted as not to draw the court's attention to him either for
excessive or for insufficient activity, an option corresponding to a view
of the court as the domain of the Goddess of the Hunt.

38. Kafka, *The Trial*, 130 / *Der Proceß*, 89.
39. Kafka, *The Trial*, 130 / *Der Proceß*, 89.
40. Kafka, *The Trial*, 134 / *Der Proceß*, 98.

During the Painter's explanation of the options to Josef K., the temperature in the artist's studio becomes unbearable, reaching its maximum as he deduces that while the latter two options will "save the accused from coming up for sentence," they may "also prevent an actual acquittal."[41] The artist seems to agree with this view, but presses K. to make a decision soon, threatening him if he delays with coming himself to hunt him at the bank. As K. struggles to leave, the painter rummages under his bed, saying "Wouldn't you like to see a picture or two that you might care to buy?"[42] Consumed by embarrassment and the blind desire to escape from the Painter's room, K. consents to look at the unframed paintings. Almost blinded by the dust blown off the canvases, K. looks at "A Heathscape": "It showed two stunted trees standing far apart from each other in darkish grass. In the background was a many-hued sunset."[43] K.'s offer to buy it unwittingly initiates the unfolding of the image-series: " 'Here's a companion picture,' he said. It might have been intended as a companion picture, but there was not the slightest difference that one could see between it and the other, here were the two trees, here the grass and there the sunset."[44] Anxious to escape, K. promptly purchases both to "hang up in his office," only to be offered a third: " 'By a lucky chance I have a similar picture here.' But it was not merely a similar study, it was more of the same old heathscape again."[45] And once again, K. repeats the gesture of buying it in order to secure his escape.

Fortunately for K., the Painter himself interrupts the unfolding of the sequence after three images, accepting to settle payment on K.'s next visit and throwing in "all the others under the bed as well. 'They're heathscapes every one of them. I painted lots

41. Kafka, *The Trial*, 140 / *Der Proceß*, 113.
42. Kafka, *The Trial*, 141 / *Der Proceß*, 114.
43. Kafka, *The Trial*, 141 / *Der Proceß*, 114.
44. Kafka, *The Trial*, 142 / *Der Proceß*, 114.
45. Kafka, *The Trial*, 142 / *Der Proceß*, 117.

of heathscapes in my time.' "[46] Much to K.'s increasingly desperate dismay, Titorelli begins to muse over the genre and his public: "Some people won't have anything to do with these subjects
because they're too depressing, but there are always people like
yourself who prefer depressing pictures."[47] K. finally interrupts the
artist's ramblings to arrange for the paintings to be wrapped up for
his attendant to collect, while Titorelli proposes to call for a porter
so that he can take them with him straight away. The negotiation is
only interrupted by K.'s horrified realization, as he climbs over the
bed to leave the studio, that all this time he had been without real-
izing it in the law courts.

The identical series of depressing heathscapes he had just purchased are not just similar but, Kafka insists, identical. Yet, even as
the same painting is repeated, the versions are also different; what is
more, there is no longer any sequential hierarchy for them as there
was with the Goddess series. Since they are identical, the place in
the image-series of the individual paintings is interchangeable, and
each is the same regardless even of its place in the sequence. In
them, the heathscape or hunting domain is divested of its presiding
goddess; they portray a hunting range at the end of the day when
the coming darkness promises to conceal the prey from the eye of
the huntress.

The heathscapes seem to contrast with the hierarchical production sequence of the portraits, marking a collapse of transcendence insofar as they neither participate in an idea nor represent an
object, but aspire only to repetition, each the same as the others. It
is not even clear that they constitute the assemblage seen in them
by Deleuze and Guattari, since although the paintings are identical,
they do not in themselves add up to a composition. It is not clear that

46. Kafka, *The Trial*, 142 / *Der Proceß*, 117.
47. Kafka, *The Trial*, 142 / *Der Proceß*, 117.

they have a referent beyond each other, for all are governed by a law of repetition and not a transcendent image, object, or rule outside their sequence, whether conceived as referent, law, or idea. They refer to each other and seem to propose a flat or even deflated sequence where each is a copy of its copy. And yet the interchangeability serves in the same way as the minor differences in the Goddess image-series to provide a source of minor, accidental differences pointing to at least the survival of the merest possibility of transcendence or an outside to disrupt the repetitious sequence. This lesson, had K. heeded it in his haste to escape Titorelli's studio, would also apply to the series of identical law offices fractally distributed across the city's attics, for as the artist explained, "There are law offices in almost every attic, why should there not be one here?"[48] The law offices are identical and repeated across the city, but their different locations serve to introduce a difference into the court that might serve as a point of distinction. The application of the law may differ according to where the court is located, which is to say that the law is not universal but, rather, that its application is governed by factors not themselves prescribed by the law. This possibility of transcendence, however frail, would be enough to give hope to anyone in a position to see it.[49] Josef K., however, in full rout, is forced to take his heathscapes and flee in a carriage, carrying his paintings with him. On getting back to the bank, he takes the precaution of locking them in the bottom drawer of his desk "to save them for the next few days at least from the eyes of the Deputy Manager."[50] He clearly learned nothing from Titorelli nor from his art of the image-series.

---

48. Kafka, *The Trial*, 142 / *Der Proceß*, 117.
49. Such as K. in *The Castle*, when he appreciates the landlady's vast collection of identical dresses.
50. Kafka, *The Trial*, 143–144 / *Der Proceß*, 117.

DANGEROUS QUARRIES

At the same time as writing *The Trial*, "In the Penal Colony," and "Nature Theatre of Oklahama," Kafka also produced one of his most remarkable contributions to the series of Annual Reports of the Workers' Accident Insurance Institute—"Accident Prevention in Quarries." Kafka had contributed a number of articles to the widely distributed Annual Reports while working at the Institute, including a well-known article on the dangers of wood planing machines, but nothing comparable with this last major contribution to the genre. At the heart of "Accident Prevention in Quarries" is an image-series of almost identical quarries, along with a commentary by Kafka. Kafka's audacity, not to say open defiance, in publishing these photographs in the Annual Report is not immediately apparent, but they date back to a fatal industrial accident in a quarry in 1911. Kafka's choice of an image-series was a direct response to an institutional and political context in which issues of truth and justice were paramount but also problematic.

Kafka was a senior official in the Institute, responsible for assessing appeals against risk assessments and thus insurance premiums. His work would later have been described as "Kafkaesque," since he was required to make judgments on individual industrial premises while being explicitly forbidden by the Worker's Insurance law to visit or assess these worksites in person. Instead, he had to rely on reports by the notoriously corrupt factory inspectors or on voluntary questionnaires returned by employers. In the case of the quarry accident in 1911, all the available information pointed to good practice at the quarry in question, most of it subsequently revealed to be false. In the months after the accident, Kafka set himself to securing the right of independent inspection for the Institute, approaching the Ministry, advocating the reform of Worker's Accident law, and even mounting a trial legal case to establish a precedent for inspection. None of these efforts proved successful, and so in 1914, Kafka used the pages of the Annual Report to publicize a series of fourteen images of dangerous quarries, rounded off by a staged artificial quarry shot as an image of good practice. The circumstances under which these images were procured were strictly *ultra vires*, and their publication constituted an open challenge to existing legislation and corrupt practice. Their publication and Kafka's commentary on them showed the readers of the Annual Report that the Institute now possessed a photo archive of dangerous quarries and had thus effectively, if illegally, constituted a regime of capillary power where previously it had been absent.

In one respect the image-series seems to differ from those evoked in the studio of Titorelli. They are all oriented toward the fifteenth and final image, which in many ways sets the visual parameters for the series while remaining outside it. It is the photograph of an artificial quarry at a permanent industrial safety exhibition in Berlin Charlottenburg that Kafka had visited during one of his ill-fated trips to his fiancée Felice, who lived in the city. Although the image is placed at the end of the series as a kind of Platonic scene of the perfect quarry—a fictional quarry—the lighting and point of view of this final photograph corresponds with the rest of the images, contributing to the sense of an identical series. The strong lighting of the industrial safety exhibit—lit from skylights above and artificial light below, fixed by the low viewpoint of the camera—is celebrated and even imitated by the other photographs in the series. They are all lit by strong, early morning light reflected off traces of snow lying on the ground; they clearly belong to the family of barren heathscapes favored by Titorelli in *The Trial* sequence. In his comment on the thirteenth image, Kafka indeed draws attention to the trees that are also prominent in Titorelli's paintings.

The impression is deceptive that the image-series of photographs is oriented toward a Platonic idea of the perfect quarry with which it concludes. While one of the characteristics of the sequence is indeed that the fourteen quarries fall short in comparison with the fifteenth image—all imperfect examples of the perfect quarry—it quickly becomes clear from the textual commentary for each image that the final, perfect quarry is not the only, or even the main, object of the image-series. In each case, the image is situated according to an accident that has yet to happen; they are images of catastrophes that are likely to take place, and that in all probability *will* take place. That is, the image-series is of accidents-to-come, and the comments for each photograph amplify the ominous sense of catastrophe in arrival. The image-series almost plays with the anticipation of where the accidents will strike first. The commentary that accompanies the images either point to Kafka as having been present at the moment the photograph was taken—whether he took them himself or accompanied a photographer on illicit raids in the early morning light[51]—or his taking pains to create the illusion of his having been there, in both cases openly breaking the law by documenting the dangerous quarries. His commentary not only evokes the coming accidents but also warns employers that he is aware of and has documented their dangerous ways, revealing the truth even if it pits him against the letter of the law.

As mentioned, each of the photographs reveals an accident-to-come. In the first photograph, the floor is scattered with debris, blocking paths of escape, which prompted the comment, "The dangers that arise when blasting is carried out under these circumstances are inconceivable."[52] The comment accompanying the third

51. As with Atget, the photographs are taken in the early morning and in most (but not all) cases in the absence of workers and their criminal employers, using the slanting early morning light to create artificial "crime scene" photographic values.
52. Franz Kafka, *Franz Kafka: The Office Writings*, eds. Stanley Corngold, Jack Greenberg, and Benno Wagner (Princeton, NJ: Princeton University Press, 2009), 285; Kafka, *Amtliche Schriften*, eds. Klaus Hermsdorf and Benno Wagner (Frankfurt am Main: Fischer Verlag, 1999), 396.

photograph contrasts the evidence of dangerous practice (overhanging) with the questionnaire that the company had returned denying any such evidence. With this, Kafka gives notice to the professional public reading the article that his office is in the process of collating questionnaire returns with photographic evidence so as to establish the truth. The fifth photograph in the series solicits Kafka's deadly humor, first reversing the photographic values established in the final photograph and copies up to now, and then confessing that this carnivalesque excavation leaves him "almost tempted to say the quarry would meet the safety regulations better if it were stood on its head."[53]

The extent to which each image is the same, depicting an accident waiting to happen, is characteristic of the temporality of this image-series, an effect compounded by the accompanying textual comment that Duttlinger aptly notes "turns the described photograph into the harbinger of a catastrophe that has already happened."[54] It is not so much that these images describe accidents or dangerous quarries than that they are potential accidents on their way to happening.

The effect of a threat or accident to come is especially marked in the comment on the eighth image, which is in many respects the most drastic in an already dramatic image-series. The photograph resembles a dismembered mountain, a moonscape or scene of trench warfare, full of pits and craters. The main danger afflicting this quarry is the level of groundwater that in some places reaches depths of between five and six meters. While the risk of death in the earlier photographs came from being buried under landslides of dirt and debris, in this picture it is death by drowning that awaits the hapless worker: "The snow points out the narrow ledges and the steep walls immediately over the water."[55] The hazards of icy paths and

53. Kafka, *The Office Writings*, 286 / *Amtliche Schriften*, 399.
54. Duttlinger, *Kafka and Photography*, 203.
55. Kafka, *The Office Writings*, 290 / *Amtliche Schriften*, 402.

hidden chutes into the freezing water evoke a lonely death by drowning. What is more, those same waters are actively undermining the quarry, hollowing out the wall separating present and past excavations, and bringing on the prospect of further catastrophe.

The largely visual regime of inspection is complemented by references to threatening soundscapes. Not only does the physiognomy of the quarry reveal its dangers, but also dangers can be heard. Unambiguously placing himself on the scene of the tenth quarry, Kafka reports on the threatening soundscape: "Shards of stone never stop rolling downward, and the echo of stones crashing against one another is a constant background noise."[56] The noise in the silent photograph is suddenly switched on, and the image-series begins to resound with it; it testifies to movements deep within the rock and in so doing also announces the coming accident. In the center of this photograph, and strangely immobilized, is the figure of a worker labeled with an "M"; visibly without goggles and as if participating in the performance of a living *Vexierbild*, this worker is camouflaged against the rock face, seeming to merge with the debris that is moving slowly to crush him.

However, as with the image-series in *The Trial*, the effect of the photo sequence is not entirely bleak—not necessarily a "depressing picture," as Titorelli would say. For each of the photographs has been captured in advance of the accident; there is still time to avert the accident, which is indeed the whole point of writing "Accident Prevention in Quarries." In spite of their relentless march through these potential accidents, the textual commentaries indicate this potential for prevention; indeed, the very existence of the series contributes to this possibility. By photographically capturing the course and many facets of the coming accidents, the image-series presents its ineluctable progress as the same as catching each

56. Kafka, *The Office Writings*, 291 / *Amtliche Schriften*, 404.

quarry at a moment of suspension, at the moment before the accident happens. As Kafka noted when reflecting on the cognitive gain of his image-series, "All these quarries share certain characteristics in spite of their individual differences,"[57] meaning that they are all theatres of industry where "accidents have not yet occurred [but] there exists a strong likelihood [*Wahrscheinlichkeit*] that they will happen any given working day."[58] This collection of suspended moments also points to the possible postponement of the court sentence in *The Trial* or, in this case, the possibility that each quarry can be suspended at this moment, not only beside the others in the photo series but also in the accidents that have so far been prevented.

Kafka's image-series from the autumn of 1914 may be viewed as a placeholder for an absent transcendence. Adorno, Calasso, Deleuze, and Guattari are right to see in it the emergence of a principle of repetition, or a flat or deflationary series that contrasts with Platonic views of a hierarchical series oriented according to an idea or ultimate referent. They also point to a vindication of art in terms of repetition that breaks with the terms of the Platonic condemnation of image-making. Josef K., however, will meet his end in a dangerous quarry, situated at the intersection of Kafka's day work in the office and his fictional writing. Perhaps it is in *The Castle*, Kafka's rewriting of *The Republic* after the death of God, that repetition, humor, and defiance point to a fictional gay science that embraces repetition and eagerly awaits the next term of the series in the landlady's new dress. The revelation of the new dress will not bring him any closer to the truth, but it will help him to pass another day while waiting to gain access to the Castle.

57. Kafka, *The Office Writings*, 293 / *Amtliche Schriften*, 408.
58. Kafka, *The Office Writings*, 293 / *Amtliche Schriften*, 408.

BIBLIOGRAPHY

Adorno, Theodor W. "Notes on Kafka." In *Prisms*, translated by Samuel and Shierry Weber. Cambridge, MA: MIT Press, 1967.

Benjamin, Walter. *Illuminations*. Translated by Harry Zohn. London: Fontana, 1992.

Blank, Herbert. *In Kafkas Bibliothek*. Praha: Nakladatelstvi Franz Kafka, 2004.

Calasso, Roberto. *Il Cacciatore Celeste*. Milan: Adelphi, 2016.

Calasso, Roberto. *K*. Translated by Geoffrey Brock. London: Vintage, 2006.

Chamayou, Gregoire. *Manhunts: A Philosophical History*. Translated by Steven Rendall. Princeton, NJ: Princeton University Press, 2012.

Corngold, Stanley, and Benno Wagner. *Franz Kafka: The Ghosts in the Machine*. Evanston, IL: Northwestern University Press, 2011.

Deleuze, Gilles, and Felix Guattari. *Kafka: Towards a Minor Literature*. Translated by Dana Polan. Minneapolis and London: University of Minnesota Press, 1986.

Duttlinger, Caroline. *Kafka and Photography*. Oxford: Oxford University Press, 2007.

Emrich, Wilhelm. *Franz Kafka: A Critical Study of his Writings*. Translated by Sheema Z. Buehne. New York: Frederick Ungar, 1958.

Kafka, Franz. *Amtliche Schriften*. Edited by Klaus Hermsdorf and Benno Wagner. Frankfurt am Main: Fischer Verlag, 1999.

Kafka, Franz. *Der Proceß: Historisch-kritische Ausgabe sämtlicher Handschriften, Drucke und Typoskripte*. Edited by Roland Reuss and Peter Staengle. Frankfurt am Main: Stroemfeld Verlag, 1997.

Kafka, Franz. *Franz Kafka: The Office Writings*. Edited by Stanley Corngold, Jack Greenberg, and Benno Wagner. Princeton, NJ: Princeton University Press, 2009.

Kafka, Franz. *The Trial*. In *Franz Kafka: The Complete Novels*. Translated by Willa and Edwin Muir. London: Vintage, 2008.

Chapter 8

Kafka's Modernism

Intelligibility and Voice in The Trial

ESPEN HAMMER

Regardless of one's favorite definition of literary modernism, it is generally agreed that it cannot be approached without paying attention to the question of language. In modernist literature, whether we are referring to Samuel Beckett, James Joyce, Paul Celan, Hermann Broch, Louis-Ferdinand Céline, T. S. Eliot, Ezra Pound, or any of the other great names associated with this movement, it seems that nothing concerning language has been taken for granted, that what it is for language to express and relate speakers and thinkers intelligibly to the world has been crucially called into question, and that literature has figured as a site for conducting radical and self-reflective experiments with language. If it is correct that such an attention to language has been an integral component of any literary project worthy of being classified as modernist, then it may not seem obvious that Franz Kafka should be considered a modernist. Kafka's specificity as a writer appears to reside in something else than his use of language, which does not in any way come across as particularly "experimental" or self-reflective. Indeed, Kafka was predominantly a storyteller.

What goes on, one might say, in a Kafka narrative is the unfolding of the story—it is the story on which we are invited to focus, not the language; and the task of Kafka's writing is to achieve sufficient transparency for the story to shine through and attain the kind of hard and precise character that readers of, say, "In the Penal Colony" or "The Metamorphosis" remember so well. Like a razor-sharp image, Gregor Samsa's transformed body leaves an indelible mark: what we remember is, as it were, the *perceptual* content.

The aim of this essay is to suggest that while Kafka's diegetic capacities were remarkable, and while he did not conduct straightforward experiments with language, there is a highly important sense in which language in his work is being called into question. Kafka's modernism, I argue, while related to his deep sense of uncertainty regarding any act of existential self-authorization, can be discerned precisely in the attention he is paying to the conditions of intelligible speech. The language in *The Trial* is only seemingly meaningful. In numerous instances, Kafka explores how utterances can be made, and in fact a whole background of crucial assumptions about what is the case be established, without any clear sense of why they should be accepted, with what authority they being received, and how their implications are to be interpreted.

Examining this topic, and in particular how Kafka's language can so successfully yet also so unnervingly rehearse the paradox of simultaneously being both intelligible and unintelligible, I argue that one of the major philosophical accomplishments of Kafka's *The Trial* consists in the way in which it depicts a state of radical estrangement— or, as Stanley Cavell would call it, skepticism—in which speech, while seeming to make sense, has lost touch more or less completely with the conditions under which it can authoritatively be accepted as meaningful. Speech in Kafka is "language gone on holiday" (Wittgenstein)—language not *meant* (Cavell) by a speaker in the sense of being properly inserted into a meaningful context.

Ultimately, it is speech for which no one is, or can be, responsible. If *The Trial* is an absurdist novel, then it is not primarily, or only, because we encounter absurd actions and events but, rather, because the novel as a whole is an exercise in unintelligible speech. Ultimately, it is intelligibility as such that is at stake here; and hence this novel may instruct us not only existentially, politically, theologically, and psychologically but also philosophically.

WHO? WHY? HOW?

In the history of the European novel, few opening lines resound with greater familiarity than these: "Someone must have slandered Josef K., for one morning, without having done anything wrong, he was arrested" (*Jemand mußte Josef K. verleumdet haben, denn ohne daß er etwas Böses getan hätte, wurde er eines Morgens verhaftet*).[1] The sentence seems to convey a somewhat complex yet perfectly transparent content. There is the modal verb *must* followed by *have* and a past participle, expressing necessity, followed by a justification, using a negative perfect-participle construction as a qualifier to a straightforward assertion of fact: one morning Josef K. was arrested. However, a fairly cursory look at this sentence seems to reveal a number of enigmas. Of course, the very assertion itself—"he was arrested"—is immediately called into question by the subsequent sentences, pages, and indeed the whole novel. Unknown men, including an "inspector" and two "guards" (none of whom is wearing a uniform) enter his room, bossing him around, and he soon discovers colleagues of his standing outside waiting for him. However, none of these people seems

---

1. Franz Kafka, *The Trial: A New Translation Based on the Restored Text*, trans. Breon Mitchell (New York: Schocken, 1998), 3. Franz Kafka, *Der Proceß: Kritische Ausgabe*, ed. Malcolm Pasley (Frankfurt am Main: Fischer, 1990), 7.

to possess the requisite authority for arresting anyone, and without any clear indication of what the arrest is supposed to lead to, and why and on what grounds it is taking place, it is far from clear what "being under arrest" means in the first place. We later learn that a case has been opened, and that court proceedings, requiring K.'s presence and council, will take place. A bell presumably signals the formal beginning of the trial; yet it remains unclear what the trial really involves. Who, exactly, stands behind the arrest?

Equally puzzling is the assertion that K. has not done anything wrong. Who says this, and with what kind of epistemic authority? To answer "the narrator" will not get us very far. To be sure, this is indeed the voice of a narrator, generally offering what Friedrich Beissner has called a "mono-perspectival narration" (being confined, temporally and spatially, to the central character's perspective), yet in some cases making statements based on observations to which K. may not have been privy. What is the narrator's identity, and why should the reader place any trust in his or her voice?[2] Is it, as some commentators have suggested, K. himself? Are we hearing, as if externalized and embodied in third-person speech, his thoughts? His self-assessment or self-justification? (It should be noted that the German subjunctive form of *getan hätte* is not adequately preserved in the English translation. The German original implies a modality related to the order of the possible (and impossible), rather than the actual. It is not that K. *has not* done anything wrong. That would be an acknowledgment of fact. Rather, K. *could not* have done anything wrong. However, we possess no disconfirmation of the claim that he has done something wrong.)

There are more mysteries here. Why is the narrator not identifying K. with his full surname? Why the strange "K.," which so easily, yet on no conclusive basis, suggests a connection between the character in Kafka's novel and Kafka himself? Did the empirical

2. Friedrich Beissner, *Der Erzähler Franz Kafka* (Stuttgart: Kohlhammer, 1952).

author want the reader to make such a connection? If so, why? And why does the narrator take for granted that the inference from "K is arrested despite not having done anything wrong" to "someone must have slandered him" is valid? Slander is an oral defamation in which someone tells one or more persons an untruth about another, thereby harming that person's reputation or standing. Something morally problematic, in other words, must have taken place in order to explain K.'s apparently unjustified "arrest." There is a morally blameworthy agent or organization somewhere, slandering innocent people. Yet why could not K.'s arrest have been instigated for some other reason? Perhaps he was just the next name on a list. Perhaps, as K. immediately starts thinking, this is all just a big mistake of some kind—a contingent event, in other words, without any morally relevant or even intentional origin.

Finally, what does "wrong" (*Böse*) mean in the opening sentence? The expression "doing something wrong" is somewhat colloquial, not necessarily indicating the breach of a legal code, and indeed neutral as between the legal and the moral registers. The German *Böse* more often means "evil" than "wrong," as in Nietzsche's *Jenseits von Gut und Böse*, which usually is translated as *Beyond Good and Evil*, a moral opposition, being contrasted by Nietzsche with the nonmoral distinction between *gut und schlecht* ("good and bad"). Should the reader, with the legally authorized operation of arresting someone in mind, infer that the accusation leveled at K. is strictly a legal one? Or is perhaps *das Böse*, of which he in the eyes of his accusers supposedly stands guilty, a moral, or, as readers since Max Brod have claimed, perhaps even theological category?

The Trial is full of these kinds of strange, slippery passages that, despite their apparent transparency, seem to resist not only the imposition of an unequivocal interpretation but also the attribution of an origin in a responsible speaker's intention. One comes across them as K. is placed before the Examining Magistrate, when he is at work, in the episode with Leni and Huld, in the visit to the painter Titorelli, and, to be sure, in the conversation with the priest.

With the possible exception of the priest, no figure seems closer to revealing the inner workings of the court than Titorelli. Yet it is never evident whether he speaks on behalf of himself or the court (he belongs, after all, to the court system). Nor is it easy, or even possible, to follow the implications of his numerous definitions, explanations, and distinctions. As an insider to the court, Titorelli *seems* to offer his assistance. He says he will try to help K. Yet K. cannot get his head around this man's real intentions. Why, he wonders, does Titorelli *both* promise to help him *and* continuously pronounce his innocence? Even worse, why does Titorelli offer assistance *on the assumption that the trial would turn out well*?

This repeated reference to his innocence was beginning to annoy K. At times it seemed to him as if, by such remarks, the painter was insisting upon a favorable outcome to the trial as a precondition for his help, which thus amounted to nothing on its own of course. But in spite of these doubts, K. controlled himself and didn't interrupt the painter. He didn't want to do without the painter's help, he was sure of that, and that help seemed no more questionable than the lawyer's. In fact K. far preferred the former, because it was offered more simply and openly.[3]

(*Die wiederholte Erwähnung seiner Unschuld wurde K. schon lästig. Ihm schien es manchmal als mache der Maler durch solche Bemerkungen einen günstigen Ausgang des Processes zur voraussetzung seiner Hilfe, die dadurch natürlich in sich selbst zusammenfiel. Trotz dieser Zweifel bezwang sich aber K. und unterbrach den Maler nicht. Verzichten wollte er auf die Hilfe des Malers nicht, dazu war*

3. Kafka, *The Trial*, 152.

er entschlossen, auch schien ihm diese Hilfe durchaus nicht fragwür-
diger als die des Advokaten zu sein. K. zog sie jener sogar beiweitem
vor, weil sie harmloser und offener dargeboten wurde.)[4]

On reflection, K. finds that he should accept Titorelli's support. (One should note the irony, though, of trusting the painter because his offer of assistance seems to have been made "more simply and openly" than that of the lawyer. Unlike the lawyer, the painter certainly belongs to the court.) However, the service is provided on the basis of a paradox. As just mentioned, Titorelli will only help on the assumption that the trial goes well. But if the trial goes well, K. will not need his help. K. understands Titorelli's words. The propositional meaning of his utterances is, as it were, comprehensible enough. The point at which Titorelli's speech becomes unintelligible has to do with the conditions under which Titorelli may successfully say what he says. For Titorelli to meaningfully communicate his proposal to K., the conditions must be such that he could find himself in need of help. Yet they are not. Titorelli, we might say, is making a claim that, while propositionally adequate, is performatively self-contradictory. He can say it, but he cannot mean it.

Performative self-contradictions are peculiar in that they seek to withdraw the speaker from any responsibility for meaningfully inserting his or her assertion into a context that can make it intelligible. In philosophy, this point has famously been put forward by Jaakko Hintikka in his account of Descartes. According to Hintikka, Descartes's *cogito, ergo sum* is usually thought of as an inference: If I think, then I exist. However, according to Hintikka's interpretation, what Descartes really does is to appeal to the unintelligibility of performative self-contradictions: thus, *cogito, ergo sum* is a performance and not an inference.[5] Descartes proves his existence *in and through*

4. Kafka, *Der Proceß*, 205.
5. Jaakko Hintikka, "Cogito, Ergo Sum: Inference or Performance?" *Philosophical Review* 71, no. 1 (1962): 3–32.

the act of thinking. Any attempt to think the denial of one's existence would involve a performative self-contradiction between the thought (of one's nonexistence) and the condition of its intelligibility, namely that the thinker exists. In this sense, skepticism about one's own existence, while "logically sound," is self-canceling. There must be someone standing behind intelligible strings of words—someone who takes responsibility for their proper projection into a meaning-giving context. With Titorelli we lack that moment of selfhood. Titorelli's words keep floating around. They are grammatically and semantically sound. Yet who is uttering them? And for what reason?

ORDINARY LANGUAGE AND THE CONDITIONS OF INTELLIGIBILITY

Many scholars have commented on the mysterious, oblique language in Kafka: on the one hand, transparent; on the other, empty, impenetrable, obscure. With reference not only to Kafka but also to a number of related modernist writers, the French critic Maurice Blanchot refers to how "The writer belongs to a language which no one speaks, which is addressed to no one, which has no center, and which reveals nothing."[6] For Blanchot, Kafka's language is thus oriented toward achieving what he calls *anonymity*.[7]

Blanchot further claims that Kafka's language has broken loose, as it were, from normal contexts of communication—contexts in which speakers stand behind their words to make sure they are addressed to someone with the intent of "revealing" some content. However,

6. Maurice Blanchot, *The Space of Literature*, trans. Ann Smock (Lincoln and London: University of Nebraska Press, 1989), 2.
7. For the complete collection of Blanchot's essays on Kafka, see his *De Kafka à Kafka* (Paris: Gallimard, 1981).

on Blanchot's reading, the achievement of anonymity is not related to a project allowing for clarification or self-clarification but, rather, to a deliberate, almost existential acknowledgment of the metaphysical distance between language and world. As the process of writerly self-divestiture gets radicalized, one is supposed to experience the fundamental nonreferentiality of all language as it unsuccessfully runs up against an incomprehensible reality—a reality that Blanchot, following Emmanuel Levinas, calls the *il y a*, the "there is." Faced with the *il y a*, the traumatic possibility of a complete loss of symbolization and reference, the writer is brought to the point of accepting a kind of unconditional responsibility for her words. The authentic writer keeps going, Blanchot claims, yet with an awareness of the essential self-referentiality of language—how the world of reference has withdrawn or been bracketed—combined with a sense of the equally essential obscurity of language as it is liberated from any illusions of "aboutness."

Blanchot's reading of unintelligibility in authors such as Kafka has achieved an almost canonical status, especially in the area of deconstruction. Blanchot starts out, however, from controversial premises about the fundamental nonreferentiality of language—premises that call for elaboration and justification beyond what we find in his work. If any, the kind of justification we do find is the nominalist claim that the particular, while exclusively real, is ineffable, that concepts can only refer to generalities (the whiteness of the white object, presumably yet falsely being "identical" with the whiteness of all other white objects), and that, as we apply concepts to particulars, we find ourselves trading in illusions.[8] Yet the claim that particulars

---

8. Blanchot develops and elaborates these ideas most explicitly in *The Infinite Conversation*, trans. Susan Hansson (Minneapolis and London: University of Minnesota Press, 1992). See, for example, *The Infinite Conversation*:

> All of our language—and therein lies its divine nature—is arranged to reveal in what "is" not what disappears, but what always subsists, and in this disappearance takes form: meaning, the idea, the universal. In this way language retains of presence only

are ineffable is hardly acceptable. Concepts do pick out properties of particulars; and if they don't, it is not because of some inherent flaw in the concepts themselves but of our inability to find the adequate predication, description, or characterization.[9] Blanchot associates responsibility with the realization of the nonreferential nature of language. However, as ordinary language philosophers emphasize, speakers have a more obvious and important responsibility for the implications of what they say. They forfeit that responsibility on pains of becoming incomprehensible. A view such as that of Blanchot, which from the standpoint of metaphysical skepticism neglects that Wittgensteinian/Cavellian responsibility, is incapable of ascertaining the subtle dialectic of meaning and nonmeaning in Kafka's work. In Blanchot, the notion of responsibility arrives too late, thereby missing the real action.

Rather than following Blanchot further, I now turn to Wittgenstein, who, while hardly a commentator on Kafka, seems to address precisely the kind of loss of meaning and intelligibility I have claimed we encounter in *The Trial*.[10] Wittgenstein's later work,

---

that which, escaping corruption, remains the mark and the seal of being (its glory as well), and therefore *is* not truly either. The drawing back before what dies is a retreat before reality. The name is stable and it stabilizes, but it allows the unique instant already vanished to escape; just as the word, always general, has always already failed to capture what it names. (34)

9. I elaborate this point in Espen Hammer, *Adorno's Modernism: Art, Experience, and Catastrophe* (Cambridge and New York: Cambridge University Press, 2015), 105–110.

10. According to Karen Zumhagen-Yekplé, "The Everyday's Fabulous Beyond: Nonsense, Parable, and the Ethics of the Literary in Kafka and Wittgenstein," *Comparative Literature* 64, no. 4 (2012), in the more than 20,000 pages of Wittgenstein's unpublished writings, there is not a single reference to Kafka. Zumhagen-Yekplé mentions, however, that Elizabeth Anscombe once "lent him *The Trial* and a collection of stories in an effort to share with him her enthusiasm about Kafka's writings" (431). Upon returning the books to her, Wittgenstein (according to Ray Monk, *Wittgenstein: The Duty of Genius* (New York and London: Penguin, 1991), is supposed to have said that "This man gives himself a great deal of trouble not writing about his trouble" (498). For the only available book-length study of how Wittgensteinian themes might apply to Kafka's works, see Rebecca Schumann, *Kafka*

including the *Philosophical Investigations,* is of course enormously complex and intriguing. In this context, I can only point to some of the most obvious ways in which it may aid us in our reading of Kafka.

It is widely accepted that the later Wittgenstein sees language use as a form of practice, involving an indefinite number of different types of speech (not just "propositions," "sentences with a definite truth-value," and so on) and an unavoidable attentiveness to the particular situation and context in which something is being said. Wittgenstein's contextualism, his view that language use needs to be studied, analyzed, and evaluated in its proper context, might seem to prevent him from formulating a normative conception. If what can be said meaningfully is a matter merely of conformity to contextual practice, then normativity seems ruled out. For Wittgenstein, however, speech is indeed normative. While there are ways to *get it right* and ways to *get it wrong,* the production of meaning is tied to the ability, often neglected by philosophers and metaphysicians searching for the abstract or ideal, to insert one's utterance into the right "language-game" or intersubjectively constituted framework in which one's words ultimately carry meaning. It is within such frameworks that we see the emergence of constraints on what can be meaningfully said. What Wittgenstein calls the "ordinary" or "everyday" is made up of the responses and sensibilities we have as competent users of a given language—knowing what to say when and under which circumstances, as well as knowing the implications of saying it in the way it is being said. Wittgenstein does not think this knowledge can be formalized, at least not to a very large extent. Rather than being based on the apprehension of rules that call for adequate application in each individual case (thereby begging for yet another normative

and Wittgenstein: The Case for an Analytic Modernism (Evanston: Northwestern University Press, 2015).

order to guide the agent in the act of application, thus creating an infinite regress), we are trained and socialized in such a way as to be *attuned* with other speakers. Most of the time, our judgments are aligned with those of others.[11] Without consulting a book of rules, or definitions, we know what counts as X in individual instances—that *this*, say, is X rather than Y or Z—thus, we know how to go on with words, projecting them into ever new contexts while continuing to make sense.

As Cavell points out, for Wittgenstein our attunement must allow for both flexibility and constraint. We need to be able to use the same words in changing situations. Yet we also need to be able to agree on what counts as violations. I can feed myself or another person. I can also feed a meter with coins or with my debit card. However, if someone purports to feed a person with coins—or a meter with foie gras—then what they do starts to become unintelligible. While the propositional content of their utterances may have a truth-value, and while the utterances may be syntactically and grammatically well formed, we no longer know why they say what they say—what the point of saying it is—and they start to become incomprehensible.

In paragraph 117 of the *Philosophical Investigations*, Wittgenstein offers an instructive example of precisely this notion of unintelligibility:

> You say to me: "You understand this expression, don't you? Well then—I am using it in the sense you are familiar with."—As if the sense were an atmosphere accompanying the word, which it carried with it into every kind of application.

11. Ludwig Wittgenstein, *Philosophical Investigations*, trans. Elizabeth Anscombe (Oxford: Basil Blackwell, 1958), §242: "If language is to be a means of communication there must be agreement not only in definitions but also (queer as this may sound) in judgments. This seems to abolish logic, but does not do so.—It is one thing to describe methods of measurement, and another to obtain and state results of measurement. But what we call 'measuring' is partly determined by a certain constancy in results of measurement."

If, for example, someone says that the sentence "This is here" (saying which he points to an object in front of him) makes sense to him, then he should ask himself in what special circumstances this sentence is actually used. There it does make sense.[12]

"This is here" makes sense when accompanied by some kind of indexical gesture made by a speaker intending to demonstrate the presence of something. Not only must the "right circumstances" occur but there must also be a reason for, or point to, the speaker's action. There must be some reason to think that the object is missing or not present where it was thought to be. Ideas of sense as some sort of "atmosphere" accompanying the word in its every application are inadequate. Rather, in order to be intelligible, words must be inserted responsibly into the right context—and thereby be used, as Wittgenstein often puts it, in the language game in which they have their rightful home.

In *On Certainty*, Wittgenstein applies this account of the "right circumstances" to philosophical skepticism, arguing that G. E. Moore, who thought he could prove the existence of the external world by holding up his arms and twice saying "I know that this is an arm," failed to make sense.[13] Assertions such as "I know that this is an arm" or "I know that this is a tree," uttered in full daylight and perfect viewing conditions by sane, undrugged philosophers, claiming against

12. Wittgenstein, *Philosophical Investigations*, §117.
13. Ludwig Wittgenstein, *On Certainty*, trans. Elizabeth Anscombe (New York: Harper & Row, 1972), §3: "If e. g. someone says 'I don't know if there's a hand here' he might be told 'Look closer.'—This possibility of satisfying oneself is part of the language-game. Is one of its essential features." Wittgenstein's point is, of course, that if uttered, as Moore did, in epistemically perfect circumstances in which it is not possible to "satisfy oneself" further, the assertions "I know that there's a hand here" and "I don't know if there's a hand here" are senseless. For Moore's anti-skepticism, see "A Defence of Common Sense" and "Proof of an External World," both in G. E. Moore, *Philosophical Papers* (London and New York: Routledge, 1959).

the skeptic to be in possession of knowledge, are empty; they do not make a point. The speaker tries to make sense outside of the ordinary or everyday. However, in doing so he brackets the responsibility that comes with being a speaker for responding properly to the phenomenon at hand. Ultimately, he excludes himself. We no longer know the speaker as a responsive subject.

In the metaphilosophical sections of *Philosophical Investigations*, Wittgenstein uses a number of figures and tropes to characterize how language can turn against itself in this way. Referring to how philosophers and others may tend to speak unintelligibly, Wittgenstein refers to "emptiness" (§107), to having gotten on to "slippery ice where there's no friction" (§107), to being "bewitched" (§109), to not knowing one's way about (§123), to language being like an "engine idling," failing to do its work (§132), but also, in what I would suggest is nothing less than a proto-Kafkean parable, to language being "a labyrinth of paths" (§203):

> You approach from *one* side and know your way about; you approach the same place from another side and no longer know your way about.[14]

In commenting on Wittgenstein's sense of how our words may become empty and detached from the ordinary, Stanley Cavell uses the term *skepticism*. It is not enough, Cavell claims, for words to make sense and be appropriately offering a response to the situation at hand that they satisfy the normative constraints—or what Cavell calls *criteria*—for their correct use. The criteria must also be *applied* by someone who stands responsible for the words being used. I may, Cavell argues, have all the relevant criteria for the correct application of mindfulness to someone and still not know with certainty that that

14. Wittgenstein, *Philosophical Investigations*, §203.

person actually possesses an inner life. What is needed is for me to acknowledge the other and, in doing that, accept that my relationship to that person, in which I am singled out as responsive (no one can substitute for me in that relation) before and to the other, is what makes it possible for me to relate to her as a mindful being. I acknowledge her as alive—and as sentient—insofar as I respond; and by responding I successfully apply the relevant criteria. The skeptic is someone who believes that words can be meaningful in the absence of such acknowledgment. The skeptic's words may seem meaningful. Yet as no particular speaker stands behind them by responsibly applying them, they no longer have any point and fail to assume meaning. There is, Cavell suggests, in those cases an absence of *voice*—and words are being said without being fully meant.

Central to Cavell's argument is the idea that philosophy, in particular, tends to create contexts of skepticism that prevent the subject from active involvement and acknowledgment. Descartes's dream argument, for example, generates a skeptical conclusion by focusing on an object about which no specific skeptical questions can be asked. Only from a best-case scenario for knowledge—an object presented in perfect lightning conditions, and so on—can a failed claim to knowledge generalize to all knowledge. In less than a best-case scenario—say, when the object is not fully in view—we might always respond to the skeptic that, rather than inferring from her failed claim to knowledge that all knowledge is defunct, she needs to take a better look, or in other ways optimize her epistemic position. However, in a best-case scenario, in which the object is supposed to represent all objects, such that if knowledge of this object fails, then all knowledge fails, it is not, Cavell argues, possible to make an intelligible claim.[15] We are—as with Moore's "I know that this is a hand"—faced with a "non-claim context."

15. In *The Claim of Reason: Wittgenstein, Skepticism, Morality, and Tragedy* (New York: Oxford University Press, 1979), 53, Cavell refers to such an object as "generic." Only skepticism

KAFKA'S MODERNISM

So what does all this have to do with Kafka's *The Trial*? The overall claim I am working toward is the following. The court system in this novel is Kafka's name for a generalized state of skepticism in which the ordinary routes to establishing intelligibility have been suspended, if not completely eliminated. The closer K. gets to the inner recesses of the court, the less he finds that people are able to establish mutual understanding on the basis of speech and action.

The scene in which Titorelli shows K. a painting suggestive of how the Goddesses of Justice and Victory are blending in with the Goddess of the Hunt has often been interpreted as the nearest one gets in *The Trial* to something like a revelation of the true meaning of the court: While at first glance pretending to represent Justice, the court turns out to be an agent of victorious power.[16] The court victoriously hunts its victims down and, as we see with K., mercilessly destroys them. This, I think, is a profoundly important comment on the court, one that almost is too directly stated to be taken at face value. However, the destructive nature of the court, as well its notorious combination of elusiveness and presence, should not preclude

---

about generic objects may extend to all objects. However, claims about such objects cannot be made intelligibly. I discuss the Cavellian distinction between specific and generic objects in Espen Hammer, *Stanley Cavell: Skepticism, Subjectivity, and the Ordinary* (Oxford: Polity, 2004), 45–46.

16. Kafka, *The Trial*, 146: "But, except for an imperceptible shading, brightness still surrounded the figure of Justice, and in this brightness the figure seemed to stand out strikingly; now it scarcely recalled the goddess of Justice, or even that of Victory, now it looked just like the goddess of the Hunt." Kafka, *Der Proceß*, 197: "Um die Figur der Gerechtigkeit aber blieb es bis auf eine unmerkliche Tönung hell, in dieser Helligkeit schien die Figur besonders vorzudringen, sie erinnerte kaum mehr and die Göttin der Gerechtigkeit, aber auch nicht an die des Sieges, sie sah jetzt vielmehr vollkommen wie die Göttin der Jagd aus." See also Roberto Calasso, *K.*, trans. Geoffrey Brock (New York: Vintage, 2006), 233: "Josef K. has lucidly perceived that the court is the place where the Goddess of Justice and the Goddess of the Hunt blur into a single figure. Titorelli suggests that the Goddess of Victory can be

us from acknowledging the extent to which the court is also a linguis-tic entity—a space, to be more specific, of linguistic degeneracy and unintelligibility.

A claim such as this may offer both an interpretive key to the novel and, in a wider sense, an account of its self-reflective, modern-ist character. I alluded in the beginning to the sense in which Kafka's *The Trial* might be viewed as belonging to a distinct lineage of literary modernism. Drawing on Cavell, I should now be in a position to fur-ther substantiate this claim.

According to Cavell, literary modernism is less a movement or a doctrine of aesthetic ideals than it is a condition in which art finds itself once it resolutely, and with the utmost sense of seriousness, comes to accept that the conventions that previously guided artis-tic creation and reflected a deep-seated agreement between artists and audiences about what counts as a successful work of art are no longer able to aspire to any obvious validity.[17] As painters, dramatists, composers, sculptors, and novelists discover that they no longer are able to view themselves as constrained by these conventions in any meaningful sense, the question arises of how, or whether, their art can at all be continued. What does it mean to continue when knowl-edge of what counts as successful art-making is up for grabs—and not only that, when it is no longer clear whether such knowledge can in fact be entertained? Moreover, in the absence of artistic conven-tions, how can artists, audiences, and critics distinguish any longer between the genuine and the merely fraudulent? In premodern art worlds, agents knew how to answer this question: fraudulent art was art that did not satisfy established expectation—the painter, say, did

---

seen in the same figure. But that's a superfluous addendum. Victory, for the court, is a given for every moment of the world's existence."

17. Stanley Cavell, "Music Discomposed," in Cavell, *Must We Mean What We Say? A Book of Essays* (Cambridge: Cambridge University Press, 1976), 167–196.

not master chiaroscuro to good effect, or the dramatist did not know how to create tension in a compelling manner. Modernist art, Cavell submits, is art that deliberately represents itself as being created and received without any guiding rails—art, therefore, whose genuineness rests exclusively on the artist's willingness to take full responsibility for every step along the way. For each move, the artist not only has to experience it as "correct" but also declare the criteria, or reasons, on which it was based. The question is what *you* can accept as continuing the process of art-making, and this question needs to be asked over and over again; indeed, this is the self-reflective, second-order injunction, as it were, of all modernist art.

Kafka's modernism is the modernism not of Cavell's cherished color-field painters (Noland, Stella), who in their semi-monochrome and wholly abstract stripe paintings do seem successfully to reveal where and on what basis they have chosen to stand. (Nothing in a color-field painting is withdrawn from this transparency; everything is, as Michael Fried would say, "present."[18]) Rather, as Kafka walks K. through the court system, he unfolds a form of modernism that hibernates in the negative and the oblique, persistently yet without any self-assurance promising itself that it will continue, despite the surrounding obscurity.

One may at this point be reminded of the final, tormented sentence of Samuel Beckett's *The Unnamable*—the famous "you must go on; I can't go on; I'll go on."[19] Unlike Beckett's prose, however, Kafka's negativity never interrupts the syntactic orderliness of individual sentences. There is in Kafka none of Beckett's tropes of direct self-negation, self-denial, or outright mockery of language itself. Rather, what is being put to the test is language as it purports

18. Michael Fried, *Art and Objecthood: Essays and Reviews* (London and Chicago: University of Chicago Press, 1998).
19. Samuel Beckett, *Three Novels: Molloy, Malone Dies, The Unnamable* (New York: Grove, 2009).

to generate intelligibility in an ordinary setting. Like Wittgenstein, Kafka provides for the reader a context of generalized skepticism in which the ultimate purpose is to stake out what it means for linguistic utterances to be responsibly used by speakers in order to create communicable sense.

A context of generalized skepticism involves alienation in perhaps its most radical form. It is not only that K. seems to have no access to the court's deliberations, decisions, and operations—and that he therefore, given that he has virtually no control over his own fate, has little or no autonomy. An alienation of this kind always seems to encourage further investigations and more conversations with lawyers, judges, accused, and other insiders of the court that may offer support. (K., of course, pursues such lines of investigations, but to no avail.) Rather, the alienation that characterizes K.'s condition is one that threatens his very ability to make sense in the first place. K.'s challenge is *transcendental*: it is the very condition of the possibility of sense-making that is at stake, and not just first-order tasks of clarification. K., in other words, rather than some sort of detective, acting on his own behalf, and in the business of solving first-order puzzles, is—via the perspective established by the narrator—a self-reflective figure, one whose struggle to understand is a struggle to understand himself and the basis of his own existence as a thinking and interpreting being.

I said that Blanchot suspends Kafka's language in a space of pure self-reflection, devoid of any ambition of achieving the kind of intelligibility that Wittgenstein associates with ordinary language. We can now see that in doing that, Blanchot ties Kafka's modernism to a perpetual skepticism and negativity in relation to which there is no possible resolution or dialectical opposition. The Wittgensteinian approach is distinct from this in that it refrains from eliminating the dialectical tension between the extraordinary and the ordinary. Blanchot sees Kafka's language as inherently extraordinary.

The Wittgensteinian Kafka, by contrast, holds open the possibility of achieved intelligibility despite the manifest lack of intelligibility throughout much of the text.

This is not to say that there are obvious instances of any "achievement of the ordinary," as Cavell calls it, in *The Trial*. However, there are passages in which some kind of hope of answerability and clarification shines through. Ironically, the best candidate may be in the final chapter, at the end of the novel, when K., as he is led by the two unknown men to his execution in the abandoned quarry, sees in a window a figure with outstretched arms:

> His gaze fell upon the top story of the building adjoining the quarry. Like a light flicking on, the casements of a window flew open, a human figure, faint and insubstantial at that distance and height, leaned far out abruptly, and stretched both arms out even further. Who was it? A friend? A good person? Someone who cared? Someone who wanted to help? Was it just one person? Was it everyone? Was there still help? Were there objections that had been forgotten? Of course there were. Logic is no doubt unshakable, but it can't withstand a person who wants to live.[20]

> (*Seine Blicke fielen auf das letzte Stockwerk des an den Steinbruch angrenzenden Hauses. Wie ein Licht aufzuckt, so fuhren die Fensterflügel eines Fensters dort auseinander, ein Mensch schwach und dünn in der Ferne und Höhe beugte sich mit einem Ruck weit vor und streckte die Arme noch weiter aus. Wer war es? Ein Freund? Ein guter Mensch? Einer der teilnahm? Einer der helfen wollte? War es ein einzelner? Waren es alle? War noch Hilfe? Gab es Einwände, die man vergessen hatte? Gewiß gab es solche. Die Logik ist zwar*

unerschütterlich, aber einem Menschen der leben will, widersteht sie nicht.)[21]

Apparently in need of some way to achieve a sense of an ending and of closure that could function as a framing device for his progress with this novel, Kafka conceived of and wrote the final chapter immediately after having drafted the first. In some readers' opinion, it comes across as slightly strained, as though Kafka could not figure out any other way of ending a story of apparently indefinite deferral than to have the main character be killed. However, as the passage I just quoted indicates, there is a certain logic (*Logik*) at stake here—a necessity: from the very first page when K. was arrested, he became a living dead, and the real question was not whether he was guilty or not (in the eyes of the court, he clearly was, and this is what matters here) but when and how the court would do away with him.

The scene with the casements of a window flying open is depicted in the free indirect mode of narrative speech: the reader sees it fully from within K.'s perspective and partakes in his thoughts as he, trying to understand its significance, already has the hands of one of his executioners at his throat. Thus, while what's occurring, whether actual or not, may seem to offer the only real glimmer of hope in the whole novel—a Messianic light, as it were, promising help or even redemption—K. is already well and truly unrescuable. Hope has rarely looked as feeble—and as hopeless!—as this, providing evidence, no doubt, for readers interested in discovering a certain theological commitment in Kafka. From several of his notes and diaries, Kafka did indeed seem to have been interested in what Adorno, in a 1934 letter to Walter Benjamin, called an inverse theology according to which whatever hope there is for man can only be discerned

21. Kafka, *Der Proceß*, 312.

by becoming aware of the complete negativity of damaged life.[22] As Benjamin himself famously put it in the concluding sentence of the essay "Goethe's Elective Affinities," "Only for the sake of the hopeless ones have we been given hope" (*Nur um der Hoffnungslosen willen ist uns die Hoffnung gegeben*).[23]

This is all very well, and K.'s sudden and unexpected leap into a universalistic, quasi-philosophical mode, pondering whether not only one person may be up there but "everyone" (*alle*), seems to provide the reader with exactly the kind of evidence that would suggest a vision of hope for man *qua* man. However, the scene may also be looked at differently. I would recommend viewing it as a fantasy of expressiveness. Unlike what seems to be the case in virtually every other sequence in the novel, K.'s "faint and insubstantial" interlocutor is here envisioned as someone who permits K. to express himself; whoever this may be, it is someone who might be sympathizing, ready to help, and prepared to actually listen seriously to the arguments at stake. It is someone, K. anticipates, whose empathy exceeds logic and the law, however "unshakable." In the original version of the novel's penultimate paragraph, we even find the narrative voice switching from third- to first-person as K., desperately yearning to be heard, utters (or merely thinks) the following two (no doubt very charged) sentences: "I have something to say. I lift up my hands."[24] Perhaps because he finds the sudden turn to the first-person voice problematic or too revealing, Kafka discards these sentences, replacing them with "He raised his hands and spread out all his fingers"

22. For the concept of inverse theology, see Peter E. Gordon's essay in this volume. See also Adorno's letter to Benjamin, December 17, 1934, in Theodor W. Adorno and Walter Benjamin, *The Complete Correspondence, 1928–1940*, ed. Henri Lonitz, trans. Nicholas Walker (Cambridge, MA: Harvard University Press, 2001), 66.

23. Walter Benjamin, "Goethe's Elective Affinities," in Benjamin, *Selected Writings, Vol.1: 1913–1926*, trans. Stanley Corngold (Cambridge, MA: Belknap, 2004), 356.

24. This deleted passage is quoted from Franz Kafka, *The Trial*, trans. Will and Edwin Muir, and with additional material translated by E. M. Butler (New York: Schocken, 1968), 263.

(*Er hob die Hände und spreizte alle Finger*).[25] The expressive intent, however, is unmistakable. K. believes, or rather fantasizes, that he is being acknowledged by this other, and that his very existence is predicated upon whether he is able to single that other out as someone who is capable of, and prepared to, listen. So far, K. has not had a real existence in this novel. The generalized skepticism of the court system—its inherent refusal to allow individuals to come forward and use language with a view to revealing themselves and their own stance—has effectively prevented anyone from being able to reveal himself or herself to others; hence, every character, and K. in particular, has been a complete mystery to every other. The utopia of this penultimate paragraph is that of being seen, being revealed, being listened to—and therefore of coming into some kind of genuinely human existence.

In Kafka, no such moment is ever allowed to be transformed into a permanent achievement of transparency and intelligibility. The unfinished chapter about the Nature Theater of Oklahoma in *Amerika* (*The Man Who Disappeared*), for example, in which the young Karl Rossmann faces the possibility of being able to escape from his ongoing experiences of alienated submission and exploitation in favor of full and free self-expression ("All welcome! Anyone who wants to be an artist, step forward! We are the theatre that has a place for everyone, everyone in his place!"[26]), turns out not to deliver on its promise of redemption. On the contrary, Karl only gets to Clayton, where a confusing and demeaning process of filing job applications ensues, and where the hornblowing angels he encounters to begin with

---

25. Kafka, *The Trial*, 231; *Der Proceß*, 312.
26. Franz Kafka, *Amerika* (*The Man Who Disappeared*), trans. Michael Hofmann (New York: New Directions, 1996), 202: Franz Kafka, *Der Verschollene. Kritische Ausgabe*, ed. Jost Schillemeit (Frankfurt am Main: Fischer, 1983), 387: "Jeder ist willkommen! Wer Künstler werden will melde sich! Wir sind das Teater, das jeden brauchen kann, jeden an seinem Ort!"

quickly give way to the familiar Kafka-style functionary. However, as Adorno remarks regarding this scene, even if Karl Rossmann does not find what he was hoping for, and the experience is no more than a dream, the proleptic moment is itself not to be ignored:

> If one wakes up in the middle of a dream, even the most troubling, one is disappointed and feels as if one had been cheated of what is best. Yet there are as few happy, fulfilled dreams as, in Schubert's words, happy music. Even the most beautiful ones retain the blemish of their difference from reality, the consciousness of the mere appearance [*Schein*] of what they grant. That is why even the most beautiful dreams are somehow damaged. This experience is unsurpassable in the description of the nature theater of Oklahoma in Kafka's *Amerika*.[27]

Damaged—yet also beautiful.

CONCLUSION

I have in this essay argued that Kafka's *The Trial* can fruitfully be studied with reference to its exploration of the conditions of linguistic intelligibility, assuming that these conditions are manifest at the level of language in its ordinary use. Pointing to insights developed in Wittgenstein and Cavell, I have tried to uncover what I see as a dialectic of expressiveness and inexpressiveness, itself suggestive of Kafka's modernism. I certainly do not think that such an approach is able to exhaust the sense most readers of this novel have of extreme alienation and confusion. Nor do I think that Kafka's modernism is

---

27. Theodor W. Adorno, *Minima Moralia: Reflections from Damaged Life*, trans. Dennis Redmond (Scottsdale, AZ: Prism Key, 2011), 116–117.

exclusively a matter of his attentiveness to ordinary language and the conditions of intelligibility. I would claim, however, that a careful study of Kafka's language is of philosophical value. If anything, it has the capacity to point us to the fragile nature of our linguistic attunement, the cost of forfeiting it, and the satisfaction involved in full self-transparency and expression.

BIBLIOGRAPHY

Adorno, Theodor W. *Minima Moralia: Reflections from Damaged Life*. Translated by Dennis Redmond. Scottsdale, AZ: Prism Key, 2011.

Adorno, Theodor W., and Walter Benjamin. *The Complete Correspondence 1928–1940*. Edited by Henri Lonitz, translated by Nicholas Walker. Cambridge, MA: Harvard University Press, 2001.

Beckett, Samuel. *Three Novels: Molloy, Malone Dies, The Unnamable*. New York: Grove, 2009.

Beissner, Friedrich. *Der Erzähler Franz Kafka*. Stuttgart: Kohlhammer, 1952.

Benjamin, Walter. *Selected Writings. Vol. 1. 1913–1926*. Translated by Stanley Corngold. Cambridge, MA: Belknap, 2004.

Blanchot, Maurice. *De Kafka à Kafka*. Paris: Gallimard, 1981.

Blanchot, Maurice. *The Infinite Conversation*. Translated by Susan Hansson. Minneapolis and London: University of Minnesota Press, 1992.

Blanchot, Maurice. *The Space of Literature*. Translated by Ann Smock. Lincoln and London: University of Nebraska Press, 1989.

Calasso, Roberto. *K.* Translated by Geoffrey Brock. New York: Vintage, 2006.

Cavell, Stanley. *The Claim of Reason: Wittgenstein, Skepticism, Morality, and Tragedy*. New York: Oxford University Press, 1979.

Cavell, Stanley. *Must We Mean What We Say? A Book of Essays*. Cambridge: Cambridge University Press, 1976.

Fried, Michael. *Art and Objecthood: Essays and Reviews*. London and Chicago: University of Chicago Press, 1998.

Hammer, Espen. *Adorno's Modernism: Art, Experience, and Catastrophe*. London and New York: Cambridge University Press, 2015.

Hammer, Espen. *Stanley Cavell: Skepticism, Subjectivity, and the Ordinary*. Oxford: Polity, 2004.

Hintikka, Jaakko. "Cogito, Ergo Sum: Inference or Performance?" *Philosophical Review* 71, no. 1 (1962): 3–32.

Kafka, Franz. *Amerika (The Man Who Disappeared)*. Translated by Michael Hofmann. New York: New Directions, 1996.

Kafka, Franz. *Der Proceß: Kritische Ausgabe*. Edited by Malcolm Pasley. Frankfurt am Main: Fischer, 1990.

Kafka, Franz. *Der Verschollene. Kritische Ausgabe*. Edited by Jost Schillemeit. Frankfurt am Main: Fischer, 1983.

Kafka, Franz. *The Trial*. Translated by Will and Edwin Muir. New York: Schocken, 1968.

Kafka, Franz. *The Trial: A New Translation Based on the Restored Text*. Translated by Breon Mitchell. New York: Schocken, 1998.

Monk, Ray. *Wittgenstein: The Duty of Genius*. New York and London: Penguin, 1991.

Moore, G. E. *Philosophical Papers*. London and New York: Routledge, 1959.

Schumann, Rebecca. *Kafka and Wittgenstein: The Case for an Analytic Modernism*. Evanston, IL: Northwestern University Press, 2015.

Wittgenstein, Ludwig. *On Certainty*. Translated by Elizabeth Anscombe. New York: Harper & Row, 1972.

Wittgenstein, Ludwig. *Philosophical Investigations*. Translated by Elizabeth Anscombe. Oxford: Basil Blackwell, 1958.

Zumhagen-Yekplé, Karen. "The Everyday's Fabulous Beyond: Nonsense, Parable, and the Ethics of the Literary in Kafka and Wittgenstein." *Comparative Literature* 64, no. 4 (2012): 429–445.

Chapter 9

Displacements on a Pathless Terrain

On Reading Kafka's Der Proceß

ELIZABETH S. GOODSTEIN

It would be difficult to find a more tempting object for a series devoted to "philosophical perspectives" on literary texts than the "novel" known in English as *The Trial*. Indeed, this work epitomizes the intriguing challenges Kafka's oeuvre poses to the dichotomy between philosophy and literature that is the organizing principle of such an undertaking. Not only, as in so much of the finest imaginative writing, does the way the text means resist reduction to clearly definable "claims." Through famously slippery prose that seems to undermine the possibility of making any assertions at all about what it says or signifies, Kafka's writing attains a kind of negative philosophical presence all its own. As its reception history amply illustrates, this "novel" can thus be brought to illustrate radically disparate, indeed contradictory, theses.

To do justice to this complexity, in which the multiplicity of the literary takes on philosophical resonance, I attempt neither to stabilize the various forms of slippage proper to the ways Kafka's writing comes to mean nor to arrive at a definitive account of the failure of strategies of reading that aim to do so. Rather, taking the author's studied pursuit of the aporetic as a point of departure, I explore the ways "literary" and "philosophical" dimensions converge in a practice of writing that calls into question the very categories and boundaries that organize and differentiate the practices of interpretation proper to these different disciplinary perspectives.

As I show, reflection on the "unfinished" text of Kafka's *Der Proceß* entangles us in philosophical questions about fiction and history, the status of authorship, and the significance of literary representation as such that are inextricable from the first-order difficulties arising out of the effort to comprehend, at the most basic level, what is happening in the story. I situate the philosophical challenges of reading Kafka's writing against the background of a vexed reception history in which modernist myth-making vies with theological speculation and literary canonization becomes intertwined with the traumas of the twentieth century. In tracing the history in which Kafka's name became a cipher for a peculiarly modern mode of experience, I foreground his importance for another master of the modernist fragment, Walter Benjamin, whose own situation as a reader at the borders between philosophy, literature, and history has generated an analogously vexed reception history. This juxtaposition—or better, constellation—illuminates how much remains at stake in both oeuvres for philosophical reflection on our own modernity.

MODERNIST MYTHOLOGY

These days, the text that goes by the name of *The Trial* is as canonical as they come. Indeed, like everything associated with Kafka, up to and including his very name, it has attained iconographic status. Josef K.'s sudden and bewildering arrest, the nightmarish bureaucracy of the court, the free-floating guilt and foreboding have come to epitomize an opaquely timeless modernism that tantalizingly blends author and protagonist. In Kafka's popular reception, the signs of historical, cultural, and biographical particularity—the cobbled streets of Prague, the vague accusations and looming violence, the lurid women, the sons betrayed and abandoned—are blurred into an existential brand, with magnetic dolls, greeting cards, and *Castle* comics depicting the angst-ridden modern artist alone in a bewildering world before a law grown alien and impenetrable.

In 1925, when Max Brod published his first version of *Der Proceß*, the iconic Kafka, our Cassandra, did not yet exist. The unfinished novel that appeared the year after its author's death was the first and most significant volley in Brod's long and arguably successful editorial campaign to establish Kafka's reputation as "one of the greatest poets and purest human beings of all times."[1] That crusade had been launched the year before in *Die Weltbühne*, when Brod revealed his intention to violate the author's explicit instructions "to burn without exception and unread" all unpublished papers and letters— instructions he had warned Kafka he would never carry out—and publish everything he could. "As far as my memory, as far as my powers extend, nothing shall be lost."

A clearer case of modernist myth-making can hardly be imagined. Placed under the magnifying glass of Brod's emphatic interventions in the name of Kafka's canonization, the sly testament kindled a controversy over the form and even the existence of this novel in particular that continues to echo through popular memory.

In 1929, Walter Benjamin, an early admirer of Kafka whose own posthumous canonization represents another variant of modernist myth-making, intervened on Brod's behalf, defending him for

---

1. Max Brod, "Franz Kafkas Nachlaß," in *Die Weltbühne* 20, no. 2 (1924): 106. The remarks in the following sentences are from 107 and 109, respectively. Translations from the German throughout are my own.

retroactively liberating the writer "from the burden of conscience of either having to give the work his imprimatur himself or burn it."[2] As Benjamin discerned, Kafka had thereby added another dimension to the challenge of reading his fragmentary texts. Nearly a decade later, however, in his review of Brod's 1937 biography of Kafka, Benjamin would harshly criticize its author's indelicacy and "lack of distance," contrasting its tone of "pietistic, ostentatious intimacy" with Brod's apparent incomprehension of his own situation vis-à-vis his friend's work.[3] Kafka, Benjamin wrote, "was evidently not willing to bear the responsibility before posterity for an oeuvre whose greatness he was well aware of." He "had to entrust his papers to someone who would not want to carry out his final will."[4] Still, their friendship was perhaps "not the smallest of the puzzles in Kafka's life."[5]

Criticism cannot be entirely disentangled from myth-making: Kafka's canonical reception is the Janus face of the modernist prophet of popular memory. The earliest commentators, disproportionately Jews for whom depictions of social alienation and looming menace and allusions to Dreyfus and Beiliss retained their immediacy, focused on penetrating the theological (and later, existential) depths of the texts. In the latter half of the twentieth century, when Kafka had long since become an icon and his macabre visions had attained all too concrete reality, the theological impulse also traveled underground, into readings centered on the peculiarly impervious purity of his writing.

Today critics must work to dislodge the specificity nestled inside the hermetic carapace of Kafka's shrewdly opaque texts.

2. Walter Benjamin, "Kavaliersmoral," in Walter Benjamin, *Gesammelte Schriften*, Vol. IV, ed. Tilman Rexroth (Frankfurt am Main: Suhrkamp, 1972), 467.

3. Walter Benjamin, "Max Brod: *Franz Kafka. Eine Biographie*," in Benjamin, *Gesammelte Schriften*, Vol. III, ed. Hella Tiedemann-Bartels (Frankfurt am Main: Suhrkamp, 1972), 526.

4. Benjamin, "Max Brod: *Franz Kafka: Eine Biographie*," 527.

5. Benjamin, "Max Brod: *Franz Kafka: Eine Biographie*," 529.

But to reconstruct the fabric of historical and cultural experience so deliberately obscured by his prose, to expose the experiential groundwork—the movies and telephones, the voyages and insurance risk assessments, the traces of politics and of Prague's winding streets—is to arrive at the materiality of a life lived in an atmosphere that has, a century later, itself become a modern parable. If, like Scholem, early readers saw "Kafka's world" as "the world of revelation" caught from a "perspective that reduced it back to its negation" (*ihr Nichts*),[6] today Kafka's modernity has itself become mythological. To penetrate his emblematic texts is to enter a lost world, a Central Europe at once Jewish and cosmopolitan, where the urgency and profundity of modernity's losses had not yet become routine. Thus in December 1927, Walter Benjamin reported that he had finished reading *Der Proceß* "practically in agony (so overwhelming is the unassuming plenitude of this book)."[7] To borrow Benjamin's own term, his response provides a historical index for critical reflection on the meaning of Kafka's writing.

I begin by exploring the vertiginous dynamic of Kafka's *Process*, showing how his modernist writerly strategies place the reader in an aporetic relation to the historical circumstances his text at once reflects and distorts into a quasi-transcendent vision of the modern. I then turn to the intriguing traces of Benjamin's encounters with Kafka, which strikingly evoke the tension between the political and the messianic—between Brecht and Scholem—that runs through his own unfinished oeuvre. Although fragmentary and in a radical sense incomplete, Benjamin's engagement with *Der Proceß* in particular led him to a distinctive and helpful recasting of the difficulties

6. *Scholem/Benjamin Briefwechsel*, 157, cited in Sigrid Weigel, "Zu Franz Kafka," *Benjamin Handbuch*, ed. Burkhardt Lindner (Stuttgart: Metzler, 2006), 551.
7. Walter Benjamin, Letter to Alfred Cohn, December 12, 1927. In Walter Benjamin, *Gesammelte Briefe*, Vol. III, ed. Christoph Gödde and Henri Lonitz, (Frankfurt am Main: Suhrkamp, 1997), 312.

involved in writing about the uncanny timeliness or timely uncanniness of Kafka's work, one that may also illuminate his own unfinished archeology of the modern.

WRITING, THE PROCESS

To read *The Process*—to take, as a point of departure, an improper and in some ways misleading departure from the tradition of referring to this work as *The Trial*—is to begin entangled in the most fundamental issues of modern criticism. These are at the same time the most pressing matters of Kafka's reception: the entwining of author and work, of writing and reading and the livability of (modern) life, matters of guilt and innocence, literature and prophecy, history and theology, not to mention sex, death, the novel, and a few other things.

"Kafka's *Proceß*" refers at once to an unfinished work—call it a novel—and to the writing of that work, to a text at once intertext and metatext, a story ended from the very outset yet drastically unfixed, one that in its unboundedness violates by slyly thematizing the accustomed ordering of author and work, object and language, story and history. To a mode of writing that recalls even as it violates Flaubert's dictum that the author should be in his work as God in the world: everywhere present and nowhere visible. Our Kafka is at once the modern(ist) hero we seek and find in an oeuvre still read with the frisson of knowledge that it had been slated by the writer himself for annihilation—and the cipher everywhere to be found in the world we, the designated fans and as it were professional readers, are so often pleased to hear others call "Kafkaesque."

Reading back, if we can, beyond modernist icon and prophet, across the fires of the twentieth century, we recapitulate even as we confront the traces of a highly orchestrated betrayal. These texts that were not to be ours create an uncanny intimacy with our very own

Cassandra, an effect intensified by the diaries and letters, by the writing of a life encircling, seeping into the fictions. Since Brod published the first selections from the notebooks and letters in 1937, readers have read of K. surrounded by these echoes of Kafka, alternating between between self-flagellation and canny narcissism, and thereby, perhaps, implicating the reader in his drama of self-betrayal. For example: "Woman, more severely put perhaps marriage, is the representative of life that you are supposed to grapple with."[8]

The text we have began to be written on August 11, 1914, a scant month after its author's return from the fateful meeting in the Hotel Askanischer Hof in Berlin that ended his first engagement to Felice Bauer. It continued to be written in the months after the beginning of the Great War, from September on in a room finally of Kafka's own, thanks to the war. By January it was over. The work was left unfinished, in fragments subsequently assembled, then reassembled, by Max Brod. Kafka's text has never since ceased being reconstructed. The pages of this modernist performance of life and work lie before us today, suitably enough, in a proliferation of editions, notably one that defers or remakes the historical-critical task by placing each of us before the profusion of possibilities, down to the most rudimentary elements of signification, even below the letter, to inscription itself, in a reproduction, larger than life, of the pages of the folios Kafka disassembled and reassembled in producing the remnants that became in Brod's hands the "unfinished" work we are still unraveling.[9]

Kafka's strategy for writing his would-be novel was formally analogous to his serial engagements: a sort of experiment in fidelity—in

8. Franz Kafka, *Nachgelassene Schriften und Fragmente I*, ed. Malcolm Pasley (Frankfurt am Main: Fischer, 1993), 95: "Die Frau, noch schärfer ausgedrückt vielleicht die Ehe, ist der Repräsentant des Lebens mit dem Du Dich auseinandersetzen sollst."

9. Franz Kafka, *Historisch-kritische Franz-Kafka-Ausgabe sämtlicher Handschriften, Drucke und Typoskripte*, ed. Rolland Reuß and Peter Staengle (Frankfurt am Main and Basel: Stroemfeld/Roter Stern, 1995).

this case, to the ideal of classical unity, the Aristotelian demand that the story, the *mythos*, imitate a unified action. In fact, Kafka's deepest allegiance remained an experiential ideal: the rush of creation reflected in "The Judgment," completed in a single sitting in September 1912. A novel cannot be written in a single night, in such "a stormy rush,"[10] and Kafka was wary of the dispersion and fragmentation, the *Auseinanderlaufen* that had befallen his first effort, the "story heading into infinity" of the unfinished novel still best known today by Brod's title, *Amerika*.[11] This time, he fixed the first and last chapters, the opening and closing of the novel's arc from arrest to death, at the outset.

That beginning and ending, *arche* and *mythos*, began, then, not long after the conclusion (provisional, as it turned out) of the tortured liaison with Felice Bauer, in Kafka's own personal "trial" on July 12, 1914.[12] In the last days of that month, so fateful for the Habsburg Empire, Kafka's crisis was personal: "If I do not rescue myself in a work, I am lost."[13] And then, August 15: "for a few days I've been writing ... I have gained a meaning, my regulated, empty, senseless, bachelorish life has a justification."[14] But unity proved elusive; the torso

---

10. In a letter written on the night of November 24–25, 1912, Kafka lamented to his fiancée Felice Bauer that "The Metamorphosis" was flawed due to the interruptions in his writing process: the result lacked the "natural stormy rush" (*ihren natürlichen Zug und Sturm*) of his original vision. Kafka, *Briefe an Felice und andere Korrespondenz aus der Verlobungszeit*, ed. Erich Heller and Jürgen Born, in *Franz Kafka/Gesammelte Werke*, ed. Max Brod (New York and Tübingen: Schocken and Fischer Verlag, 1967), 125.

11. On November 11, 1912, Kafka used the epithet "ins Endlose angelegt" in a letter to Bauer to describe the story (*Geschichte*) he himself called *der Verschollene*: "The Man Who Disappeared," literally, "The Missing One." On January 26, 1913, Kafka complained to her that the novel was "unraveling" in his hands ("er läuft mir auseinander"). Kafka, *Briefe an Felice*, 86, 271.

12. Kafka describes this "tribunal in the hotel" in a diary entry of July 23, 1914. Franz Kafka, *Tagebücher*, ed. Hans-Gerd Koch, Michael Müller, and Malcolm Pasley (Frankfurt am Main: Fischer, 2002), 658.

13. July 28, 1914. Kafka, *Tagebücher*, 663. Kafka reflects on his feelings about the war, comparing their "tortuousness" to his earlier preoccupation with Felice Bauer (677).

14. Kafka, *Tagebücher*, 548–549.

failed to take form even when Kafka extrapolated his vision of long nights of pure writing into a consecrated staycation, an entire week, then two, of time at his own disposal.[15]

In one reading, the novel's writing becomes an emblem of a life lived as constant deferral: engagement unconsummated, the torrent of words turning in various directions. . . . A writing flowing (leaving aside the letters and diaries) most essentially into that anatomy of judgment, "In the Penal Colony," likewise composed during these weeks away from his official desk. A writing fueled, like Flaubert's, by a coquettish bachelor's ambivalent pursuit of a woman, call her a colleague, who thereby came to be remembered as an unworthy aggressor against literature itself. The mystery, unclarified still in the case of Emma and Louise, is recapitulated, or perhaps reinscribed, in K.'s Fräulein Bürstner and even more in the tangled collective postmemory of Kafka's literary life. January 20: "Writing at an end. When will it take me up again?"[16] A few days later, January 24, poor Prussian Felice, having ventured to the border zone for yet another meeting with her erstwhile beau, would be in a hotel room, "lying on the settee with her eyes closed," listening, unsatisfied, bewildered perhaps: the first audience of the most famously Kafkaesque of Kafka's texts, "Before the Law."[17]

Kafka is remembered, then, as modernist hero, as the suffering genius par excellence. Lost without a work; beset like his Josef K. by women, rivals, superiors, family demands; aspiring to transcendence, timelessness, fame; and paring it all down to sentences of a purity that

15. Beginning on October 5, 1914, Kafka took vacation time from his position at the state insurance agency where he worked, the Arbeiter-Unfall-Versicherungs-Anstalt. The entries referring to the vacation and its extension; Kafka, *Tagebücher*, 678.
16. Kafka, *Tagebücher*, 721.
17. Kafka describes the occasion in *Tagebücher*, 721–724; here, 723. For a synthetic overview of the course of events, see Roger Hermes, Waltraud Johns, Hans-Gerd Koch, and Anita Widera, eds., *Franz Kafka: Eine Chronik* (Berlin: Wagenbach, 1999).

becomes thematic in the novel's pages. Here everything is "the proc-ess," a proceeding, as we both read and experience, that turns imper-ceptibly into a verdict. For improbably, perversely, Kafka wagered the success of his text on the specific delight of a well-wrought imitation. *Der Proceß* describes, to invoke the passage in the *Poetics* once again, not what has in fact happened but what might happen: "what is pos-sible as being probable or necessary." Kafka thereby took aim at the very thing that makes poetry, as Aristotle puts it, "more philosophi-cal and more serious than history" by laying claim to universal rather than singular truths.[18]

What appears as nightmarish universality is, though, itself contin-gent, historical, emergent: modern, even if the problem is not, strictly speaking, modern at all. The reader, reading (and all the more, the editor-reader, assembling) confronts what K., poor, foolish, obtuse K., disoriented and preoccupied with the challenges of maintaining his composure, refuses to grasp, or cannot understand, or simply fails to see. In every way, Kafka places us before the omnipresent respon-sibility to venture to understand the meaning, to grasp the unity and, perhaps, universality of a story poised between the historical and the ahistorical, the phatic and the apophatic. At the same time, his text goes out of its way to suggest what may be its own teaching: "cor-rectly understanding a thing and misunderstanding it are not entirely mutually exclusive" (*richtiges Auffassen einer Sache und Mißverstehen der gleichen Sache schließen einander nicht vollständig aus*)[19]—and thus that the reader, no less than the protagonist, is condemned to failure, or if that is too much said, to the uncertainty that plagues all mor-tal knowledge. All this is delivered to the reader darkly shadowed by

18. Aristotle, *Poetics*, Book 9, 1451b.
19. All citations are to Franz Kafka, *Der Proceß*, ed. Malcolm Pasley, in *Franz Kafka: Schriften Tagebücher Kritische Ausgabe*, ed. Gerhard Neumann, Malcolm Pasley, and Jost Schillemeit, Vol. I (Frankfurt am Main: Fischer, 2002), 297.

what, in living memory, had not yet ceased to seem divine guarantees of meaning. This not-quite-a-novel is, then, Kafka's oeuvre at its most Kafkaesque: fragmentary, evocative, portentous, hermetic, tantalizing with would-be symbols, yet rigorously resisting definitive interpretation.

The difficulties extend to the text itself. Five years after Kafka gave Brod the manuscript in 1920, it was stripped of "unfinished" chapters and irregular German to become the first volume of his first edition. For the second edition, Brod fitted the manuscript out again just a few years later with fragments he had removed, only to remake the novel yet again, revealing new fissures, this time in the very ordering of the chapters, in the third edition in 1945.[20] Brod's editorial efforts, the object of attacks by generations of Germanists, were eventually supplanted by competing versions (and visions) of historical-critical editions. The second and more recent of these, located, as noted, at the contemporary radical end of the *via extremis* of the democratization of historical-critical scholarship, commenced with a facsimile version of *Der Proceß* that places the urtext before us literally in fragments, in the digitally reproduced traces of the repaginated notebooks that bare the traces of Kafka's painful, ecstatic production process.[21] Now we can each spread out this *Proceß* on our own tables and floors and attempt to reassemble it for ourselves in a self-relativizing literalization of scholarship's claims for itself.

This text has long since become a modernist exemplum, with the author everywhere intricated in its reception: K. as Welles's everyman, guilty as charged; K. as Existential Man searching his Truth;

---

20. Osman Durrani provides a helpful English overview of "Editions, Translations, Adaptations," in *The Cambridge Companion to Kafka*, ed. Julian Preece (Cambridge: Cambridge University Press, 2002), 206–225.

21. For more detail and references to the extensive literature on the editorial controversies, see Manfred Engel, "Ausgaben und Hilfsmittel," in *Kafka Handbuch: Leben, Werk, Wirkung*, ed. Manfred Engel and Bernd Auerochs (Stuttgart/Weimar: Metzler, 2010), 517–527.

K. the mystic god-seeker placed before the mysteries of the law—
and of course, K. the emblematic first victim of fascism *avant le lettre*,
Kafka clairvoyant. For Kafka, sly Kafka, has us read what K., preoccupied like every accused subject with matters of guilt and innocence
and legality, misunderstands in confronting the shadow system, the
dream-mirror in which no defense is admissible save the perhaps
indiscernible vindication of forthright deeds. For his part, the protagonist, his attention (mis)directed toward the past, preoccupied
with maintaining appearances, yet ever falling sideways into the arms
of women of dubious virtue, fails, must fail, to grasp the mystery of
a proceeding that is never other than its outcome at every moment,
even as the text progresses—or rather, does not progress but leaps
inexorably toward the final scene, toward the chapter marked
"Ending." The conclusion, foregone at the outset of Kafka's writing,
ensues anything but organically even as, in the course of reading, "the
procedure gradually gives way to the judgment."[22]

To read *Der Proceß* is to suffer this mimetic transformation in
and through the double-binding of K.'s encounters with an unsus-
pected shadow-world concealed in dusty attics and dubious quar-
ters and opening onto unimagined dimensions beneath the smooth
surface of his banker's life. Kafka's reader thereby undergoes what
Benjamin called *Entstellung*, the disfiguration or distortion—or better, more literally, the displacement—that he identified as Kafka's
ownmost movement. In a series of notes from the early 1930s,
Benjamin explores this concept, which becomes a reflexive switching point between the metaphysical and the political in his unfolding
reading. These end by invoking a phrase from a fellow early critic of
Kafka's: "Entstellung—'derangement de l'axe' sagt [Félix] Bertaux."[23]

---

22. "Das Verfahren geht allmählich ins Urteil über." Kafka, *Proceß*, 289.
23. Walter Benjamin, *Gesammelte Schriften*, Vol. II, ed. Rolf Tiedemann and Hermann
   Schweppenhäuser (Frankfurt am Main: Suhrkamp, 1977), 1200. Benjamin emphasized

To read, to submit to, *Der Proceß* is indeed to experience a fundamental disturbance, a disfiguring derangement of the axis of orientation, of reflection, of interpretation itself. It is to encounter, or uncover, in K., Kafka's everyman, the merging of the utterly universal and indelibly specific that is the very logic of the text and of the history of the reading of the text and, perhaps, the logic of the law. This moment, this movement, is described, or announced, to K. at the very outset: since the authorities are, as it were, magnetized by guilt, that he has attracted their attention is proof enough.[24] As Benjamin describes it, in Kafka's texts, appearance "compromises" essence when "essence becomes that which appears" (*das Wesen bei Kafka zum Scheinenden wird*). Justice itself undergoes a similar distortion: "its decisions are unfathomable. That is what the proceedings [*Prozeßverfahren*] in Kafka bring to expression. But in the form of corruption." *The Process* appears as mimetic disfiguration, as an anamorphic image of the modern: "The way law and the court here permeate all the seams of social life, that is the inverse side of the lawlessness in our social relations."[25]

The distorted appearance of Kafka's *Process* is the externalized logic of the self-fulfilling prophecy. But the system's compromising self-purification is enacted via a process of identification that draws the reader into its vortex. Attracted, as it were, by the possibilities of the universal—of the most diverse varieties, as Kafka's storied reception history confirms—the reader is seduced into affirming the displacement through which innocence comes to an end at the very moment a suspicion is issued:a process complete, like K.'s story itself, at its inauguration and repeated, reiterated, in every incident.

the centrality of *Entstellung* for his approach to Kafka in a letter to Scholem of August 11, 1934: "That I do not disavow the aspect of revelation for Kafka is clear from the fact that by declaring it to be 'displaced,' I recognize it as the messianic." Benjamin, *Briefe*, IV:479.

24. Kafka, *Proceß*, 14.

25. All the remarks in this paragraph are from the same (undated) note series. Benjamin, *Gesammelte Schriften*, II:1200.

READING, THE PROCESS

To read *Der Proceß* is to experience the insidious operations of the ubiquitous bureaucracy it portrays. To be sure, that experience is quite unlike that of Josef K., who is revealed—not in a "trial" but rather (to translate the title more precisely) via "proceedings" that follow on his arrest on unknown and perhaps nonexistent charges— to be fatherless, friendless, self-deluded, prey to dubious passions, and condemned to death. What is by turns illuminating, horrifying, darkly comic, and tragic in K.'s story lies in his failure to grasp (though, to be sure, Kafka never allows us to forget how impossible it would be for him *not* to fail to grasp) what lies on its very surface: the way K.'s efforts to defend himself become proofs of guilt, how the proceedings gradually give way to judgment.

The reader is destined not just to see but also to (re)enact the judgment on which that process depends: to witness how K., with all the confidence of the privileged male subject of the *Rechtsstaat,* misrecognizes the negative purity of the law, which in its (bureaucratic) operation can traffic with the ideal of justice only as an instrumental end. Thus the reasons for his arrest are immaterial for the "low-level employees" who invade K.'s rooms. Not only does it go without saying that "the authorities" have been informed as to the "grounds" and "person" in question when an arrest order is issued. "Our authorities," K. is assured, "do not seek out guilt in the population but are, as it states in the law, attracted by guilt and must send us guards out."[26]

To be sure, the absurdity of this "process" and the self-exculpatory circularity of such accounts of the law's operation on the part of those who "belong to the court" is as evident to the reader as to K. On Benjamin's incisive reading, "*The Process* is a hybrid of satire

---

26. Kafka, *Proceß,* 14.

and mysticism"—a novel "with its failure inscribed on its countenance."[27] So it is that the fissure between law and justice, absolute from the outset, is played for laughs: "'Look,'" one guard says to the other, "'he [K.] admits that he is ignorant of the law and at same time claims to be innocent.' 'You're right, but one can't get him to understand anything.'"[28] But to follow (or rather, to construct) what is happening, the reader is constrained to mimetically enact the very operation K., being subjected to it, fails to grasp—which reveals his self-understanding as (autonomous, legal, moral) subject as a (perhaps necessary) illusion.

Before the law, then, K. becomes an object, a case, whose very efforts at self-assertion inadvertently suggest his guilt. Like the nameless condemned man of "In the Penal Colony," K. is directly subjected to the very material, performative mechanism of the law we witness through the prism of Kafka's fiction. But the experience of the reader is barely less sinister. Like the Forschungsreisender, the researcher-voyager who witnesses the operation of the "strange apparatus" of judgment in the colony, thanks to a mode of writing defined by a self-eliding clarity, the reader becomes implicated in judging the process witnessed in the medium of fictional representation. That position, like K.'s, is anything but transparent to itself.

This *Entstellung* becomes apparent through a paradoxical decentering that only appears to be at odds with the forward movement of the narrative. It is thematized, or more precisely, activated, in the "First Hearing." Even if Josef K. had, as perhaps suggested, been mistaken for an unknown "house painter," he quickly becomes an illustration of the infallibility, the tautological totality, of the law when, seduced by the applause of the dimly unrecognized crowd, he attempts to

27. Benjamin, *Gesammelte Schriften*, II:3, 1258. This conception dates from sometime after 1935.

28. Kafka, *Proceß*, 15.

exploit his moment in the spotlight to call its operations into question. By then, K.'s self-defensive mendacity in the very smallest details has probably already aroused the reader's dismay and, indeed, retroactive suspicion that Kafka's opening gambit—"someone must have slandered Josef K., for without his having done anything wrong, one morning he was arrested"[29]—had not, after all, suggested his protagonist's innocence. The scene that ensues in response to K.'s putative misrecognition by the court illustrates that the logic in play is quite different than K., with his vision of himself as the autonomous legal subject of a "constitutional state" (*Rechtsstaat*),[30] imagines himself to be upholding—that our own anti-Oedipus is blind to his own blindness.

Insisting that "it is only a proceeding if I recognize it as such,"[31] K. flouts the advice he had received on the first day to be "more discreet in speaking" and not to "make so much noise about his feeling of innocence" because this tended to "disturb the not entirely poor impression" he was making in general.[32] Instead, he asserts his objectivity, his capacity to "calmly judge" the operations of the court[33] that has only seized upon him, as it were, by accident. "What has happened to me is but a single case and as such not very important," K. declares, save as a characteristic example of the flawed procedures many others had also been subjected to: "I stand here for them, not for myself."[34] But such representing is subject to the derangement, the *Entstellung*, of exemplarity that turns K.'s fate not into the exception but the rule. In the scene that follows, this agonizing movement becomes unmistakably palpable for the reader.

29. Kafka, *Proceß*, 7.
30. Kafka, *Proceß*, 11.
31. Kafka, *Proceß*, 62.
32. Kafka, *Proceß*, 22.
33. Kafka, *Proceß*, 68.
34. Kafka, *Proceß*, 64.

K. proceeds to work himself into a state of righteous indignation about what we would call the justice system, eventually declaring that an "organization" devoted to "arresting innocent persons and beginning senseless and generally, as in my case, fruitless proceedings against them" can hardly "avoid the worst corruption of the officials, given the senselessness of the whole."[35] K. then vehemently denounces his guards' attempt to garner personal profit from his arrest, with unintended consequences he will soon unsuccessfully attempt to circumvent by availing himself of the very corrupt means he has so bitterly critiqued.

Only after all this speechifying does K. suddenly discover the insignia worn by the judge on the collars of every member of his audience. In a parodic version of Aristotelian *anagorisis*, he is infuriated into what sounds unfortunately like a paranoiac vision: "You are yourselves the corrupt gang I spoke against . . . you formed pseudo-parties and one applauded to test me, you wanted to learn how one seduces the innocent."[36] Attempting to storm out, he is stopped by the Examining Magistrate, who alerts K. that through his conduct, he had "robbed himself of the advantage that an interrogation in any case signifies for the detainee."[37] K.'s "First Hearing" perfectly captures the self-affirming and self-regulating operation of the law, how encounters with its bureaucratic instantiations empty out the liberal understanding of justice, of representation, of the very meaning of legal process. As the Chaplain puts it later on, *Das Gericht will nichts von dir*: "The Court wants nothing from you."[38] K. becomes an example by evacuating the logic of exemplarity. Here as elsewhere, the novel is in a sense complete without its (missing) parts.

35. Kafka, *Proceß*, 69.
36. Kafka, *Proceß*, 71–72.
37. Kafka, *Proceß*, 72.
38. Kafka, *Proceß*, 304.

Benjamin, thinking of other texts, wrote that Kafka had composed "Fables for dialecticians."[39] Thus K. returns unsummoned to the erstwhile courtroom or becomes embroiled with a series of dubious "helpers" whose advice only deepens the opacity of the law. Thus the bailiff, while acting (like everyone else associated with the court) as though the universal corruption of its officers were "self-evident," first declares that "as a rule, we don't pursue futile cases here," then assures K. with a "friendliness" as dubious as the applause that had met his oration: "one does always rebel."[40] So, too, the reader is kept acutely aware that K.'s acts of self-assertion and appeals to universal rights only reinforce their own futility since, as the seemingly unending thrashing of the guards he had denounced vividly illustrates, every such gesture embroils K. more deeply in an apparently absolute, labyrinthine system. Its emblem, "Justice and the Goddess of Victory in one," appears in Titorelli's deceptive, ritually flattering portraits of judges—where it actually looks to K. more like "the Goddess of the Hunt."[41]

Perhaps the advice K. keeps receiving is impossible to heed. Certainly he seems to have difficulty following—a hard time getting it. Much of the book's humor is rooted in this circumstance. Thus when Titorelli, "half joking," explains that "everything belongs to the court," K.'s response is radically indeterminate: "I had not noticed."[42] Kafka makes clear that such insider knowledge might not help K. in any case. In the same scene, Titorelli, poised between "conviction" and "indifference," assures him that "the court can never be dissuaded" of the guilt of anyone who has been accused.[43] A court that cannot recognize innocence without calling its own

39. Benjamin, *Gesammelte Schriften*, II:415.
40. Kafka, *Proceß*, 91–92.
41. Kafka, *Proceß*, 196, 197.
42. Kafka, *Proceß*, 202.
43. Kafka, *Proceß*, 201.

authority into question has no—or only one—exit. But when K. objects to the contradictions that he feels he has discovered "not in the painter's words but in the court procedure itself,"[44] Titorelli explains that actual practice diverges from the law. "Naturally on one hand it states that the innocent will be acquitted, and on the other it does not say that judges can be influenced. But I have experienced just the opposite. I know of no actual acquittals, but of many influencings."[45] Since the court's records remained inaccessible even to the judges, the many legends of innocents being freed could not be confirmed.[46]

In 1931, Benjamin, already insisting that the dominant theological line of interpretation was untenable, declared: "That they remained unfinished—that is how mercy actually prevails in these books. That the law itself never speaks in Kafka, that and nothing else is the merciful dispensation [*Fügung*] of the fragment."[47] In a fragmentary notation of his own connected with the 1934 essay that is his fullest completed statement about Kafka, Benjamin went on to speculate that the court's corruption was perhaps a "figure for mercy"—a "*Sinnbild der Gnade.*"[48] But it remains unclear whether the distortion, the *Entstellung,* of the absolute expressed in the *aporiai* K. repeatedly encounters is a consequence of the pretension of the legal apparatus to represent the Law—or simply represents, imitates, the internal dynamics of a corrupt process as such. Like all dialectical fables, Kafka's turn on the question of differentiating meanings and the meaning of the moment of indifferentiation. What Titorelli presents as K.'s strategic options: the choice between *Verschleppung* (indefinite delaying, though the word can also mean "being carried

44. Kafka, *Proceß,* 206.
45. Kafka, *Proceß,* 207.
46. Kafka, *Proceß,* 208.
47. Benjamin, *Gesammelte Schriften,* II:679.
48. Benjamin, *Gesammelte Schriften,* II:1215.

off") and *Scheinbefreiung* (apparent, which turns out to mean merely provisional, acquittal) forms the most extreme example.[49]

K.'s efforts at self-defense keep transmogrifying into self-incriminations that loop back against him, rendering the once-vigorous banker's (self-vaunted) worldly strategic skills far worse than useless. This dynamic threatens to immobilize him: his uncle arrives to find his former ward in a state of apparent "indifference" in the face of a proceeding that, he warns, could lead to K.'s being "simply rubbed out. . . . Looking at you, one almost wants to believe the saying: 'to be in such a process means to have already lost.'"[50] Perhaps even Titorelli's alternative is an illusion.

The omnipresent aporetics, the insistent, vaguely nightmarish mixing of public and private, day and night, friend and foe, guilt and desire, that suffuses K.'s story is at once form and content: Kafka's Kafkaesqueness. The subtly woven textual web or, perhaps better, montage of operations—what Benjamin called the "unassuming plenitude" of *The Process*—becomes ever more apparent in the course of reading and, especially, rereading. For as already noted in the case of the opening sentence, Kafka's text demands rereading as the increasingly palpable dynamic of K.'s self-incrimination recursively implicates the reader in a tangle of interpretation and retrospectively recognized error parallel, analogous, or perhaps even identical to K.'s.

Thus while the circumstances of K.'s arrest had made amply clear that, as he put it to his uncle, these were "by no means proceedings before the ordinary court,"[51] at this juncture the text quite overtly refers the reader back to the beginning, or rather the *arche*: "'How did it happen?,'" his uncle asked, "'Such things don't come suddenly,

49. *Wirkliche Freisprechung*, "genuine exoneration," being beyond Titorelli's influence. Kafka, *Proceß*, 205.
50. Kafka, *Proceß*, 126.
51. Kafka, *Proceß*, 124.

they have been preparing themselves for a long time, there must have been signs of it.' "[52] The reader who has witnessed K.'s obliviousness can hardly fail to agree, and returning to the initial scene suggests grounds for an even more profound uncertainty about his innocence.

K. is barely awake, struggling to understand what is happening; he is uncomfortably aware that his neighbor across the way has the whole scene under observation, yet remains peculiarly concerned, given the goings-on, with his missing breakfast. At this point, the guards attempt to get him to turn over his linens with a seemingly unvarnished account of corrupt practices at the court. "K. hardly paid attention to this speech"; instead, as the passage continues, an eerie narratorial middle voice opens within K.'s own thoughts:

> the right to dispose of his things, which he perhaps still had, he did not hold in high esteem, it was far more important for him to achieve clarity about his situation; in the presence of these people he could not even think [nachdenken]. . . . What sort of human beings were they? What were they talking about? What sort of authority were they part of? After all, K. lived in a state ruled by law [Rechtsstaat], there was peace everywhere, all the laws were standing, who dared to ambush him in his apartment? He always inclined to take things as lightly as possible, not to believe the worst until the worst arrived, and to take no care for the future, even when everything was threatening. Here though that did not seem right to him.[53]

It is at this point that K. comes up with his theory that the whole thing may be a big practical joke, "perhaps because his thirtieth birthday was today."[54] Fearful of losing what he imagines to be his upper

52. Kafka, Proceß, 125.
53. Kafka, Proceß, 11.
54. Kafka, Proceß, 11.

hand, he weighs the risk that he may later be ridiculed for not getting it. In what follows, Kafka exposes K.'s stunningly superficial form of self-consciousness:

> he recalled well—not that it had generally been his habit to learn from experiences—a few occasions [*Fälle*], insignificant in themselves, in which he had, unlike his friends, deliberately [*mit Bewußtsein*], without the slightest feeling for the possible consequences, acted carelessly, and been punished for it by the consequence. That should not happen again, at least not this time, if it was a comedy, he would play along.[55]

Upon rereading, the treacherousness of K.'s self-understanding as a liberal male subject whose rights will always be assured by the smoothly functioning legal system of the state is all too apparent. Despite his vague misgivings, K.'s deeply internalized confidence in his own future, the successful businessman and upstanding citizen's inclination to "take things as lightly as possible" and trust that everything is ultimately going his way, persists long after it becomes apparent that everything is not.

As Kafka makes emphatically clear, all K.'s actions, including his fitful attempts to counteract his own habitual self-satisfaction and "learn from experiences," spur on the process. It is immaterial whether he sees himself as deliberately "playing along" or acts out of his habitual expectations and self-understanding—as when, "irritated [*befremdet*] and hungry" because his breakfast has not appeared, he rings the bell and inaugurates the sequence of interactions that reveal that he is being held prisoner.[56] That this omnipresent double-binding is constitutive for K.'s identity is conveyed with searing economy in the sentences that follow immediately upon his dubiously

55. Kafka, *Proceß*, 12.
56. Kafka, *Proceß*, 7.

motivated decision to "play along": "He was still free. 'Allow me,' he said, and went hurriedly between the guards on into his room."[57]

K.'s apparently boundless capacity for self-delusion is propped up by what appears to the reader as a tragi-comically carefree confidence not just in himself and in the prerogatives of status and position but in the apparatus of legality itself. Yet—as Kafka pointedly underlines by inserting "Before the Law" into the text—what interferes with K.'s ability to grasp what is happening as the proceedings unfold is constitutive of the *mythos* itself. With a Flaubertian twist, the opaque ordinariness of the protagonist becomes an entry point into abyssal questions. Before K., unsurprised and even accepting—"so you are here for me?"[58]—arrives at the ending toward which his story has moved so relentlessly, Kafka presents him, and us, with a final word about its meaning in the form of a sort of koan: "Logic is surely unshakeable, but it cannot resist a human being who wants to live."[59]

READING KAFKA

Der Proceß exposes the irrationality generated in and through the (bureaucratic) rationalization of the law. Yet by inscribing the reader into the process it describes, it also turns the paradigmatically modern operation by which the self-creation of the social converges with the negation of the subject it posits into a seemingly self-sufficient spectacle. Kafka thereby presents his reader with the seductive possibility of absolutizing K.'s experience—as existentialist paradigm, apophatic revelation, allegory for modernity itself. But such modes of reading should be rejected. They elide the distinctions between judge and victim, witness and bystander, and so reify and reinforce the very operations of

---

57. Kafka, *Proceß*, 12.
58. Kafka, *Proceß*, 305.
59. Kafka, *Proceß*, 312.

the law Kafka dissects. If there is to be a position of judgment that does not, as it were, belong to the court, it is necessary to theorize and problematize the reader's experience in ways that better resist the insidious temptation of submission to the modernist spectacle that construes a process at once absolute and arbitrary as the modern (subject's) fate.

Benjamin's insights into the abyssal dimensions of *Der Proceß* found highly enigmatic expression in a series of fragmentary and unfinished texts whose often aporetic riches are intricated with his own work—and life. The images they throw up may perhaps serve us as "historical index," for they bespeak, as Benjamin puts it in a famous passage in the monumental fragment that is the *Das Passagen-Werk,* a constellation of something hailing from a definite historical moment that is "coming to legibility in a certain time."[60] They may thereby help us discern what Benjamin's claim that "Image is the dialectic at a standstill"[61] means for us by reminding us that "every now is the now of a certain knowability" even, or even especially, in modernity.[62]

Der Proceß was published the year after its author's death, in 1925. In July, Walter Benjamin wrote Scholem that he planned to review "a few posthumous things of Kafka's. Today, as ten years ago, I regard his short story 'Before the Law' as one of the best that exist in German."[63] Something must have intervened, for no such review was ever written, and it appears to have been more than two years before Benjamin actually began the task of writing up "what I have to say about Kafka."[64]

This extended deferral is the mark of an engagement far more significant for Benjamin's thinking than the modest sum of finished

---

60. Walter Benjamin, *Gesammelte Schriften*, Vol. V, ed. Rolf Tiedemann (Frankfurt am Main: Suhrkamp, 1982), 577 (Convolut N 3,1).
61. Walter Benjamin, *Gesammelte Schriften*, V:577 (Convolut N 2 a,3).
62. Walter Benjamin, *Gesammelte Schriften*, V:577–578 (Convolut N 3,1).
63. Benjamin to Scholem, July 21, 1925, Benjamin, *Briefe*, III:64.
64. Letter to Alfred Cohn of December 12, 1927. Benjamin, *Briefe*, III:312.

pages on Kafka might suggest.[65] Benjamin left voluminous notes and reflections devoted to the writer, for whom he imagined a starring or supporting role in a series of possible books he began to envision at least as early as 1927. We have his notes from crucial conversations with Brecht beginning in 1931, as well as a series of very significant letters, most notably exchanges with Scholem and Adorno, that attest to the links between Benjamin's deepest philosophical, cultural, and political concerns and his engagement with Kafka's oeuvre.

The posthumously collected fragments and letters in which Benjamin's life and work, too, lie before us in a modernist palimpsest track a slow evolution, but also a circling and rethinking, a series of variations on themes, in his engagement with Kafka between 1927 and 1938. As his letters, but also the long essay written as he began to come to terms with life in exile after 1933, attest, Benjamin's engagement with Kafka became entangled, like all else, with his struggles—intellectual, psychic, material—to realize *Das Passagen-Werk*.[66] It will be impossible here to do more than gesture toward a way of understanding the significance of that entanglement.

Consider, by way of orientation, this profound remark, from the earliest phase of Benjamin's work on Kafka, in notes probably related to his 1931 radio address:

"The court wants nothing from you. It accepts you when you come and releases you when you go" [*Das Gericht will nichts von*

65. Leaving aside remarks scattered in other writings, these were the brief pieces from 1929 defending Brod's actions as literary executor ("Chivalric Morality"); the review of Brod's biography; a radio address of 1931 in which Benjamin read from a sketch for a review of Kafka's posthumous writings ("Franz Kafka: At the Construction of the Great Wall of China"); and, finally, "Franz Kafka. On the Tenth Anniversary of his Death," partially published in 1934.

66. There are almost no references to Kafka in the convolutes themselves, but Titorelli's proliferating, identical "heathen landscapes" serve Benjamin as a sort of cipher for reproduction as eternal return. *Gesammelte Schriften*, V:675–676, 680, 686 and (in "Pariser Passagen I") 1010.

Dir: Es nimmt dich auf, wenn du kommst und entläßt dich, wenn du gehst (304)]. What is actually expressed with these final words that K. experiences is that the court is no different from any given situation.[67]

Benjamin's reading of Kafka's ending returns us from *The Process* to reality while gently indicating the chilling silence of K.'s executioners.

Benjamin's thinking of modernity, his reflections on the categories of history, tradition, and experience, on the antinomies of the new and the eternal, the messianic and the profane, is embedded in a history of living conversations and exchanges only partially documented or documentable. Dense with the political and personal traces of exile, war, and historic loss, this thinking stands on the other side of a caesura that we cannot truly bridge, a distance that is itself constitutive of our deep interest in Benjamin's radically unfinished oeuvre today. The question of Kafka's meaning, not least for Benjamin's thinking of the modern as eternal return, is decisive.[68]

The concept of *Enstellung* first enters the traces of this lived encounter in his June 6, 1931 notes from a conversation with Brecht, in remarks Benjamin recycled, virtually verbatim, in his radio address that year.[69] In these notes, partially composed in the middle voice, Benjamin explicates Brecht's view that Kafka was "a prophetic writer" whose only theme was his "astonishment" (*Staunen*) at the "gargantuan displacements" (*Verschiebungen*) under way—consequences, for the masses and individuals alike, of the "dialectical laws" of history.[70]

67. Benjamin, *Gesammelte Schriften*, II:3, 1203.
68. In "Pariser Passagen," among his earliest notes for *Das Passagen-Werk*, a sentence that will recur: "The sensation of the newest, most modern, is namely just as much as the eternal return of the same, the dream-form of what happens." Benjamin, *Gesammelte Schriften*, V:1023.
69. Benjamin, *Gesammelte Schriften*, II:2, 678–679.
70. Benjamin, *Gesammelte Schriften*, II:3, 1203–1204.

But the individual as such must respond to the nearly incomprehensible displacements of existence [*Entstellungen des Daseins*] that betray the rise of these laws with astonishment, mixed, of course, with panicked horror . . . Everything that he describes bears witness to something other than itself.

For Brecht, Kafka had broken with "a purely narrative prose"; his unflinching vision made him "the only genuinely Bolschevist writer."[71]

After the 1931 address, Benjamin continued to read Kafka as forging a new kind of writing, a break with mimesis that opened a new dimension of reflection on contemporary existence. However, keeping his distance both from a "progressive" alignment with the laws of history and from Scholem's apophatic take, he ceased to call Kafka "prophetic." In May and June of 1934, the fruits of Benjamin's efforts to bring the years of reflection on a still-emerging oeuvre to expression appeared in two remarkable installments in the *Jüdische Rundschau*. Here Benjamin's innovations—notably his conception of "dialectical fables" and examination of the role "gesture" plays in Kafka's texts—remain poised between the political and the metaphysical.

Benjamin's penetrating, hermetic text was under epistolary attack from all sides even before this "provisional completion" and partial publication in honor of the tenth anniversary of Kafka's death. By the fall of 1934, he was moving on again. With a most characteristic mélange of modesty and pride, Benjamin wrote Carl Linert that while he had not "arrived at a definitive fixing of its object," he hoped his critical efforts would be recognized as having "disclosed

---

71. Benjamin, *Gesammelte Schriften*, II:3, 1204. In the radio address, Benjamin amended to "a purely poetic prose"—and omitted Brecht's political claim entirely. Benjamin, *Gesammelte Schriften*, II:679.

the proper terrain [*eigentliches Terrain*] for the discussion of Kafka."[72] Today, Benjamin's "proper terrain" is itself displaced. We encounter that disclosure against the backdrop of events that turned Kafka into a transnational literary mega-phenomenon even as they undermined the ambiguities of that dialectical witnessing to "something other than itself" that had both tormented and enchanted Benjamin.

It is all the more crucial, then, to attend to the critic's own view that with this fruit of his (and the) first two decades of engagement with Kafka, Benjamin had (as he put it to Werner Kraft a few months later) at least arrived "at a carrefour of my thoughts and reflections," a space where "continued observations promise to have the value for me of a compass direction on a pathless terrain" (*weglose Gelände*).[73] The "animated and so very heterogeneous reactions that this work called forth from friends" had assured him of its significance. The text he had at long last produced clearly needed to be reworked, but, Benjamin insisted, even if its deliberately open form might seem "problematic," it was necessary.

> I did not want to conclude. And historically speaking, it may not yet be time to conclude—least of all then if one, like Brecht, views Kafka as a prophetic author. As you know, I have not used the word, but there is much to be said for it, and perhaps that will yet take place from my side.[74]

Benjamin went on to insist on the importance for Kafka of "the motif of being a failure" (or perhaps better, "having foundered," *Gescheitertseins*). The writer's own "incorruptible and pure" conviction of his failure had to be trusted if readers were to avoid "false

72. Benjamin to Carl Linert, September 5, 1934. Benjamin, *Briefe*, IV:489. He refers to the essay's *provisorischen Abschluß* in the second paragraph.
73. Benjamin to Werner Kraft, November 12, 1934. Benjamin, *Briefe*, IV:525.
74. Benjamin, *Briefe*, IV:525.

profundity" and access his oeuvre's "historical conjunction [*histo-rische Knotenpunkt*]." Benjamin promised he would someday show that "in Kafka, the concept of the 'law' has a primarily illusory [*schein-haften*] character and is actually a prop [*eine Attrappe*]." [75] This remark opens onto an abyss.

In 1938, with the perils of life in Nazi Europe taking on ever more desperate contours, Gershom Scholem asked his friend for a "pre-sentable letter" to help him persuade the magnate Salman Schocken to fund Benjamin's long-contemplated book on Kafka. In response, Benjamin rehearses his recently published critique of Brod's biog-raphy, then pronounces it unsuitable for conveying his "image of Kafka."[76] In attempting to capture a "new aspect, one more or less independent from my earlier reflections," Benjamin arrives at a com-plex image that places Kafka's writing at the heart of the force-field proper to his thinking of the modern:

> Kafka's work is an ellipse whose distant focal points are deter-
> mined by mystical experience (which is most of all the experi-
> ence of the tradition) on the one hand, and on the other by the
> experience of the modern metropolitan human being.[77]

It is not that Kafka is prophetic, but that the intensity of his experi-encing opens beyond itself. According to Benjamin, Kafka's modern subject is not just "the modern citizen who knows himself to be at the mercy of an unfathomable apparatus of officials, whose functions are steered by entities that remain uncertain to the executive organs themselves, not to speak of the ones being handled by them." He is also, "just as much, the contemporary of today's physicists" who have

75. Benjamin, *Briefe*, IV:525–526.
76. Benjamin to Scholem, June 12, 1938. Benjamin, *Briefe*, VI:106–110; remark on 109–110.
77. Benjamin, *Briefe*, VI:110.

transformed lived experience itself into a "physicalistic aporia."[78] Oriented at once to (the disappearing) tradition and the psychic and physical realities of modern metropolitan experience, Kafka had "perceived what was coming to be without perceiving that which is today, but he saw it essentially as the individual affected by it. His gestures of terror benefit from a wonderful *latitude* [*Spielraum*] that will be unknown to the catastrophe."[79]

Today, after the catastrophe, Kafka's prescience has become a commonplace, and Walter Benjamin has himself acquired a quasi-iconographic status as tragic seer of the modern. To be sure, in a world of burgeoning bureaucracies and ever more opaque systems of regulation, where "culture" increasingly designates the ever-same, ever returning as the new, and sensory experience itself has become so highly mediated and subject to reproductive manipulations that the distinction between lived experience and mechanistic and reductive simulacra threatens to dissolve, Kafka often reads like nonfiction. But as Benjamin's cautiousness regarding the category of the prophetic underlines, we do well to resist the temptations so vividly placed before the reader of *The Process*.

Situated before the events (and the mountains of criticism) that threaten to obscure the texts themselves today, Benjamin's critical strategy for responding to the challenge of Kafka's modernity epitomizes a thinking that remained persistently unfinished in the face of an aporetic dialectic that was perhaps but a piece of stage machinery. The difficulties Benjamin encountered in writing about what is opening in Kafka cast light on his own unfinished *Das Passagen-Werk*. Not only are his philosophical concerns mirrored in the hermetic dialectical fable of *Der Proceß*, in which a subject incapable of learning from experience encounters the traces—or remnants—of the universal in

78. Benjamin, *Briefe*, VI:110, 111.
79. Benjamin, *Briefe*, VI:112.

282

the guise of an illegible social apparatus. Kafka's own uncanny historicity provided an image of incompletion of unparalleled importance for Benjamin's thinking of the modern, returning him to his search for unrealized possibilities in the ruins themselves. Reading his reception of Kafka's *Trial* as historical index thus helps render legible the potential value of Benjamin's strategic reconfiguration of the boundaries between philosophy, literature, and history for navigating the "pathless terrain" of our own modernity.

BIBLIOGRAPHY

Benjamin, Walter. *Briefwechsel 1933–1940*. Edited by Gershom Scholem. Frankfurt am Main: Suhrkamp, 1980.

Benjamin, Walter. *Gesammelte Briefe*. Edited by Christoph Gödde and Henri Lonitz. Frankfurt am Main: Suhrkamp, 1995.

Benjamin, Walter. *Gesammelte Schriften*. Edited by Rolf Tiedemann and Hermann Schweppenhäuser. 7 Vols. Frankfurt am Main: Suhrkamp, 1972–1999.

Benjamin, Walter. *Gesammelte Schriften*, Vol. II. Edited by Rolf Tiedemann and Hermann Schweppenhäuser. Frankfurt am Main: Suhrkamp, 1977.

Benjamin, Walter. *Gesammelte Schriften*, Vol. III. Edited by Hella Tiedemann-Bartels. Frankfurt am Main: Suhrkamp, 1972.

Benjamin, Walter. *Gesammelte Schriften*, Vol. IV. Edited by Tilman Rexroth. Frankfurt am Main: Suhrkamp, 1972.

Benjamin, Walter. *Gesammelte Schriften*, Vol. V. Edited by Rolf Tiedemann. Frankfurt am Main: Suhrkamp, 1982.

Brod, Max. "Franz Kafkas Nachlaß." *Die Weltbühne* 20, no. 2 (1924): 106–109.

Durrani, Osman. "Editions, Translations, Adaptations." In *The Cambridge Companion to Kafka*, edited by Julian Preece, 206–225. Cambridge: Cambridge University Press, 2002.

Engel, Manfred. "Ausgaben und Hilfsmittel." In *Kafka Handbuch: Leben, Werk, Wirkung*, edited by Manfred Engel and Bernd Auerochs, 517–527. Stuttgart/Weimar: Metzler, 2010.

Hermes, Roger, Waltraud Johns, Hans-Gerd Koch, and Anita Widera, eds. *Franz Kafka: Eine Chronik*. Berlin: Wagenbach, 1999.

Kafka, Franz. *Briefe an Felice und andere Korrespondenz aus der Verlobungszeit*. Edited by Erich Heller and Jürgen Born. In *Franz Kafka/Gesammelte Werke*, edited by Max Brod. New York and Tübingen: Schocken and Fischer Verlag, 1967.

Kafka, Franz. *Der Proceß.* Edited by Malcolm Pasley. Volume I of *Franz Kafka: Schriften Tagebücher Kritische Ausgabe,* edited by Gerhard Neumann, Malcolm Pasley, and Jost Schillemeit. Frankfurt am Main: Fischer, 2002.

Kafka, Franz. *Historisch-kritische Ausgabe sämtlicher Handschriften, Drucke und Typoskripte.* Edited by Rolland Reuß and Peter Staengle. Frankfurt am Main and Basel: Stroemfeld/Roter Stern, 1995.

Kafka, Franz. *Nachgelassene Schriften und Fragmente I.* Edited by Malcolm Pasley. Frankfurt am Main: Fischer, 1993.

Kafka, Franz. *Schriften Tagebücher Kritische Ausgabe.* Edited by Gerhard Neumann, Malcolm Pasley, and Jost Schillemeit. Frankfurt am Main: Fischer, 2002.

Kafka, Franz. *Tagebücher.* Edited by Hans-Gerd Koch, Michael Müller, and Malcolm Pasley. Frankfurt am Main: Fischer, 2002.

Weigel, Sigrid. "Zu Franz Kafka." In *Benjamin Handbuch,* edited by Burkhardt Lindner, 543–557. Stuttgart: Metzler, 2006.

INDEX

accusation, 10, 19, 24–41, 121, 129–32, 149,
  168, 176, 190, 201, 206, 210–17
  false, 132
  groundless, 132
  guilt of the, 270
  legal, 231
  of self, 131–33
  vague, 255
Adorno, Theodor W., 17, 19–20, 23, 27, 29,
  32–45, 49, 51–52, 99, 116–18, 119n14,
  124, 129, 133, 143, 146–47, 162,
  202–4, 247
aesthetics, 86, 121–22
  and art, 102
  and ethics, 87n3
  See also ethics
Agamben, Giorgio, 20, 129–33
alienation, 18, 42–43, 139–70, 194, 245.
  See also skepticism
allegory, 2, 9, 58, 122–23, 133, 162n49, 203,
  275. *See also* literature; parable
ambiguity, 139–70
Antonioni, Michelangelo, 21
Aristotle, 262, 269
art, 86–87, 94, 97, 99–104, 201, 214, 219
  attitudinal models of, 87–92
  ethical dimensions of, 87n3, 89, 102
  literary work of, 114
  modernist, 244

representational, 89n5
  and truth, 113
  See also literature; paintings; Titorelli
atheism, 29
attitude, 26, 74, 86–92, 99–100,
  103–6
attunement
  linguistic, 251
  for Wittgenstein, 238
Auden, W. H., 111
authority, 66, 119, 179, 190, 228
  epistemic, 230
  inscrutable, 11, 149, 230
  institutional, 48, 271, 273
  law and, 152–53
  male, 184
  religious, 68
  the source of, 31
  symbols and, 16, 194
autonomy, 7, 37, 86, 106–7, 184, 190,
  194, 245
  aesthetic, 106
  critical, 107
  ethical, 107
  political, 106
  See also ethics

Barthes, Roland, 66–67
Barth, Karl, 40–41, 44

INDEX

Bauer, Felice, 14, 14n17, 15n19, 50–51, 115, 170, 173, 177–78, 221, 260
Beckett, Samuel, 15, 17, 35, 244
Beissner, Friedrich, 230
Benjamin, Walter, ix, 19–31, 34, 40, 80, 139, 156, 201, 203, 248, 254–57, 266–67, 271, 276–83
Bergman, Ingmar, 21
Binet, Alfred, 192–93
Blanchot, Maurice, 5, 21, 134, 234–36, 235n8, 245
Bloch, Grete, 173
Boa, Elizabeth, 183
Brecht, Bertolt, 10, 278–79
Bresson, Robert, 21
Broch, Hermann, 15
Brod, Max, 3–4, 12–13, 24–27, 30–33, 38, 55, 58–59, 65, 93, 126, 176, 255–56, 263
bureaucracy, 48, 92, 185

Calasso, Roberto, 9, 9n9, 201, 210–12, 211n28
Camus, Albert, 152n30
capitalism, 178, 203
Cassandra, 255, 259
Cavell, Stanley, 228, 238, 240–46
Celan, Paul, 17
Christ, 39, 46, 68. *See also* God; religion; theology
comedy, 131–32, 203, 274
  bad, 196
  classical, 6
  and tragedy, 7
  See also tragedy
commodity, 203–4, 206
Conrad, Joseph, 7
Corngold, Stanley, 3n2, 14–15
Crary, Jonathan, 192
crime novel, 7
  metaphysical, 8–9
  standard, 7
  See also literature; novel
culture, 93, 95, 97

Deleuze, Gilles, 204, 218
DeLillo, Don, 21

de Man, Paul, 125–26
Derrida, Jacques, 125–26
Diamant, Dora, 14
Duttlinger, Carolin, 203, 223
dyschronia, 177–96. *See also* time

education, 141
ekphrasis, 93
Emrich, Wilhelm, 203
Enlightenment, 40–41
epistemology, 193
estrangement. *See* alienation
ethics, 20, 47, 87, 98, 103–6, 141
  and aesthetics, 87n3
  Greek, 152
  and society, 96
  See also aesthetics; autonomy; philosophy
exegesis, 72–80. *See also* interpretation

fate, 154
film, 21
Flaubert, Gustave, 258
forms of life, 92, 103, 105
fragment, 5, 5n5, 6, 6n6, 114, 122, 134, 148, 150, 155, 167–69, 191, 271
  Benjamin and the, 276
  Brod and the, 259–63
  modernist, 254, 259–60, 277
  reading of the textual, 256–57
  See also literature; Kafka, Franz; novel
freedom, 107, 169
Freud, Sigmund, 11
Fried, Michael, 244
Fuchs, Anne, 20

Gibson, John, 20
Gnosticism, 30, 33, 33n15
God, 41–42, 44, 51–53, 93. *See also* theology
Goethe, Johann Wolfgang von, 122
Goodstein, Elizabeth S., 20–21
Gordon, Peter E., 19–20
Guattari, Felix, 204, 218
Guess, Raymond, 99
guilt, 7–11, 14, 19–21, 37, 49, 81–82, 121, 129, 131–33, 150–57, 161, 168
  of the accused, 216, 231, 247, 263, 266–67, 270